Murder Files from Sc
and the Black M

ALSO BY R. MICHAEL GORDON

*The Infamous Burke and Hare: Serial Killers
and Resurrectionists of Nineteenth Century Edinburgh* (2009)

The Space Shuttle Program: How NASA Lost Its Way (2008)

*The Poison Murders of Jack the Ripper:
His Final Crimes, Trial and Execution* (2008)

The Thames Torso Murders of Victorian London (2002)

Alias Jack the Ripper: Beyond the Usual Whitechapel Suspects (2001)

Murder Files
from Scotland Yard
and the Black Museum

R. MICHAEL GORDON

Exposit

Jefferson, North Carolina

LIBRARY OF CONGRESS CATALOGUING-IN-PUBLICATION DATA

Names: Gordon, R. Michael, 1952– author.
Title: Murder files from Scotland Yard and the Black Museum / R. Michael Gordon.
Description: Jefferson, North Carolina : Exposit Books, 2018 | Includes bibliographical references and index.
Identifiers: LCCN 2018016405 | ISBN 9781476672540 (softcover : acid free paper) ∞
Subjects: LCSH: Great Britain. Metropolitan Police Office. Criminal Investigation Department. | Murder—Great Britain—Case studies. | Murder—Investigation—Great Britain—Case studies.
Classification: LCC HV6535.G4 G674 2018 | DDC 364.152/3094109034—dc23
LC record available at https://lccn.loc.gov/2018016405

BRITISH LIBRARY CATALOGUING DATA ARE AVAILABLE

ISBN (print) 978-1-4766-7254-0
ISBN (ebook) 978-1-4766-3127-1

© 2018 R. Michael Gordon. All rights reserved

No part of this book may be reproduced or transmitted in any form or by any means, electronic or mechanical, including photocopying or recording, or by any information storage and retrieval system, without permission in writing from the publisher.

Front cover image of Big Ben in London © 2018 okeyphotos/iStock

Printed in the United States of America

Exposit is an imprint of McFarland & Company, Inc., Publishers

Exposit
Box 611, Jefferson, North Carolina 28640
www.expositbooks.com

To all those hardworking men and women of the London police and gatekeepers of the "Black Museum" who take their tradition of service back to the days of horse-drawn carriages and London's fog-filled cobblestone streets and cool gas-lit nights. May your most difficult cases always end with "case closed." Cheers to one of the finest police forces in the world—London's Metropolitan Police, better known as the venerable Scotland Yard.

Table of Contents

Introduction   1

Section I: Scotland Yard and Its Museum of Crime
   History of Scotland Yard   3
   The Black Museum   7

Section II: The 19th Century—The Victorians
   James Greenacre, the Dismemberment Killer of Edgware
      Road (1837)   13
   William Sheward and the Tabernacle Street Murder (1851)   19
   Dr. William Palmer, the Rugeley Poisoner (1856)   26
   Madeleine Hamilton Smith, Arsenic "Not Proven" (1857)   37
   Constance Emily Kent and the Road Hill House Murder (1860)   45
   Dr. Edward William Pritchard, Death by Antimony (1865)   51
   Christiana Edmunds, the Chocolate Cream Poisoner
      (1870–1872)   57
   Mary Ann Robson (Cotton), the Dressmaking Serial Killer
      of Durham (1873)   63
   Kate Webster (Catherine Lawler) and Her Bloody Little Axe
      (1879)   71
   Charles Frederick Peace and the Banner Cross Murders (1879)   79
   Percy LeFroy Mapleton and Murder on the Brighton Line
      (1881)   88
   John Henry George Lee, the Man They Could Not Hang (1885)   96
   Adelaide Blanche Bartlett and the Pimlico Mystery (1886)   104
   Florence Maybrick and a Little Arsenic with Breakfast (1889)   111
   Mary Eleanor Wheeler Pearcey, a Woman Scorned (1890)   120
   Dr. Thomas Neill Cream, the Lambeth Poisoner (1891–1892)   127
   Amelia Elizabeth Dyer, the Baby Farmer Most Foul (1896)   136
   Samuel Herbert Dougal and the Moat Farm Murder (1899)   143

Section III: The 20th Century—A New Era for Murder

The Stratton Brothers and a Thumbprint to the Gallows (1905) 151
Dr. Peter Hawley Harvey Crippen and Miss Ethel Clara
  Le Neve (1910) 157
Mr. and Mrs. Seddon and the Death of Miss Barrow (1911) 166
George Joseph Smith and the Brides in the Bath Murders
  (1915) 171
The Murder of Police Constable George William Gutteridge
  (1927) 177
Cecil Louis England (Toni Mancini) and the Brighton Trunk
  Murders (1934) 183
Gordon Frederick Cummins, the Blackout Ripper (1942) 189
Neville George Clevely Heath, the Gentleman Vampire
  of Bournemouth (1946) 195
John George Haigh and the Acid Bath Murders (1949) 201
John Thomas Straffen, British Serial Child Killer (1951–1952) 209
John Reginald Halliday Christie and His Special Gas (1953) 219
Ruth Neilson Ellis and the Public House Murder (1955) 230
Peter Thomas Anthony Manuel, Scottish Serial Killer
  (1956–1958) 235
Edwin Bush and the Antique Shop Murder (1961) 241
Peter William Sutcliffe, the Yorkshire Ripper (1975–1980) 245

Bibliography 259
Index 263

Introduction

In the long history of British justice, many strong personalities come to the fore. Some have the best intentions of fighting crime and serving the public. Others, however, are just as determined to commit criminal acts, some of which would make even the strongest person reel with shock. Max Haines of the *Toronto Sun* wrote about British crime in an October 7, 2001, article: "There is something about the British Isles that compels murderers to commit horrible acts with a certain élan, which seems to be absent in other locales. What these killers lack in volume, they make up in quality. It has always been thus."

Macabre examples of this élan may be seen in the 1837 murder of Miss Hannah Brown by James Greenacre, the Dismemberment Killer of Edgware Road; George Joseph Smith and the Brides in the Bath murders of 1915; and of course the brutal murders committed by Jack the Ripper in 1888–1891. Brutality, of course, was not limited to days long past, as the more recent example of Edwin Bush and his 1961 Antique Shop Murder attests. This book will examine many of these cases.

Even today, when one thinks of Scotland Yard, images come to mind of smartly dressed officers on unarmed patrol, and detectives in brown suits amid scenes of London's fog-shrouded cobblestone streets. It is difficult not to imagine gaslights, rain-soaked streets, horse-mounted officers and police call boxes mixed in with an always moving and ever-changing population.

It is historically interesting to note that the "Yard" was not always as respected as it is today. The early Victorian London populace was hard up, as it would be throughout the entire Victorian period; at times the police were thought of as being just another gang but with better political connections. However, it would not take long for the people of London to realize the wisdom of having an organized and professional law enforcement arm which not only arrested the criminals but also came when called to protect the lives and property of Londoners. More often than not the police put their very lives on the line and stood their ground when others of less sterner stuff would have fled.

There would of course be some missteps, as well as out-and-out corruption, but even those problems would be openly dealt with, and with an even hand, as the vast majority of those who chose to serve were honorable, determined and diligent in their work. The worldwide reputation of the "Yard" would flow from them.

In addition to the cases studied, this work will take a peek into the mysterious world behind the walls and into the case files of Scotland Yard's Museum of Crime, better known worldwide as the Black Museum. Never meant to be a proper museum, these two rooms nevertheless hold artifacts and files related to many of Britain's most famous crimes, infamous criminals and victims. Officially, the Black Museum's files are held for the research and training of officers, though civilians on occasion are allowed in.

So put on your trench coat against the cold and foggy night, turn on your bull's-eye lantern, light your pipe, grab your magnifying glass and come along for a little page-by-page visit with some of the most memorable cases from Scotland Yard and its mysterious Museum of Crime. Your theatre of the mind waits in *Murder Files from Scotland Yard and the Black Museum*.

Section I

Scotland Yard and Its Museum of Crime

History of Scotland Yard

"Their basic mission would be the prevention of crime and disorder."

Scotland Yard, the popular name for the Metropolitan Police of London, is arguably the most famous law enforcement agency on Earth. It is also considered by many to be one of the finest at the job. (Apologies to the Royal Canadian Mounted Police.) But even the best at times are not able to get their man, or woman. Over the years there have been spectacular successes, some of which remain government secrets in the face of modern terrorist realities. However, examples of the Yard's tenacity and determination to close a case may be found in Inspector Richard Tanner's 1864 pursuit of a murder suspect all the way to the United States, and in the efforts of Chief Inspector Frank Froast, who traveled to South America in pursuit of a fraud suspect. Inspector Thomas Butler (1913–1970) would gain fame and the nickname "Gray Fox" for his relentless tracking down of all 15 men who had pulled off the Great Train Robbery of August 8, 1963.

Created by Parliament with the Metropolitan Police Act of June 19, 1829, the force commenced with nighttime street patrols on September 29, 1829 (some accounts say it was September 25). Training for this work had only begun days earlier, on September 21. Uniforms included a smart tailcoat and top hat. The uniform had a distinctly civilian look to it, as the authorities wanted to avoid any impression that this was any type of military force. Set up by Sir Robert Peel, the original salaries for the new force can still be found on a handwritten memorandum dated July 20, 1829. By 1839 the police force could boast some 3,350 steady members covering an area of 700 square miles and serving a growing population of around 2,500,000.

By 1862 Scotland Yard was forming their first "Rogues Gallery," using the recently perfected art of photography. Photographs of convicted prisoners held in several British prisons at the time were forwarded to the Yard by prison governors. The gallery soon included those who were held by Scotland Yard itself. However, it was not until 1901 that an official photographer was added to the police force. That gallery quickly expand, as London seemed well placed to provide a never-ending number of subjects for the file, which of course continues to this day.

By 1900 the Metropolitan Police force had grown to almost 16,000 men divided into 21 divisions. The modern force was beginning to take shape and would continue to grow as the population increased.

The original Scotland Yard headquarters were located at 4 Whitehall Place, with a much used rear entrance on a street named Great Scotland Yard. The site during the medieval period held a royal palace, used to house Scottish royalty during their visits to London. From this came the name Scotland Yard.

The use of fingerprint evidence would find its way into Scotland Yard's arsenal of crime detection by the turn of the century. Credit for this discovery, at least in the Western world, would go to a Scotsman named Dr. Henry Faulds (1843–1930). However, the use of chops to identify an individual was well known in Asia. Certainly the ancient Chinese were well aware of this method of identification. Before them the Babylonians had scribes press their fingerprints into clay cuneiform tablets to identify the individual who had done the work and as a method to prevent forgery. The Western world was far behind in this area of investigation. Dr. Faulds had been working in Japan in 1880 and teaching in Tokyo when by chance a neighbor's home was robbed. The thief had left sooty fingerprints on the walls, which Dr. Faulds compared to those of a man who had been arrested for the crime. His work cleared the suspect and led to the real thief being convicted. Dr. Faulds would later publish his account in the British magazine *Nature*, which reported his "scientific detection." The man responsible for bringing this advancement to Scotland Yard was Major Sir Edward

Richard Henry (1850–1931), who served as commissioner from 1903 to 1918. Henry had served in Bengal, India, where he became familiar with the procedure and soon saw to it that London's finest were well versed in the method after having formed the Fingerprint Bureau in 1901.

The new fingerprint science (dactyloscopy) recorded its first success on June 27, 1902, when Harry Jackson was convicted of burglary primarily on the fingerprint evidence he had unknowingly left behind. He was sentenced to seven years penal servitude for his trouble. Only three years would pass before fingerprint evidence would be used to convict a man, or rather, men, for murder. It would be the Stratton brothers who could claim the rather dubious honor of being the first to be hanged on the evidence of a fingerprint one of them had left at the scene of the crime. By that time the new Fingerprint Bureau boasted 80–90,000 sets of prints in its files. Scotland Yard's fingerprint system would soon find favor with the Americans and in the early 1900s would be adopted by the newly formed Federal Bureau of Investigation (FBI). The Yard's system now holds fingerprint records for all of England, Ireland and Scotland.

When telephones eventually became part of the Yard, Londoners in need of Scotland Yard's services could reach officers by dialing *WHI-1212* (Whitehall 1212). Even today many police stations in London use 1212 as their last four digits, including Scotland Yard.

By 1906 Scotland Yard had five well-respected top detectives that the general public could count on. The "Big Five" included chief inspectors Charles John Arrow, Paul Cane, Walter Dew, Frederick Fox and Frank Frost. These men and their subordinate inspectors and detectives were often seen working high profile murder cases throughout London as well as in other areas of the British Isles.

When manpower shortages became critical during World War I, the first women began patrolling the streets of London. This inspired painter Walter Richard Sickert (1860–1942) to place their images on canvas, some of which are held today in the Metropolitan Police Museum.

After World War I the force created the Flying Squad, which was dedicated to combating criminals and road bandits who used automobiles during their criminal pursuits. (And pursuits they were!) The Flying Squad's first motor car was a 1927 Lea Francis. In 1933 the squad acquired a Fordson van, which is said to still be in service as of this writing. The Forensic Science Laboratory was open for business on April 10, 1935, originally at the Police College at Hendon. The lab was later transferred to better quarters at Lambeth.

After World War II the Yard's Flying Squad added members of the Ghost Squad to their ranks. The original members of the Ghost Squad were Detective Inspectors John Capstick and Nobby Clark and Detective Sergeants John Gosling and Matthew Brinnand. The Ghost Squad were undercover men and women who went easily in and out of London's criminal environments as they passed along details of criminal or planned criminal activity to headquarters at the Yard. After World War II, London was awash in crime. Efforts to stem this criminal tide were difficult due to problems associated with the war, which came not only from the confusion and destruction brought on by German bombers on entire areas, but were also caused by the lack of manpower due to the large number of men who had once again volunteered for military service.

In 1963 Parliament passed the London Government Act, which increased the area covered by Scotland Yard to 786 square miles, serving a population of 8 million with a force of some 18,000 officers. Today the Yard boasts its own forensic laboratories, criminal records office, fraud and drug squads, photography section, flying squad, police criminal laboratory, intelligence branch, and a school dedicated to training some of the world's best detectives. In addition, the Yard handles the 999 emergency telephone system, traffic and crowd control, regulates the buses and cabs as well as licenses for the British public.

In 1967 the Metropolitan Police Headquarters would move to newer digs at a 20-story concrete and glass office building. Still called New Scotland Yard, the headquarters is now located off Victoria Street at 10 Broadway, S.W.1. London, near the Houses of Parliament, but a new building was not required for the move. The Yard was moved into an existing office block, which is now leased by the Metropolitan Police on a long-term basis.

The earlier New Scotland Yard headquarters building is now known as the Norman Shaw Building, and due to its history and prized location it did not stay vacant for long after it was vacated by the Metropolitan Police.

The Black Museum

"...contains an extensive collection of weapons..."

There is a certain underlying mysticism and dark mystery etched into the very fabric of the Black Museum, and it begins with the name itself. The officers who developed the museum were not the ones who named the rooms and files, which hold Scotland Yard's artifacts of crime. History records that on April 8, 1877, a reporter from *The Observer*, a London newspaper, had requested a tour of the museum in Scotland Yard's headquarters from Inspector Neame, who promptly refused the request. Nevertheless, the reporter was able to pen his article and in his report to the people of London he referred to the collection of files and criminal artifacts as the Black Museum. Much later, the people of London found that the powers-that-be had changed the name to the Crime Museum. However, to most, these macabre exhibits displayed in their "Gallery of Death" still ring true to the original and more popular name—the Black Museum.

The authority to retain what was in effect the property of those who had been convicted of crime, and some who had not, came in 1869 with the passage of the Prisoners' Property Act. However, it was not until April 25, 1874, that the Central Prisoners' Property Store opened its doors and Police Headquarters had the opportunity to begin properly storing items that had been collected. The Property Store was assigned to No. 1 Great Scotland Yard just behind the Commissioner's Office at No. 4 Whitehall Place.

Credit for the idea of transforming a simple storage facility into a proper crime museum goes to Inspector Neame, who had already selected a number of items which he thought would be of most interest to those in the business of crime detection. The inspector's original intent was to use these items to instruct and inform police officers during a practical course focusing on how to detect and prevent burglary, a not uncommon crime at the time. Strange as it may seem now, many burglars came to that criminal occupation through the tools of the trade that were passed down from father to son.

Scotland Yard lore has it that it was in late 1874 when official recognition of the museum effort came, and with that the authority and funding to keep the new museum in operation. With funding the museum would open its doors in the latter part of 1875. There is, however, no actual date when the museum can be said to have been in operation as it was meant to be a fully internal matter for Scotland Yard. Nevertheless, April 12, 1875, is when Inspector Neame and Police Constable Randall were permanently assigned to the Prisoners' Property Store, so that is as good as any date to use as its official starting point. Months later, after Neame and Randall had properly collected items and placed them in their appropriate places in the storage area, the museum opened its doors to its first visitors. In doing so it became the world's first and now oldest museum dedicated purely to the display, instruction and very possibly the investigation of crime.

On October 6, 1877, the first visitors were recorded in the guest book in the guise of Police Commissioner Lt. Col. Sir Edmund Henderson accompanied by Assistant Commissioners Lt. Col. Labolmondiere and Captain Harris, along with other unrecorded guests. These names were recorded in the museum's first visitors book, which spanned the years from 1877 to 1894. By this time the museum exhibits were in constant demand and became a regular part of instruction by officers assigned to CID. By then it was generally referred to as the Black Museum.

Henderson had a long history of police work and had served as Comptroller-General of Convicts when the far outpost of Western Australia became a penal colony in 1850. He arrived on June 1 of that year aboard the *Scindian* along with the first convicts sentenced to the new crude facility. After securing the convicts he began construction of what would become Fremantle Prison. He would serve there from 1850 to 1863. Henderson would later establish the fixed-point system for police as Commissioner of Police of the Metropolis, as well as starting the Habitual Criminals Register. He would serve as Commissioner of Police from 1869 to 1886, but he would eventually resign on February 8, 1886, as a direct result of his commanding officer's mishandling of the Trafalgar Square Riot.

Despite the public's outrage at the time of the riot, there was a successful end to the tense situation, which seems to have been overlooked. The Yard having been forewarned of a potential riot, 500 constables were put in reserve. However, aging Superintendent Walker dispatched only a token force to the area, which soon lost control as the rioters pushed on. Walker then sent most of the reserves to Pall Mall, but the mob had reached Oxford Street and its many shops. It was at this point that Inspector Cuthbert out of Marylebone Police Station moved into action with a sergeant and a squad of 15 constables armed with only batons. Facing the raging mob Cuthbert and his small force of very determined officers stood their ground against overwhelming odds. Amazingly, the rioters were turned away, not wanting to do battle with even a small force of London's finest. Order was once again established on the streets of Victorian London. Henderson would be replaced by General Sir Charles Warren (1840–1927) who would himself be confronted by a major riot in 1887 (Bloody Sunday) as well as a brutal murder spree in Whitechapel, East End of London, in 1888.

When Scotland Yard headquarters moved in 1890, naturally, the museum moved with it. This time, however, a proper set of rooms, located in the basement, were assigned to the exhibits, which also included files to be used for reference, along with the items used in crimes. It is interesting to note that even though there was no official curator at the time, Police Constable Randall was still listed on the staff with the responsibility of keeping the small but growing internal museum in good working order. He was also responsible for adding new exhibits to the museum as well as approving requests for museum visits. The only times the museum has not been in operation since 1875 were during World Wars I and II when operations were temporarily suspended. The only other time the museum closed its doors for a brief period was in 1967 when it was moved to the new Metropolitan Police Headquarters off Victoria Street. At this move the museum was housed on the second floor in much better digs than its former basement area. In 1981 Scotland Yard redesigned its Museum of Crime and moved it to a prominent place on the first floor. Form was now following fame as more visitors came by for a bit of a look-see.

Even though Scotland Yard makes it clear that the Black Museum "is a Private Museum … not open to the general public" it is also quite clear that those with enough political power or celebrity can be given private tours of the museum's exhibits even today. Crime writers please take special note.

Those invited to browse around the dusty stacks and macabre exhibits have included such notables as Sir Arthur Conan Doyle of Sherlock Holmes fame, master escape artist Harry Houdini (1874–1926), comedic actors Stan Laurel (1890–1965) and Oliver Hardy (1892–1957), librettist William S. Gilbert (1836–1911) and composer Arthur S. Sullivan (1842–1900), members of the royal family, and of course Orson Welles (1915–1985), who would go on to develop a 1952 radio series of the same name based upon exhibits at the museum.

Possibly due to the ongoing visits by those and other individuals of note, the present manifestation of the museum has a distinct museum quality to its dusty shelves even though it is still primarily used to instruct police officers in the techniques of crime prevention and detection, law, forensic science and other matters related to criminal investigation. The new museum, we are told, has been divided as before into two rooms. The "old room" has the feel and perhaps even the taste and smells of how the original museum would have presented itself in the late 1880s. It is in this room one would find an impressive collection of weapons and other artifacts for the most part used in the commission of violent assaults or murder. On the Metropolitan Police Service website we are informed that these items are part of the "old room [which] contains an extensive collection of weapons, all of which have been used in murders or serious assaults in London, and displays items from famous cases, generally, prior to 1900, such as *Jack the Ripper* and Charlie Peace."

We are also informed by the museum website that "a morbid display, which attracts comment, is the display of the death masks of people hanged at Newgate Prison which adorn a high shelf of honor and look down on visitors." Naturally the masks are displayed to impress all visitors who may gather.

We then move on to the second room, which by its very nature appears more sterile and certainly has a modern bent with its many steel file cabinets. The contents of these cabinets would whet the interest of any crime buff as in them are the files of some of the most interesting cases in British history. Again from Scotland Yard's website we learn that the categories held in these files include:

> Famous Murders, Notorious Poisoners, Royalty, Murders of Police Officers, Bank Robberies, Espionage, Sieges, Hostages and Hi-jacking, as well as cabinets on particular cases. Famous cases shown in the museum include Ruth Ellis, John Reginald Halliday Christie, The Stratton Brothers, John George Haigh, Neville Heath, Dennis Nilsen, Dr. Neil [misspelled on the website] Cream, Mr. & Mrs. Seddon, Dr. Crippen, Craig and Bentley, and many, many others.

As with the first room, the second most surely holds a mystery or two among its dusty files, many well over 100 years old. Clearly, there is still much to learn from those old case files, now thought to be closely held in Scotland Yard's very private Black Museum.

SECTION II

The 19th Century— The Victorians

James Greenacre, the Dismemberment Killer of Edgware Road (1837)

"...and after considerable difficulty he was at length taken into custody."

Mr. Bond was a bricklayer working on a new series of dwellings called the Canterbury Villas, located about a quarter of a mile from Regent's Canal on old Edgware Road, London. On December 28, 1836, Mr. Bond could be found walking towards Kilburn at around two o'clock in the afternoon, having finished his work for the day. At a point where his path emerged from under Regent's Canal, something caught his attention. This looked to be a coarse cloth package or sack which appeared to have been purposely placed behind a large paving stone resting against the wall. When he removed the heavy stone he saw what appeared to be a frozen pool of blood. Mr. Bond was soon on his way to summon the superintendent of the job site, Mr. Samuel Peglar, who rushed to the canal site along with a second man to examine the find. Together they opened the package and discovered to their amazement the partial remains of a woman. The trunk of the woman was in the sack, but the head and legs had been crudely removed and were not found in the sack or anywhere in the area, which was searched by the men and later by police investigators.

The torso, found at the Pineapple Toll-Gate building development site, was soon in the hands of London police authorities. The medical examination showed that the head had been severed from the trunk, but not completely cut through to allow for removal. It had been a crude cutting job, as the neck bone had been only partly cut before being broken off at the cut point. Both legs had been removed in a similarly crude manner, indicating that the amputations were not performed by anyone with medical training. It was also discovered that the work had been speedily done for the purpose of quickly disposing of the body. The police would be looking for a killer, but not a doctor. What was strange about the discovery was the fact that the killer had certainly carried the body parts for disposal away from the murder site, but he had not done a very good job of hiding the crime. The killer had not even tried to bury the evidence.

On December 31, 1836, a coroner's inquest was held at the White Lion Inn on Edgware Road, near the site of the discovery. It would not be long before the jury returned a verdict of "Willful murder against some person or persons unknown." The police now needed not only to discover who had murdered the woman, but also identify the victim of what would soon be reported by the press as the Edgware Road Tragedy.

Ten days later a human head was found by lockkeeper Mathias Ralfe at the canal's Ben Johnson Lock. This new discovery precipitated the exhumation of the torso, which had already been buried, so that a proper comparison could be made with the earlier find. Newspapers would continue to report on the parts being discovered. "[Ralfe] found the head of a female in the canal, which he wrapped up in a cloth, and took it [to] the bone-house. It appeared to have had [a] violent blow struck on the forehead. One of the eyes was knocked out. The left jawbone was broken." It would not take long for the surgeon of the district, Mr. Girdwood, to declare that the torso and head had come from the same woman. There was a brutal killer to be found and just because this latest discovery was not a new murder, no one could guarantee that the killer was finished. However, there was little to go on at the time other than the body parts. The police would need more information to advance the case.

In order to support the investigation, Mr. Girdwood placed the head in a jar of spirits, which would preserve it for possible later identification. The torso was then re-interred as investigators believed that it could not possibly aid any further in the investigation. Girdwood kept the head at his office with the generally published information that anyone who felt they could identify the victim would be welcome to inspect the artifact. In the meantime, the police did their best to track down any missing woman who could possibly fit the description. In an area the size of London this would be no easy task and in fact was fully unsuccessful. No missing woman seemed to fit the description of the head. The investigators could go no further at that time.

Thursday, February 2, 1837, found a laborer named James Page cutting osiers (willow reeds used in making baskets) for Mr. Tenpenny in a patch at Cold Harbour Lane in Camberwell. He stepped over a small drainage ditch to afford a better position to do the work and as he did Mr. Page spotted what seemed to be a large bundle enclosed by a piece of old sacking. The bundle was partly covered by water in the ditch. Mr. Page's curiosity got the better of him and he decided to have a closer look. When he picked it up for his closer examination he saw the toes from a human foot sticking out. He soon dropped the package and called another workman who was close by to see what he had found. Both men carefully opened the package, which soon revealed two legs looking very much to have come from a woman. Once again the remains were taken to Mr. Girdwood's office, which was soon able to declare that the body parts fit with the torso and head. There had not been another murder. The cold weather, it would be declared, had preserved the parts well enough to make the identification possible. Nevertheless, they still had no clue who the victim was.

The solution to the identity of the victim came after March 20 when Mr. Gay from Goodge Street, Tottenham Court Road, London, applied to "inspect such of the remains of the deceased woman as had been preserved above ground." His request was sent to the churchwarden of the parish of Paddington: one Mr. Thornton. Mr. Gay was concerned that the remains could be his sister Hannah Brown, who had disappeared on the afternoon of Christmas Eve 1836. Upon viewing the preserved head he immediately declared that it was indeed the remains of his missing sister. Now the police had a name and could proceed with their investigations. It would take a good deal of effort by Inspector George Feltham and Police Constable Peglar out of T Division to dig out the details of just who had last been seen with Hannah Brown.

It would not take long for the authorities to discover that the unfortunate woman had been engaged to one James Greenacre. Their investigation found that Hannah Brown had left her lodgings in Union Street, Middlesex Hospital, accompanied by Mr. Greenacre and that both had made their way to his home in the Carpenter's Buildings, Camberwell (Camberwell House), London. This was the last time she had been seen alive so naturally the police were quite anxious to discuss the matter with Mr. Greenacre.

From the *Newgate Calendar* we may read:

> A warrant was granted by the magistrate of Marylebone police office for the apprehension of this man; and after considerable difficulty he was at length taken into custody, on the 24th of March 1837, at his lodgings at St. Alban's Place, Kennington Road, together with a woman named Sarah Gale, with whom he cohabited, and her child.

The End Game

James Greenacre (1785–1837) and his "wife" Sarah Gale were soon questioned and in a short time both were arrested by Inspector Feltham. They were taken into police custody, having been found together in bed at No. 1 St. Alban's Place, Kennington Road, London. As would be expected, both Greenacre and Gale denied any knowledge of the murder. In fact, Greenacre at first forcefully denied even knowing who Hannah Brown was. He may not have known that the body had been identified and that he was known to have last seen the victim just before she disappeared. Once Greenacre's denials were destroyed by the inspector, Greenacre began to fill in part of the story. He related that he had in fact intended on marrying Miss Brown; however, because of a lack of funds (both expecting the other to have money) the wedding had been called off. Greenacre then denied that he knew what had become of Miss Brown and that he was just as concerned as the officers as to what may have happened to the young lady.

As the suspects were dressing for their transportation to police headquarters Greenacre remarked that the police were very fortunate to have come that evening as he and Miss Gale were in the process of moving to America. In point of fact, there were several boxes in their apartment which had been packed, corded and prepared for the move scheduled for the very next day. Greenacre however, would miss the boat, and Miss Gale would eventually be rescheduled on a different ship for a much different destination. The trunks, however, would stay in London in the good hands of Scotland Yard.

A search of the trunks yielded a good deal of evidence for the prosecution. The authorities found several items which could be traced directly to Hannah Brown. The woman's earrings were another matter. They were being worn at the time by Sarah Gale! The trunks also held a section of an old cotton dress, which matched exactly the same dress fragment which had been used to wrap up pieces of Brown's body. There was no doubt that the police had their man.

Final Days

The two-day trial, which drew large crowds to the Old Bailey, began on April 10, 1837, with Greenacre charged with "willful murder of Hannah Brown" and Gale charged with being an accessory after the fact in her death (officially listed as "consorting, aiding and assisting"). Broadsheets were soon available on the streets showing sketches of both of the accused with details of the case and trial. Reporters would follow the events of the trial very closely and reported on most of the details in the local papers.

> Trial commenced Monday, April 10, 1837, at the Central Criminal Court, before the Chief Justice Tyndall, Mr. Justice Coleridge, and Mr. Justice Cottman. Mr. Adolphus, Mr. Clarkson, and Mr. Bodkin were council for the prosecution. Mr. Price and Mr. Payne stood for the prisoners. Mr. Adolphus opened the case and in addressing the jury, gave a comprehensive detail of the principal features of this extraordinary affair. In the course of the learned gentleman's argument he expatiated forcibly on the confession of Greenacre.

The fact that there were so many judges hearing the case shows the level of importance given the case by the authorities.

Both surgeons who had examined the remains were called to discuss the horrendous damage done to the victim while she was alive. The prosecution wanted to demonstrate how brutal the crime had been. "Mr. Birtivistle, a surgeon, said he had examined the head and that the blow on the eye was done during life; and on being shown a saw, said he had applied the saw to the neck, and it fitted exactly. Mr. Girdwood, surgeon, deposed that the wounds around the eye were inflicted during life." The jury took careful note of this examination. Nevertheless, it did not show by any means who the killer had been.

"The Lord Chief Justice summed up, which occupied two hours and a half." Fifteen minutes would be all the jury would need to bring verdicts of guilty to both prisoners at the bar. It was noted that "the prisoners did not appear to be much surprised on hearing the verdict." Greenacre was immediately sentenced to death and Miss Gale was sentenced to be "transported for the rest of her natural life."

As to Greenacre's exact sentence: "It only remains for me to pronounce the awful sentence of the law, which is, that you, James Greenacre, be taken to the gaol [jail] from whence you came to a place of execution, and there hanged by the neck until you are dead; and that your body be buried within the precincts of the prison. May the God of all grace have mercy on your soul."

Murderers did not hang around for very long in Victorian London, so his time in the condemned cell would be a short one. His appeals were quickly and easily dismissed and on May 2, 1837, Greenacre took his well-deserved drop on the gallows at Newgate Prison by the skilled hand and rope of Chief Executioner William Calcraft as Sarah Gale made preparations for her long voyage to the very far off penal colony in New South Wales, Western Australia. Her story would end in Australia many years later. Reports on Greenacre, however, make mention of the fact that his drop into the abyss was not a smooth one. It seems that the old rope used for his drop had broken as his neck was not so cleanly snapped. Nevertheless, the work of the executioner was completed so Calcraft was able to collect his fee! But what of Sarah?

From the State Library of New South Wales we learn what life was like when Sarah Gale arrived at her new home.

> Between 1788 and 1868, 165,000 convicts were transported to Australia. Transportation in New South Wales officially ceased in 1840, although there was a short-lived revival in 1849. Under Governor Phillip and the early governors most convicts were employed on public works constructing roads, bridges and public buildings and cultivating government farms. Female convicts were generally employed as domestic servants to the officers. As the colony developed and free immigration increased, convicts were assigned to work for free settlers and small landholders. In addition, the growing number of freed convicts or emancipists were given positions of trust and grants of land. By the mid-1830s the vast majority of convicts were assigned to private employment.

As a postscript to these events, it is said that for years after his execution with the broken rope that stevedores who worked the London docks adopted Greenacre's name to indicate when a rope sling was breaking loose while goods were being loaded or unloaded. The cry "Greenacre!" could be heard as a warning along the busy docks as their fellows warned each other of a coming danger from above. It would seem however, that those who would kill as Greenacre did would not hear the cry of "Greenacre" and as such many would end their days on the very same gallows at Newgate Prison which had taken the measure of the "Dismemberment Killer of Edgware Road."

William Sheward and the Tabernacle Street Murder (1851)

"I have nothing to say."

William Sheward (1816–1869) could not be considered by any measure to have been happy with his 54-year-old wife Martha (1797–1851). She was 19 years his senior and, if reports may be relied upon, his very disagreeable wife had driven him to despair and then to the temporary escape found only in drink. On the Sunday evening of June 15, 1851, things had gone about as far as they could for William as his wife continued to argue with him about money problems. It would later be found to have been a rather common friction between the two of them. William decided that he had finally had enough that evening as he found himself slowly walking the few steps towards the bathroom to retrieve his straight razor. From the bathroom he quietly crept towards the bedroom where he found his still-complaining wife. William would see to it that she would not complain for much longer.

Coming up behind Martha, William drew out his razor, held her head and slit her throat from ear to ear! As she struggled to speak, he simply allowed her to drop to the floor while he stood over her and watched her quickly bleed to death. Her final attempts to speak were no longer loud enough for him to hear. The terraced house on Tabernacle Street, built in 1753 by architect Thomas Ivory, now contained a body to dispose of. William had not given himself enough time to plan the disposal since the murder was committed in the heat of the moment rather than being planned. There was blood all over the floor and the clean-up would take a good deal of time. But then again no one had heard a thing so he would have the time he needed to work. However, William remembered that he had an appointment in Great Yarmouth for a job interview.

When he returned from his appointment, William discovered that he was up to the task of disposal and was soon at work tackling the problem a piece at a time—literally! Deciding that small pieces were easier to dispose of than a rather large body, he began his cutting up. First came the head which seemed as good a starting point as any. No sense staring at the wife's face all night long. This was quickly followed by the hands, feet, arms, and legs. Parts of these were chopped into even smaller pieces. The fingers of course needed to be cut off for easy disposal. All in all it would take the good part of four evenings (he still had a day job to do) to complete the cutting up. He was now ready for part two—cooking the meat! For the next three days William worked his small saucepan over an open fire in the living room, reducing the bits and pieces of his late wife as he went along. Once cooked, the meat was dropped into a nearby bucket. This part of the work however, was not without its problems. The stench of his cooking the bones and flesh which had begun to decompose and putrefy began to overpower him and could have alerted the neighbors. The solution was to toss lavender leaves into the pan and the fire. It seems to have worked, as no one came by to complain and he would continue his task.

With the main work done, the final task had arrived. William put on his coat, grabbed his bucket and began nightly trips around Norwich depositing Martha's pieces—a little here and a little there. Out of the way places such as gullies and water drains soon held parts of Mrs. Sheward. It would take a week of wandering around town with his tea-towel-covered bucket, but in time Martha was completely out of his life—at least for the time being. All he would ever say for a very long time was that Martha had finally left him, which did not surprise their friends as she had often spoken of just such an event. It appeared that he had committed the perfect crime as no one seemed to have missed the wife, at least not enough to do a proper search. There were after all many other more pressing problems to deal with in 1851 Victorian England than one complaining old woman.

"Is this a joke?"

Naturally, with so many pieces deposited in so many areas around town it did not take long for the locals to run into Martha—at least parts of her. The first piece to be found was a hand, closely followed by a piece of a foot, a leg and then a section of well-cooked arm. The authorities first thought that because so many body parts were turning up that this was some kind of macabre joke being played on the town by some local medical students. This theory was soon dispelled by the fact that more and more parts continued to be found and they were clearly from the same body. This was no joke. This was murder, but the police had no idea who the victim was as no one had found the head and the body did not seem to match anyone on the local list of missing persons. At the time it was extremely difficult to identify an individual without the head. Police science was not yet advanced enough to make a confirmed and positive identification of every corpse, particularly one sans head. It should also be recalled that dogs and rats also scavenged pieces of Mrs. Sheward for a tasty little cooked treat, but they never consumed her entrails, which had been pushed into a drain by William; they were recovered!

One area which had played host to a piece of Martha was Deepdene Lane, which seemed for some unknown reason to draw William night after night. Taking note of William's poking around in the dark with a stick, a patrolling constable began to get suspicious. He soon discovered that William's wife was missing, and he formed the opinion that just possibly he had killed his wife. Searching the area with his own dog the constable located a hand and was certain that he had discovered a part of Martha Sheward. Luck, however, was on William's side as the police surgeon made his report on the remains so far discovered. The official report noted that the victim was "female, between 25–30 years at death, light brown hair and medium build." Mrs. Sheward was 54 years old, with a heavy build and black hair. As far as science could report at the time—and with no head to help in the identification—this was not a match for Mrs. Sheward. There would be no charges filed as the police simply did not have a case to prosecute. But William was certain that his dead wife was not really that far away. He would later report that her ghost was a constant presence; that killing her did not keep her quiet. Eventually William discovered that the murder had been a big waste of time; her somewhat irritated spirit had not been removed from his life, at least in his troubled mind.

Attempting to move on with his life and improve his situation, 1868 found William Sheward living comfortably over the Key and Castle public house in St. Martin at 105 Oak Street, Norwich, England. He had become the landlord and proprietor of the popular pub. With him was his new wife and according to William, his wife's ghost. In December of that year, seeing that her husband looked worn-out, the new Mrs. Sheward suggested a small vacation in London. William quickly agreed, but upon entry into the London hotel he began to feel uneasy. It seems that they had taken rooms near where he had met his first wife Martha some 30 years earlier. On December 31, 1868, William Sheward could not sleep, and found himself wandering the cold and wet gas-lit streets of South London. He was quite convinced that he was being closely followed by his wife's ghost. He decided that he had had enough of this spectral nagging. He had to end his misery and the only way was to go to the police and confess to murder.

On January 1, 1869, William walked into a Walworth police station where he found Inspector James Davies on duty at the desk. Davies would later relate that a very calm Sheward simply walked up to his desk and stated that he wanted to bring a charge against himself. The inspector's response was simply, "What is it?" To which Sheward replied, "For the willful murder of my first wife in Norwich." For the next hour the inspector questioned Sheward and received a general confession, but the murderer was unwilling or unable to go into great detail as he said the events were "too terrible" to speak of. Within days Sheward was in the Norwich jail and charged with murder. Whether his wife, or rather her ghost, was by his side in the jail cell was never established. But perhaps the fact that Mr. Sheward was reported to be very calm in jail tells part of that story.

On Trial for Murder

March of 1869 found Sheward on trial for his life. By this time, he had completely contradicted his confession with the statement that he had been drinking heavily at the time, was depressed and confused and thus did not know what he was saying. He further stated that his wife was yet alive, as far as he knew, and further that she had gone off to Australia with another man those many years ago. Where she was now, he could not say, having "not seen her since she had disappeared."

The case itself was very weak and indeed the only real evidence the prosecution had was the signed confession, now retracted, by Sheward. The medical evidence of a body of course was still in the murder file, but other than the victim being female there were no factors which matched Martha Sheward. The police surgeons who took the stand stood by the original report that the pieces that had been gathered around town were of a much younger woman. Defense council was also able to show that nothing in the original confession was new or unknown and that all of it could have easily been taken out of local newspaper reports, which at the time had been very detailed regarding not only the discoveries, but also which parts were found. In effect, there was no evidence of murder. Even the recovered body parts could not relay to the authorities how the victim had met her death. The body parts were not in good enough shape for any positive conclusions in that regard. It would be the judge himself who reminded the jury that no new information had been submitted by Sheward and further that the defendant had a right to be believed as much when he confessed as when he withdrew that very same confession. On the other hand, the judge asked the men of the jury to consider who would go to the trouble to invent such a story if it did not hold some truths within those troubling words. The problem came down to one simple fact—there really was no evidence that Martha Sheward was dead or that William Sheward had killed her. The only relevant fact was that no one had seen Martha for a very long time.

The jury took the case at 3:05 p.m. and returned with a verdict at 4:20 p.m. When the clerk asked the foreman to stand and deliver the verdict, with a clear voice the foreman said, "The jury find him guilty!" With that Sheward was asked if he had anything to say and he replied, "I have nothing to say." The judge then donned the black cap and passed the expected sentence that the prisoner was to be "taken to a place of execution and there be hanged by the neck until your body be dead." Needless to say, there were those in the press who would question the verdict and the sentence as the case, which was closely followed by the local press, seemed even weaker after the trial had ended. Despite efforts to remove William from the death cell, there would be no reprieve and the execution date would stand.

The Gallows

As he waited for his final walk to the gallows at Norwich City Gaol, Sheward decided that he had a great deal to say. He took the opportunity to unburden himself of the events which occurred some 18 years earlier. On April 15, 1869, the day before he was to be hanged (some reports put his hanging at April 20, 1869), Sheward requested a meeting with the prison governor. In the late afternoon, as the state executioner began preparations for his work, Sheward ended speculation that he had been wrongly convicted. He wanted to tell the full story, at least as much as his mind would allow. It seems he was still troubled by the ghost of his wife who he said was still at his side.

Relating the events which drove him to kill, Sheward explained that there had been an argument over money. William had lent money to his employer and this had enraged his wife. She threatened to demand that the money be repaid. Sheward, for whatever reason, felt he had to stop her at all costs. He told the governor how he had come up behind his wife, quite enraged, and slit her throat from ear to ear. Sheward then described in detail how he had dismantled, cooked and then scattered his wife's remains around town. The only surprising part of the story was how he was able to continue to walk around town with his small bucket of body parts and simply drop off a piece of Martha here and a piece of Martha there even as the earlier pieces were being discovered and the police were on the lookout for the possible killer.

Soon enough the time came for his final few steps. He had written a letter to his new wife apologizing for what he had done to her and asked for her forgiveness. As the execution party moved towards the hanging shed, the bells of nearby St. Peter Mancroft and St. Giles could be heard in the distance. The party had to move slowly, as Sheward's rheumatism in his ankles had flared up, requiring him to be supported by two warders. In the pinioning room the party was met by the under-sheriff, a local police surgeon and the prison governor. Sheward could walk no further and needed to sit down for a while. After the pinioning he was again supported as he slowly shuffled to the gallows and was for the most part carried up the 13 steps to the wooden beam and single hanging rope which had been in place since late the day before. The hood was placed over his head and the bolt was withdrawn from its usual place. His executioner was William Calcraft, a long-serving executioner who invariably used a painful short drop method. The same was used to dispatch Sheward. As he fell to his death, his supporters let go and he took his drop to a less than exact finish. It was reported that a "brief struggle brought life to an end." We will never know if Sheward saw the ghost of his wife watching as he was prepared to take his drop. Perhaps he saw a smile on her face!

One hour later, after the hangman had finished his tea, the corpse was cut down and examined. It was determined that the execution had been successful and the executioner could collect his fee. Dropping into the waiting hole in the ground within the prison walls, the corpse was covered over and a small brick was placed nearby with W.S. cut into its surface. Sheward had become the second man to be hanged at Norwich Prison and as records show, would be the last.

The Remains of the Day

With Sheward's confession came official closure to the mystery of who had been the victim dismembered and found 18 years earlier in and around Norfolk, but there were one or two items which were never cleared up. William Sheward never reported what he did with Martha's head or where some of the other undiscovered body parts rested. He had stated that he cut off the head and then proceeded to cook it in his saucepan along with other bits and pieces. Speculation, and it was nothing more than that, ran to a very interesting possibility. Sheward mentioned that he had worked very hard on his wife and that the disposal caused him to work up a very good appetite. Perhaps in the end they remained together after all! But when all is said and done, this was only speculation and has never been proved or disproved. There is also the possibility that even though Sheward's feelings for his wife were overwhelmingly negative and he had been nagged into killing her, he may have had some remaining feelings for her. Perhaps this led to him keeping her head around to take out every once in a while to see how she was doing. This of course is also just speculation.

One other matter came to light during the investigation into his wife's murder. It seems that had Mr. Sheward waited for three more months before dispatching his wife she would have inherited a considerable fortune. This event would have ended any problems brought on by their recent money shortages. Of course if Martha had known of the coming funds perhaps they would not have argued so much over money and he would not have been driven to murder. Timing, it would seem, is everything.

Dr. William Palmer, the Rugeley Poisoner (1856)

"I am innocent of poisoning Cook by strychnine."

William Palmer (1824–1856) could never be accused of having a nurturing or ordinary home life as a young man growing up in the small town of Rugeley, Staffordshire, in central England. He had an older brother who had been fathered by a man other than his mother's husband, which seems to have bothered his father little. She was said to be "no better than she should be." As for Palmer's wandering father, he seemed no better than his wife, gaining a reputation for dishonest dealing, which allowed him to acquire a considerable fortune. It would not be a long life; he died relatively young, leaving his ill-gotten gain to his seven recognized children. The children would receive the considerable sum of £7000 when each turned 21.

William's mother lost no time whatsoever in acquiring new men friends, but she could not remarry, as any union would cause her to lose her considerable inheritance, which included money and other property. As long as she stayed "Mrs. Palmer" her lavish way of life was secure. Against this background of lust and greed William seemed to be for the most part immune. People in the small town viewed him as being always friendly, generally honest and rather generous when it came to helping his less fortunate friends. He was in a word a "good" person—at least on the surface.

Despite the large sum of money to be had William needed to make a living, at least for a few years until his inheritance came in. With this in mind, at age 17, young William became apprenticed to a local wholesale chemists company. It was the first step towards a possible career in medicine or surgery, which in and of itself could be very rewarding financially. It would also keep him in the eyes of some less than savory young ladies who saw young William as their way out of poverty for themselves and their families. One such somewhat older yet still quite attractive woman was Miss Jane Widnail.

Widnail was a local redhead who would be hard to miss in any crowd. She had heard of William's windfall and could soon be found in his company. Before long she was with child and making demands on William Palmer. These demands came in the form of monetary "requests," which, as Jane discovered, he could not deliver on. Young William would have no money of his own for nearly four years until he

Dr. William Palmer (1824–1856) was known as a womanizer and gambler who lived far above his means.

turned twenty-one. That revelation did not end her demands on William, who looked for a way out of his problem. He decided that in order to pay for an abortion he could acquire the necessary funds from his employers, without their consent, of course. He failed in these attempts and came close to prosecution for the crime until his mother came forward to replace the missing funds. He did, however, succeed in ridding himself of one Jane Widnail.

Putting this incident well behind him, William at age 20 was studying at Stafford Infirmary. By that time he had acquired a solid reputation as a womanizer and gambler. It was said at the time that he had his eye on the wife of a man named Abley. William was not looking for marriage, but a mistress would do just fine. One evening, as the two men were having their brandy before the fireplace, Abley fell ill after consuming two full tumblers. He was later found dead and, naturally enough, suspicion fell on William. No charges were ever filed in this death but William decided that things were becoming far too untenable so he left Rugeley for London.

It was 1845 when William entered studies at Bart's Hospital in London to study the fine art of surgery. At Bart's his reputation continued as a gambler and ladies' man, as did his efforts at spending too much money on high living. He had acquired many friends during his studies, but most of them it can be said were friendlier to the money than to the man. Nevertheless, he did manage to stay out of trouble long enough to finish his medical studies and return to Rugeley a full-fledged surgeon. By that time however, he needed an infusion of cash.

He was not above marrying for money (taking after his mother), so he began to search for a suitable young lady. It would not take long for his eye, and his slim purse, to sight one Annie Brooks. Annie was the illegitimate daughter of a Colonel Brooks, who had decided early in life not to marry or to ever have children. The colonel's family had a long history of suicide, four of his brothers having killed themselves, so he decided not to pass on the family trait. However, he did have a young mistress and she eventually became pregnant with Annie. In time, Colonel Brooks did marry his mistress and adopt Annie, but not before Annie's mother had become a hopeless drunk.

Before long, Annie's father followed his brothers by shooting himself, leaving young Annie in the care of her mother. Her mother was soon declared unfit and Annie was sent off to live with a guardian named

Mr. Dawson. Her father had acquired a large estate and all was put in trust for Annie to receive on her 21st birthday. William Palmer, newly appointed town surgeon, began to court the beautiful and soon-to-be-rich Miss Annie Brooks. Mr. Dawson, however, would prove to be a careful guardian of Miss Brooks' affairs, and he was well aware of Dr. Palmer's reputation. Dawson was not about to allow his ward to court the young surgeon as long as he had any say in the matter. However, Annie Brooks was a very determined young lady who had become infatuated with the young doctor. Annie went so far as to hire solicitors who brought her cause to the attention of the Court of Chancery. Before long she was declared fit and responsible for her own affairs and was given permission to marry Dr. Palmer.

In 1847 William and Annie married in St. Nicholas Church, Abbots Cromley, and for a while seemed to settle down to a comfortable life. William had developed a well-paying surgical practice and had for the time being given up his gambling and running around. Annie, it would seem, had many charms, which kept William firmly planted at home and soon enough Annie became pregnant with her first child.

It would not be long after that that Annie looked up her mother who became part of her life again even though she would never give up the bottle. Young Willy was born and all seemed to be going well, but the reentry of Annie's mother into the situation seemed to have affected William in a bad way. William began to gamble once again and invested in a series of horses and racing stables. The money, however, was flowing out of the family coffers faster than it was being replaced. Something would need to be done—and with speed—as William's mistresses were also costing him a good deal of money. He was not about to give up his re-kindled roving eye.

Let the Killings Begin

It was at this point that Annie persuaded her now continuously drunk 49-year-old mother to live with her and William. William, it would seem, did not argue against his mother-in-law moving in with the growing family despite the fact that she needed constant care. Within two weeks his mother-in-law was dead, and with her "unexpected death" the young couple inherited nine houses once owned by Annie's father.

Despite the delirium tremens caused by constant drinking and her premature aging, "old" Mrs. Brooks' death was viewed by many in the small town as somewhat suspicious. However, no one openly accused the good doctor or Annie of anything underhanded in the woman's death.

A few months later found Dr. Palmer visiting his uncle whom he had not seen for a while. The next day the man was dead and again people began to talk. The suspicious death did not seem to bother Dr. Palmer's friend Mr. Blandon, who accepted the doctor's invitation for a visit. This visit had a business purpose as well since the good doctor owed Blandon a gambling debt. Blandon was dead within the week and the effect on Palmer's reputation was not lost on his wife: "My poor mother died here last year and now this man. What will people say?" Indeed, the townspeople had much to say, but nothing was done in the way of investigating the local surgeon who seemed not to notice the controversy. It was time to bury Mr. Blandon along with the debt and get on with other business.

Palmer's children did not seem to survive any better, as one after another died. The next four children with Annie lasted only a few weeks each, as all four died of convulsions. His illegitimate children did not fare any better, as both of them died soon after their births. By this time no fewer than ten individuals had died after coming into contact with Dr. Palmer and yet there was no solid evidence that any of them had met their fates at the doctor's hands—not yet at least. For a while Palmer would remain a successful for-profit serial killer.

Palmer continued to practice medicine and gamble a great deal, for the most part on the losing side of the equation. The doctor's true passion was gambling on the horses and making risky business speculations which caused him to use credit extensively. Death continued to follow the doctor as an £800 debt vanished with the untimely death of one Mr. Bly. The young Mr. Bly had met with Palmer to arrange payment and was dead the next day. At the funeral Palmer would explain to the young widow that it was Bly who owed him the money. "Of course I should not dream of pressing for payment now." It was not the only debt owed, as other creditors began to press for payments. It was then that his wife became ill.

It was 1854 and Annie had traveled to Liverpool to enjoy a concert. During the trip she caught a chill. Before long the chill worsened, and Dr. Palmer decided to call on an old doctor named Bamford. Dr. Bamford was an old family friend and Palmer felt he could be trusted. The old man came to the conclusion that Annie was suffering from "English cholers" (cholera). He prescribed calomel pills that accomplished nothing. Within a week Annie Palmer was dead. She had "gone to join her maker," reported Dr. Palmer, as the townspeople again began to speculate on another death close to the local doctor. This time however, the people had something substantial they could point to as a possible motive—Annie had a £13,000 insurance policy, which her husband cashed in on soon after her death. Nine months later the family housemaid gave birth to Palmer's son. It was clear that Dr. Palmer did not mourn for his dead wife for long, but when the child died weeks later very few in the small town thought that he was anything more than a serial killer. Yet even with his latest child's death he was not charged with any crimes!

Before long he was again deep in debt, having gone through all of the insurance money. He was also being blackmailed by one of his lady friends, who was, incidentally, the daughter of a Staffordshire policeman. He fell upon a new plan to enhance his monetary situation; this involved the cooperation of his alcoholic brother, Walter. Walter, it seemed, needed little of substance, but heavy drinking was a way of life for him, and one which had cost him his health and his wife. Walter eagerly agreed to have his life insured for around £400 or £500 in exchange for a never-ending supply of alcohol. He did not find out that he was actually insured for some £13,000. Nor did he realize that his brother William was deeply in debt. At a rate of five pints a day of hard drink it did not take long for brother Walter to become the latest to die in the general vicinity of Dr. Palmer. His death certificate noted that Walter Palmer had "died from apoplexy." Despite the certificate, the insurance company decided that poor Walter's not untimely demise was just a little too convenient and a detective was dispatched. For a while at least Dr. Palmer's money worries would continue.

It was at this point that an old friend named John Parsons Cook entered the scene. The two men had met at the horse races at Shrewsberg while Dr. Palmer was attempting to recoup his losses with a big day. It would not be a good day for Palmer, but his friend Cook came away with a considerable amount of cash. Naturally John Cook invited Palmer and a few other friends to dinner at his hotel for a little celebration. After dinner the brandy was served, it was later reported by Dr. Palmer, that Mr. Cook soon fell ill. Not one to miss an opportunity to aid a "dear old friend," Palmer insisted that his friend go with him to Rugeley, where Cook was put up at the Talbot Arms in town under the ever-watchful eye of his friend the doctor.

It did not take long for Cook to become violently ill. Not wanting his friend to miss out on any of his winnings as his health continued to deteriorate, Dr. Palmer asked a friend to forge Cook's signature on a document in order to help collect the funds: "He's too ill to sign it himself and I need the money now, desperately." Soon old Dr. Bamford was called to look in on John Cook and he ordered morphia pills. The prescription was given to Dr. Palmer who medicated his friend Cook—by noon John Cook was dead!

Despite the loss of his friend, Dr. Palmer decided that he should continue to collect the debt owed, which drew the suspicions of Cook's stepfather Mr. Stevens. Stevens at once suspected some type of foul play and demanded to see Cook's betting book in which Cook had kept very close track of his wagers. Palmer informed him that the book was missing, but the chambermaid told Mr. Stevens that Palmer had gone through Cook's pockets and other possessions. This was enough for Stevens, who promptly informed the authorities. An inquest was soon held. The post-mortem evidence given at the inquest found no strychnine or any other poison in the body but testimony was given that strychnine could cause death by tetanus, which was what the formerly healthy Mr. Cook had died from. It was also discovered that Palmer had purchased strychnine not long before Cook's death. With only circumstantial evidence to go on, a verdict was returned of "willful murder against Dr. William Palmer."

A Trial at Long Last

By the time the trial was underway the authorities had unearthed both Palmer's wife and brother. Investigation proved inconclusive in brother Walter's case and absolutely no poison was found in his wife's body. In a news report published in 1903 during the Borough Poisoner case, it was said that "the body of Ann Palmer, wife of William Palmer, who died in 1854, was found in a mummified condition 18 months later." In the 1850s the medical men did not seem to know that certain poisons would preserve a body after death. Palmer would not be charged in the cases of his wife or brother. He would only be tried for a single murder—that of John Cook.

At his murder trial six government witnesses stated that strychnine had been found in Cook's body while eleven fully qualified medical men testified on behalf of Dr. Palmer that no poison of any kind could be found. The prosecution could not bring forward a single witness to show that Dr. Palmer had given any poison at all to Mr. Cook or anyone else for that matter. From Susan Steinback we read:

> In the courtroom, [Ian] Burney (author of *Poison, Detection and Victorian Imagination*) argues, the status of toxicological evidence itself was on trial; [Britain's foremost toxicologist Alfred Swaine] Taylor, called on as an expert witness, argued that chemical evidence was limited and subject to interpretation, and found himself having to defend not only himself but his field.

Dr. Taylor would state: "Poison in a small dose is a medicine, and a medicine in a large dose is a poison." The bottom line to this case was the fact that without any clear evidence of poison, the murder was circumstantial,

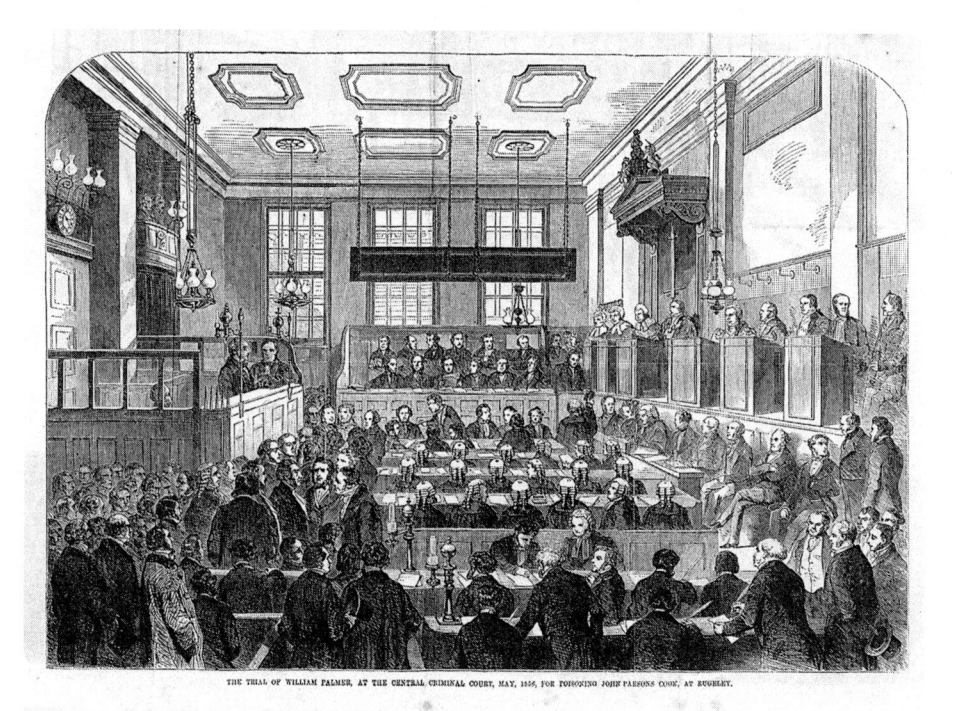

The trial of Dr. William Palmer, for the poisoning death of John Cook, was held at Rugeley in May 1856.

Dr. William Palmer was tried and executed for only one death, that of John Cook, but he was suspected of many more killings, including those of his mother-in-law, wife and several children.

as was all of the evidence against Palmer. Nevertheless, Palmer was found guilty of a single murder by poison in the Cook case by a jury and was sentenced to death. All in all Palmer could very well have murdered 14 during his career as a serial killer.

The Execution of William Palmer

It would become a memorable event for the people of Stafford on June 14, 1856, as some 35,000 to 40,000 people would witness the death drop at the gallows for the Rugeley Poisoner. All the doctor would ever say about the matter would be a comment to his solicitor Mr. Smith the night before he was hanged: "I am innocent of poisoning Cook by strychnine. All I ask is that you have Cook's body exhumed and that you will see to my mother and boy." It was hardly a glowing endorsement of his innocence. Perhaps he had really used antimony to dispatch his many victims, which would have been much more difficult to detect at the time, or perhaps he was just an innocent man in the wrong places at many very wrong times. Some legal scholars have looked at the case and wondered whether an innocent man went to the gallows. But then again, there was that mummified corpse of his wife to explain and of course all those other deaths!

The execution had been set for the usual 8 a.m. drop. During a meeting with his solicitor, Palmer gave him a copy of *The Sinner's Friend* on which he wrote: "The gift of William Palmer June 13th 1856." Palmer was also visited by his sister and two brothers who would later report that he had accepted his fate and was for the most part calm. At 1 a.m. he took some brandy and slept but only for a short while. At 2:30 a.m. he awoke and received a visit from the Reverend R.H. Goodacre, the prison chaplain. Goodacre would stay with Palmer until 5 a.m., all the while trying to get Palmer to confess to the murder to which he had been convicted. The priest failed, but returned for a second try from 6:30 to 7:30 a.m. All Palmer would say is that Cook had not been murdered by strychnine. At 7:30 a.m. Palmer had some tea and brandy.

By 7:40 a.m. it was getting close to the final event in Palmer's life as the prison governor, the High Sheriff Lt. Col. Dyott and Under Sheriff R.W. Hand entered the condemned's cell to inform him that it was time to carry out the death sentence. From the cell Palmer was led to the pressroom where he was introduced to the hangman George Smith. As Smith tied Palmer's hands, Palmer asked Smith to be sure to not draw the rope too tight around his neck before he sent Palmer on his way. Smith, the hangman from Dudley in the Midlands, held the office from 1849 to 1873 and was said to be very good at his work. He would also be credited with helping William Calcraft from Little Baddow near Chelmsford, Essex, hang serial killer Mary Ann Robson in 1873.

Palmer, now tightly bound, was taken to the small prison chapel where he was asked if he was satisfied with his sentence. Palmer's answer was firm and clear. "No!" The priest asked one more time for Palmer to confess that he was a murderer. When he refused, the priest walked away with the words, "Then your blood be on your own head."

At 7:53 a.m. Palmer was paraded in front of the other prisoners. He was accompanied by a large group of prison officials, including the chief constable, the Head Turnkey Mr. Chidley, warders George Plimmer and George Roberts, the Reverend H. Goodacre, the High Sheriff Lt. Col. Dyott, Under Sheriff T.D. Atkinson as well as the governor and deputy governor of the prison.

The group then walked out of the prison gate to where the portable gallows had been erected at 4 o'clock a.m. that morning. It had been raining heavily that night and early morning so the procession had to avoid several puddles of water. As he made it to the gallows the crowd began to cry "Murderer" but soon the crowd became hushed in anticipation of what was to occur. Many of the spectators had walked 10 miles from Rugeley to view the hanging and special trains had been put up from Birmingham, Stoke-on-Trent and London to satisfy the large crowds expected to arrive at the prison. The heavy drizzle did not seem to affect the mood of the crowd, and the mood was almost certainly bolstered by the fact that the local public houses had stayed open all night to accommodate the crowds. It was reported that the Greyhound Inn, just across the street from the prison, "did a roaring trade."

The local constabulary supplied 160 men, to which an additional 150 special officers were added for crowd control. Platforms had been set up to allow a clear view of the execution for those who could afford the front row price of a guinea. Rooftops were also rented out for a price to see the hanging.

It did not take long for Palmer to climb the ladder, which he was reported to have taken with a firm step. He was centered by Smith, and a white hood was soon covering Palmer's face, much to the disappointment of the crowd. Palmer made no death speech. He shook hands with the hangman who was quick to leave the platform and take his place at its side. The crowd was silent as the chaplain was reading and the only other sound the crowd heard was the bolt being slipped out of place to allow Palmer's body to drop. A gasp from the crowd overrode the chaplain's words as Palmer struggled for a short period and then nothing. The crowd did not witness a great death struggle.

The still warm corpse of Dr. William Palmer was allowed to hang from the gallows for the customary hour before it was cut down on that gray and rainy day and disposed of in the usual manner.

After Days

As for Dr. Taylor, he would continue his work in toxicology. Earlier, in 1848, he had published a book, *On Poisons in Relation to Medical Jurisprudence*. Considered an expert in poisons, he would revise his book based on his testimony and trial records of the Palmer case, which at the time had only served to destabilize the English courts when it came to relying on expert witnesses in poison cases. The controversy would surface again three years later as Dr. Taylor stepped forward to testify during the poison murder trial of Dr. Thomas Smethurst. Once again the new science of forensic medicine would be severely tested.

As a postscript to the murders of William Palmer the good citizens of Rugeley petitioned the prime minister for permission to change the name of their town, which was now linked closely to the killer. The prime minister was more than happy to give his permission for the name change, but with the stipulation that the new town would be named after him—Palmerston! The townsfolk declined the generous offer.

Madeleine Hamilton Smith, Arsenic "Not Proven" (1857)

"Had known each other as husband and wife."

Madeleine Hamilton Smith (c. 1836–c. 1920s) was a soft-spoken and refined beauty, there was no doubt of that. She was also as deadly as a viper with the poison to match. This combination of grace and lethality would hold the public's fascination for weeks as the British press closely followed this latest case of Victorian poison. Imaginative and secretive poisoning seems to be part of the Victorian landscape as once again the public was invited to read all about a young lady and her little bottle of arsenic.

Madeleine was the eldest child of an upper-class family from Glasgow, Scotland. As she entered her early teens she was sent to London to learn how to be a proper Victorian lady. It would be at Mrs. Alice Gorton's Academy for Young Ladies that Madeleine would learn how to properly walk and talk as well as practice the refined arts that come from exercise, piano lessons and "womanly crafts." The art of poisoning, however, was not on the list of approved subjects at Mrs. Gorton's academy. Madeleine would mention at a later date that there she had learned how to mix arsenic with water as a cosmetic to wash her face and arms.

In 1853 at the age of 18 she returned to her home, ready to challenge the world. Although she was a young socialite in Glasgow's polite society she was not above having a secret love affair or two with those "beneath her station." Thus in 1855 we find the lovely Madeleine engaged in an affair with a man who was not only a simple gardener and seed man's assistant (apprentice) named Pierre Emile L'Angelier (1823–1857), but also "foreign-born." This torrid affair could not be allowed to stand. Something would need to be done if her reputation was to be saved.

Emile had been born of French parents on the Channel Islands. Naturally, the family seed business was mostly directed towards the French-speaking population, but expansion was the way to increased sales and a better way of life for the family. His father decided that Emile should be apprenticed to a nearby nursery which had for a time catered to a small British clientele who visited the island. In 1842 Sir Francis Mackenzie took notice of young Emile's work and offered him a job on his estates in Scotland. Emile's father agreed, feeling that not only would his son be able to continue his education in the business, but his English would improve, allowing for greater business contacts for the family. However, when Mackenzie died not long after Emile arrived in Scotland, the young man was suddenly stranded in Edinburgh. Nevertheless, the new nursery liked his work and kept him on for the next few years. His job there included trips within Scotland as well as to his home in the Channel Islands and even over to France. He would finally settle in Glasgow where he would meet a delightful young lady named

Madeleine Hamilton Smith was a great beauty who, when she found a suitable man to marry, rid herself of her lover, Pierre Emile L'Angelier, using arsenic. She was released in 1857 following a verdict of "not proven."

Madeleine. At the time he was working as a simple warehouse clerk, but it would seem that he was just what Madeleine was looking for.

An Affair to Remember

Trial testimony would reveal that the couple would often meet late at night with the two carrying on long conversations as Madeleine leaned out of her bedroom window. Letters they exchanged would also reveal that they would plan to meet each other on the street in a casual manner or in nearby shops. Thanks to Emile's friend, one Miss Mary Perry, the couple also spent time together at Perry's home—secretly of course. Before long Emile would find himself invited into Madeleine's room and the affair began in earnest. It was a situation which would cause some papers covering the later trial to refer to her as a "naughty charmer." Certainly she reveled in thumbing her well-shaped nose at the locals in her well-heeled group. Her trial for murder would be another thing entirely.

Madeleine's first note would set the tone of the relationship.

My Dear Emile
I do not feel as if I were writing you for the first time.
[We] have become as familiar friends.
May we long continue so.
Madeleine

Her earlier affairs had apparently not caught the attention of Madeleine's parents, who surely would have put an end to them at once. When they found out about Emile they thought they had put an end to Madeleine's indelicacies. Therefore they felt free to search for a suitable man from Glasgow's upper class to court their daughter. In fact, a suitor would be forced upon her. Madeleine's father, James Smith (1808–1863), chose a young businessman named William Harper Minnoch. Mr. Smith had met the young man through his work as an architect, a profession which had made Mr. Smith quite wealthy. September 1856 found Minnoch staying over at Mr. Smith's summer home on the Clyde where he and Madeleine could become better acquainted, spending a great deal of time together. This arrangement seems to have worked at least for a while. In January 1857 William proposed to Madeleine who perhaps simply gave in to her father.

At this point Emile became expendable, as Madeleine seemed to accept her father's choice, which held the promise of a good and proper life ahead. However, it would not be quite that easy to dispose of the very determined Pierre Emile L'Angelier. After all, Madeleine had promised to marry him and he had a large number of letters from the young lady to prove it. He had also been informed that the young lady's mother, Janet, had approved of their union, which of course was one of many little white lies told by Madeleine to keep Emile in the picture as long as she wanted him—and not a day longer. Even though Emile had kept all of Madeleine's letters she had followed his instructions and had burned all of her correspondence.

Madeleine would write:

> I trust your honor as a gentleman that you will not reveal anything that may have passed between us. I shall feel obliged by your bringing me my letters and likeness on Thursday evening at seven. Be at the area gate and [the housemaid] will take the parcel from you. On Friday night, I shall send you all your letters, likeness, etc.

The critical point in the now broken relationship came when Emile threatened to tell her father that they had "known each other as husband and wife." In his mind they were already married and would state that this was true "in the eyes of god." Emile had heard the rumors that an engagement had been made between Madeleine and Minnoch. Madeleine wrote a heated denial, but Emile knew that his situation had indeed changed. Madeleine was convinced Emile would show the letter to her father. Something had to be done! And Miss Smith, being a very proper Victorian young lady, knew just how to dispose of the situation.

> As there is coolness on both sides, our engagement had better be broken. Altogether, I think owing to coolness and indifference—nothing else—that we had better, for the future, consider ourselves as strangers.

Despite the tone of the new letters, the evening of March 22, 1857, found Emile once again secretly below Madeleine's window at Number 7 Blythswood Square, held in a long conversation. During that conversation his lady love served him cups of coffee and hot chocolate. It did not take long for Emile to begin to complain of stomach pains and he begged off the conversation to return home. The very sick Emile barely made it back to his lodgings in great pain as he stumbled along the dark streets of Glasgow. He would make it to his room in Franklin Place at a little past 2 a.m. He was helped to his room by his landlady who inquired if he had eaten anything which may have caused the problem. Emile told her that he had not, but the landlady would recall that this was the third such attack of stomach pains in the past two months. It seemed that Madeleine needed a bit of practice before she found just the right amount of poison to finish the job. This was, after all, if reports are correct, her first murder! He soon collapsed on his bed. At 5 a.m. the landlady saw that her boarder was not getting any better so she went out to find a local doctor. She was told by the doctor to simply give the young man laudanum with water along with a poultice, not suspecting that a poisoning had occurred.

The doctor would see his patient at seven that morning and again at 11 a.m. Upon the second visit the landlady would report that her boarder was quiet and resting well. When the doctor examined Emile he exclaimed, "The man is dead!" Emile had died with what was reported by a coroner's inquest to be enough arsenic in his body to kill 40 men!

A close examination of the evidence in Emile's room, which included young Madeleine's letters and Emile's diary, showed that there really was only one suspect in his death—the lovely Madeleine Smith. On March 31 Madeleine was arrested by the sheriff-substitute of Lanarkshire. She reported that she did indeed know the victim quite well and had in fact purchased poison. She was calm and clear in her statement and was for all outward appearances cooperative. But murder was another thing altogether and she was not about to admit that to anyone. "I never administered, or caused to be administered, to M. L'Angelier arsenic or anything injurious—and this I declare to be truth." Nevertheless, the coroner's jury delivered a verdict of "Willful murder against Madeleine Hamilton Smith in the death of Pierre Emile L'Angelier." A jury would have to sort all of this out.

The Trial

One of the greatest legal minds in Scotland at the time was hired to represent Madeleine. John Inglis, a well-known defense counsel, knew that he had a tough job ahead and he would use every method he could to cast doubt on the prosecutor's case. He would, however, not be able to call Madeleine to the stand, as British law at the time would not permit it. Madeleine's letters would be admitted as evidence, as would Emile's papers found in his room. Inglis argued successfully that Emile's diary, on the other hand, could not be used in court, as Scottish law demanded the ability to cross-examine witnesses. This could not be done with the entries in Emile's diary, of course. The jury would not hear from Emile.

The public's clamor for details of the case was intense and crowds gathered daily outside the courthouse in Edinburgh. Needless to say, the press reported on all aspects of the trial, much of which was mere speculation as the penny flyers flew off the presses. Special note was made of the defendant's remarkable calmness throughout the trial. She also refused all food and drink during the trial, but did keep a vial of smelling salts nearby, which she never used.

During her nine-day trial it was shown that she had made several purchases of arsenic in the weeks before Emile had been murdered. Indeed, Madeleine did not deny that fact, but she stated in her police interrogation report that she was somewhat vain about her appearance and had purchased the poison to use as a face wash. Although the jury felt that the fact that she did not attempt to conceal her purchases stood well in her favor they did not believe that her purchases were to be used in this way. With this in mind the defense would go on the attack, calling several expert witnesses to testify that arsenic was indeed used as a cosmetic. They also testified that its use was not unusual. The defense further attacked the arsenic found in Emile's body, bringing witnesses to the stand who testified that Emile had made several suicide attempts prior to his eventual death. The defense was also able to show that Emile's first attack had come at least two days before Madeleine's first purchase of arsenic.

The defense team led by Inglis would also attack claims by the prosecution that Emile had met with Madeleine on the night of his death. No one could testify that they had seen the couple together for at least three weeks before his death. This part of the defense case ended with Madeleine's sister Janet testifying that Madeleine had not gotten out of bed the night of March 22, the evening that stood as Emile's last. The prosecutors could show no evidence to the contrary.

Even though all of the circumstantial evidence seemed to point towards Madeleine Smith as the killer, the jury felt that a strong enough case had not been made against her.

The Surprise Verdict

After nine days of testimony the jury would spend a mere 30 minutes in deliberation on July 9. There was silence in the courtroom before the verdict was read, but a gasp was heard when the results were read in court. The jury voted a purely Scottish verdict of "not proven," which freed her from the gallows. Not proven in Scottish law means that the jury did not believe that she was innocent, but could not convict on such a small body of circumstantial evidence. It was simply not a strong enough case. Madeleine was sent home that afternoon, still as calm as ever.

After her sensational trial and unexpected release, *The Scotsman* continued to follow the story and ran an article which stated that a witness had come forward with critical evidence in the case. The witness was reported to have seen a young man outside of Madeleine's house talking with her on the night before Emile died. This was *the* critical evidence which had been missing in the case, but because the trial was already underway when the witness came forward this testimony was not allowed to be brought forward. If this evidence had been allowed, Madeleine Smith may very well have made her way to the gallows with her pretty neck lengthened by the sharp snap of a sturdy hemp rope! But alas, most of the press was certainly not to be found on her side.

The *Scotsman* would print that Madeleine Smith is "either the most fortunate of criminals or the most unfortunate of women."

The *Examiner* would print a slightly different view of her case: "To Madeleine Smith alone his horrible death seems to have been no shock, no grief, and she demeaned herself [at] her trial as if L'Angelier had never had a place in her affections. If it had been a trial for poisoning a dog the indifference could not have been greater."

From the *Glasgow Sentinel* we may read that Smith was "as much the seducer as the seduced. And when once the veil of modesty was thrown aside, from the first a very frail and flimsy one, the woman of strong passion and libidinous tendencies at once reveals herself ... one of those abnormal spirits that now and then rise up in society to startle and appall."

The Glasgow Citizen took a decidedly different look at the matter, siding with the young lady: "In her first efforts at retrieval [of her letters], she found herself not in the arms of a protector, but in the coils of a reptile."

Life Goes On

Madeleine's life after she was released from jail has become confused over the years. Because of the great notoriety of her trial and the scandal it brought to proper Scottish society, she left her home in Scotland and eventually settled in London. William Harper Minnoch was long out of the picture by then, but there really was no real love lost there as it would have been an arranged marriage at best. In London she would eventually marry an artist and draftsman named George Wardle on July 4, 1861, and in time she raised a family which included two children. Even at this distance the men of the newspapers never stopped seeking her out for details of the death and her newfound life. That however, is not the final mysterious word on Madeleine Smith.

The beginning of the 20th century found Madeleine, at over 60 years old, no longer the great beauty she had been. It seems she had separated from her husband and this is where the official trail ends. Rumor and speculation then take the fore as she is reported to be found as far afield as Australia, France, New Zealand, New Orleans and finally New York City, reportedly dying in her early 90s in the late 1920s. There is even a report that she was approached by a film company to appear in a film based upon her most interesting life. The truth is that there are no confirmed reports of what actually became of Madeleine (Smith) Wardle, who seems to have been able to finally escape the notoriety of a verdict of "not proven" which had haunted much of her life. "Not proven" had become "unknown" for the once beautiful yet very deadly young socialite from Glasgow, Scotland. One thing, though, is very clear—Madeleine never admitted to poisoning Emile, taking anything she knew about those long-ago events to the grave. So there will always be that part of the case, at least as far as the law is concerned, which forever will remain "not proven."

Constance Emily Kent and the Road Hill House Murder (1860)

"The magistrates directed Constance's arrest..."

When nursemaid Elizabeth Gough went to look in on four-year-old Francis Savile Kent at 7:15 a.m. on June 29, 1860, she found the child was missing. She soon raised the alarm and informed Mr. and Mrs. Kent that the child was gone. An immediate search located the child in an outside toilet in the garden area with his throat cut and a stab wound to the chest. Clearly the child had been murdered. It was discovered that there was no trace of blood in the home, but there was a window open in the drawing room near where the little boy had been put to bed. The servants were clear that it had been closed that evening so the child could not have crawled out of it. He had been taken from the bedroom of his nursemaid sometime during the night. Focus of the investigation would be on the nursemaid; only later would investigators take a very careful look at the little boy's half-sister Constance Emily Kent. When she was arrested for murder the press would report that she was "a difficult child." This was Victorian press speak for "she was not right mentally."

The small village of Road (Rode) in Wiltshire had a murder to investigate and the local police superintendent Foley soon found that this case was more than he was prepared to handle. Foley began to investigate the nursemaid who was responsible for Francis. Local town magistrates became impatient due to what they perceived as a very slow-moving investigation. The magistrates contacted the Home Office for assistance from Scotland Yard. However, this request went forward without the chief constable's agreement that assistance was needed. The forces of money and power were beginning to be felt very early in this case and because of it justice would certainly be delayed. Proper channels were being bypassed and it was only after a second request that Scotland Yard sent their most senior detective, and by 1860, one of their best-known, Detective Inspector Jonathan Whicher. Whicher requested that he be accompanied by a detective sergeant which was a first using this teaming of investigators on a case. After this case it would become the standard for Scotland Yard investigations.

The Ambitious Samuel Kent

Samuel Savile Kent was an ambitious factory inspector in Road who pushed himself for promotion and better prospects for his family in the small town. His personal efforts to promote himself along with his locally-known family problems made the family subject to much gossip. This community disapproval had caused Mr. Kent and his growing family to move several times. There was never much of a serious problem and it could have been that the people in Road with "small town ways" simply did not like Samuel Kent. Kent had married his first wife Mary Ann around 1828 and between 1829 and 1845 she would have ten children. Her daughter Constance Emily was born in February of 1844.

Naturally, with all of these children around Mr. and Mrs. Kent, now doing quite well in their large home, decided that the children needed a resident governess. Before long Mary Drew Pratt was living in the home and taking care of the children. Not long after that Miss Pratt was sharing a bed with Mr. Kent. Once again the local tongues were wagging as it did not seem to be all that much of a secret to the pub-going townspeople. This was not the proper thing to do in a proper Victorian home.

In May of 1852 Mrs. Kent suddenly died, which devastated 8-year-old Constance. Constance would blame Miss Pratt, suspecting subpar nursing of Mary Ann during her short illness. She would also

Sixteen-year-old Constance Emily Kent killed her four-year-old stepbrother in 1860 but nothing came of the scant evidence in the case until Miss Kent came forward five years later and confessed to the crime.

resent the fact that in August of 1853 her father married Mary Pratt, moving her from sleep-in governess to stepmother to Mr. Kent's ten children. If later reports are accurate Constance hated what had happened, but could do nothing about it—for the moment.

The marriage of Samuel and his new wife would produce five more children including Francis in 1856. All of this time Constance's hate for her stepmother continued to grow until 16-year-old Constance could stand it no longer. She wanted revenge for the unexpected death of her mother and her father's infidelity. Her focus fell on four-year-old Francis.

The Murder and Investigation

When the child was first reported missing that June morning, the actions of Mr. Kent seem, on the surface at least, to have been somewhat strange. Rather than rely upon the local police he personally drove across the county boundary to Trowbridge to speak directly to Superintendent Foley. He did not seek help from the local police, at least at first, though they were notified. It was noted at the time by investigators that perhaps Mr. Kent knew a good deal more about the events which had occurred in the home than he would or could later admit. It is possible that he knew that his daughter Constance had committed the murder and he may have even been part of a cover-up. Mr. Kent reported to Foley that the little boy had been taken or "lost wrapped in a blanket." However, until the body was found there was no evidence that a blanket was involved. Mr. Kent would never be questioned properly as to how he knew critical details of the incident before they could properly have been known.

The coroner's inquest that followed the murder was controversial. Money and power seemed to be in play as the coroner originally restricted the witness list to police offices, medical examiners and the servants in the home. Only upon the insistence of the jury would the family be questioned and even that was of a limited nature. Clearly, something was being covered up. Nevertheless, the coroner did travel to the Kent home to interview Constance and her brother William. He did not ask any questions of Mr. or Mrs. Kent under oath. Only a brief conversation—off the record—occurred.

As Detective Inspector Jonathan Whicher stepped into the investigation he found that there was a great deal which had not been done and that powerful people were interfering with the case. He and Detective Sergeant Williamson felt that a good deal of the investigation was being unfairly subjected to the direction of and interference by local magistrates. He and his fellow officer were not allowed to work the case effectively as should have been the case. Whicher would concentrate his inquires upon a missing nightdress belonging to Constance. Along with other circumstantial evidence the inspector felt that the nightdress would have been blood-soaked and thus clearly expose Constance to murder charges. The laundress for the Kents reported that she normally washed three nightdresses for Constance. Whicher, during his investigation, established that Constance took a nightdress from the laundry basket as a ruse to blame the local laundry woman for the lack of the proper amount of nightwear. This flimsy excuse by Constance for not being able to account for the missing nightdress did not impress the inspector, who promptly reported his suspicions to the local magistrates. The magistrates would proceed in the proper direction, but Whicher would have precious little time to solve this case.

From the Metropolitan Police website on the Kent case we learn that "the magistrate directed Constance's arrest and gave Whicher seven days to prepare a case. Mr. Kent provided a barrister for his daughter who dominated proceedings. Constance was released on bail and the case was later dropped." In court her counsel T.B. Saunders would declare that "from first to last there was not the slightest ground for justifying suspicion against her." It was also suggested that she could not have "carried the heavy lad single-handed." There must, according to her defense, have been two others or a stronger person to do the crime. As the investigators continued and Constance's release was reported, the newspapers began rather sympathetic coverage of Constance though the *Times* would report that "public interest had manifestly decreased." The press was also very critical of Inspector Whicher, who continued to look closely at the 16-year-old. Unfortunately, even though Whicher was able to locate the nightdress, the good inspector was soon back in his office at Scotland Yard. A half-burned nightdress, bloodstained of course, had been found in the basement boiler, but it was not enough for those in power to close this case.

After Scotland Yard withdrew, the local police two months later, under the direction of the magistrates, arrested nursemaid Elizabeth

Gough for a second time. Their efforts would eventually fail, as the prosecution was never able to bring forward any evidence that she had been involved in the murder or the cover-up in any way. They had gone after the lowest and weakest rung on the ladder and they had failed.

A Postscript to Murder

It was five years before the Road Hill House murder was definitively solved. An investigation did not ultimately solve the case; a confession brought it to a close. However, even then there would be a good deal of the case which would not make sense. At the time Constance wrote: "It has been stated that my feelings of revenge were excited in consequence of cruel treatment. This is entirely false. I have received the greatest kindness from both the persons accused of subjecting me to it. I have never had any ill-will towards either of them on account of their behaviour to me, which has been very kind."

In April of 1865, Constance Kent went with her attorney to the Bow Street magistrate's court to confess to the murder of Francis Savile Kent. She had spent some time in a religious institute in France as well as in a religious institution in Brighton St. Mary's Home for Penitent Females in the south of England. While there she had confessed to the Mother Superior, who directed her to cleanse her soul of her guilt. Other reports would state: "Constance has come under the influence of the Anglo-Catholic priest, the Rev. Arthur Wagner, and it was in making her Easter duties that she felt the need to confess to the reverend gentleman." Wagner held the post of principal at the religious institution in Brighton which Constance was attending at the time. At the Court she would plead guilty to murder and was sentenced to death. Her sentence would soon be commuted to life imprisonment and later to 20 years penal servitude. She then faded from history, taking with her the real story of what happened during the Road Hill House murder of 1860.

From the October 24, 1865, *Times* of London we may read a report some five years after the murder. "The circumstances of this mysterious murder have never been forgotten,—how, nearly five years ago the body of a male child, which had been missed from its cot, was found in a privy outside the house, and how, suspicion having been directed towards Miss Kent ... she was examined before the local magistrates, at the instigation of Inspectors Whicher and Williamson, and acquitted of the charges."

The Confession

Constance wanted to relieve her mind and a full confession was the only way. She would tell the court that she had waited that evening until all of the family and servants were in their rooms and surely asleep. She then silently walked downstairs to the drawing room where Francis was in his cot. She opened the closed shutters and window and from there took the child, wrapped in a blanket, leaving the bedsheet still in place as cover. Earlier she had placed matches in the privy as well as secretly taking her father's razor. She then walked to the privy and killed Francis. This act was clearly, by her confession, one of premeditated revenge and not a spontaneous act taken in a rage.

After the murder Constance returned to her room. At this point she discovered that the murder had left two distinct bloodstains on her nightdress. Removing her nightdress, she washed the stain and set it out to dry. However, in the morning she found that the bloodstains had not been fully removed. Hiding the nightdress, she eventually made her way to the kitchen boiler where she burned the only real evidence which could connect her to the murder of her half-brother. She was of course not fully successful in her work. There would be no mention of anyone helping her either with the murder or her cover-up.

By the time news of Constance's confession to the Road Hill House murder reached London, Inspector Whicher had retired from Scotland Yard due to ill health. Once again we may read from the Metropolitan Police website.

> The confession from Constance came too late to save the career of Jonathan Whicher who had been pensioned before Constance's appearance at Bow Street confirmed his original suspicion. It is a classic illustration of how early investigations were directed heavily by magistrates, of the influence which well-to-do people could exert over local police officers, and of the importance of immediately searching and questioning the whole household at the scene of a crime, regardless of social status.

Nevertheless, Inspector Whicher was able to read published editorials from some of the newspapers, which had at one time been so critical of his investigation into this case. This served to completely vindicate his original suspicions in the Kent murder. The only problem with the accepted final solution to this murder is the very real possibility that Mr. Samuel Kent, although not suspected of the murder of his son Francis, may very well have been involved in the cover-up. And what of her brother William? Did he know more than he was willing to admit about the murder? Was he fully involved? We shall never know as by confession Constance, who had been suggested after the murder to have been at times "mentally unbalanced," was the only one to step forward and confess to the murder.

Dr. Edward William Pritchard, Death by Antimony (1865)

"I acknowledge the justice of my sentence."

The dubious but well-earned honor of being the last man hanged before a public crowd in Scotland goes to one Dr. Edward William Pritchard (c. 1825–1865) after his trial and conviction for (at least) two murders by poison. And to say the least it was a grand and noisy affair with some 100,000 in attendance for this final "Gala Day." The public evidently did not want to miss this last event, as they came early and stayed late.

Born around 1825 in Hampshire, England, to a naval family, Pritchard's early life is not well documented. Even his medical education has a limited paper trail and he is said to have "questionable medical qualifications," most often said to have been obtained from Leyden University, yet there is no documentation of his obtaining a degree. He also claimed to have studied at Kings College Hospital in London, under "two eminent surgeons." There also seems to be some claim by Pritchard to have graduated from the college hospital in 1846, but again there is no real paper trail.

In 1846, despite his rather questionable references, he was somehow able to obtain a commission in the Royal Navy as an assistant surgeon. During the last operational days of the HMS *Victory* he served onboard her in that capacity. In 1850 while still serving in the Navy and based in Portsmouth he met and married Miss Mary Jane Taylor. Mary Jane was well off at the time, being the daughter of an Edinburgh silk merchant who was quite prosperous in the trade. A year later Pritchard resigned his commission and took a position as a general practitioner in Hunmanby, Yorkshire, Scotland. He was shortly after appointed as governmental medical officer to an area known as the Bridlington Number Three Area. Before long he had established surgeries in Filey and Hunmanby as well as a third office in Bridlington across from Lloyd Hospital. He was soon making a good but not rich living as a doctor, but he wanted much more.

Not a man to miss Sunday church services, he would nevertheless create a good deal of commotion whenever he received a call from his groom that his services as a doctor were required. It was noted that he would loudly bolt from the church in a great disruptive manner before riding away dramatically and quite noisily—more suggestive of a hack movie plot then would be called upon in real life. In a word his dramatics was his way of proclaiming his importance to the community.

Nevertheless, Pritchard found that he despised the life of a simple country doctor. He found the long hours, low pay, and little fame was none to his liking. In addition, it is said that his local colleagues were somewhat less than satisfied not only with his lack of medical skills and demonstrated weak character, but they also tired of his boasting, which included tall tales and outright lies about his military service. The fact that he considered himself to be a great lover, constantly and loudly boasting of his conquests, certainly made him the butt of jokes among his medical colleagues. They seemed to know better as they laughed and related stories of Pritchard behind his back.

Dr. Edward William Pritchard was the last man to be publicly hanged in Scotland when his sentence for two poisoning deaths was carried out on July 28, 1865.

Needless to say, he had few if any real friends in the area. With his somewhat indifferent reputation and a growing debt, Pritchard began to look to other areas for income. All things considered, the good doctor decided that he had had enough of country life and moved back to the Berkeley Terrace section of Glasgow, Scotland, in 1860. The wagging tongues were left behind, but not his need for attention and money.

Dr. Pritchard soon made himself a good life in Glasgow with his wife Mary Jane and their five children to the point where the now respectable doctor was able to afford servants to help manage his home. He now had the money that he felt was rightly his. After setting up his practice he attempted to enhance his reputation by joining several learned societies, including the Athenaeum Club and the Masons. He also began a series of public lectures on his reported travels, most of which never occurred. This included a tall tale of a close and continuing friendship with Italian patriot Giuseppe Garibaldi (1807–1882). His bragging had not stopped, only increased in tone and tale. It was at this time that he purchased a Doctor of Medicine diploma which was prominently displayed in his office. If it was not mentioned by visitors he would certainly mention it himself.

However, all was not as well as surface appearances would have indicated. Pritchard was alleged to be having relations with other women in town, including, according to some reports, the servant girl he had living in his home. Any problems she may have caused were soon removed in 1863 when a small fire mysteriously broke out in her upstairs room. After the fire was put out the girl was found dead in her bed. An investigation into her death showed that the girl had made no attempt to leave her room or for that matter get out of her bed. Investigators suspected that she had been murdered where she lay. Suspicion was naturally laid at the feet of Dr. Pritchard, but there was no real evidence of foul play so the death was ruled accidental. With this ruling Dr. Pritchard was able to win a claim against the insurance company as he had been "generous" enough to the young lady to make certain that her life had been insured. With the help of the insurance money Pritchard moved his family to 22 Royal Terrance and then further on to Clarence Place. It would be Mary Jane's mother who would help the family purchase their house on Clarence Place. Pritchard, despite his good income, was still spending more than he was able to take in.

Naturally, with the "unexpected" loss of the servant girl, the family would soon need to hire another. Pritchard would do the hiring. This became another opportunity for Dr. Pritchard to try out his charms on 15-year-old Mary McLeod, which became complicated in 1864 with the young girl becoming pregnant. There are some reports that both his wife and mother-in-law knew about his relationship with Mary and this was later brought forward as a possible motive for murder. The secret that he shared with Mary McLeod was that he had promised to marry her, but only upon the condition that his present wife passed away. With this in mind he was able to convince the servant girl from Islay to undergo an abortion, which of course he was happy to perform himself being that he was a doctor and all. It was a successful operation and the secret arrangement was still in place.

A Death or Two

This of course did not remove the problem of having a wife who was stubbornly healthy and showing no signs of dying any time soon. If this kept up she could very well outlive him and that would simply not do at all! He still wanted the servant girl, so he needed to develop a new plan since his wife and mother-in-law were both in the way. In November of 1864 things seemed to turn in a different direction. His wife Mary Jane had started having dizzy spells accompanied by fits of vomiting. The doctor, it would seem, had decided to trade up and keep his promise to the young, still available and seemingly willing Mary McLeod.

In order to present a good front, Dr. Pritchard called in another doctor to see to his wife. This new doctor soon came to the conclusion that Mrs. Pritchard was being poisoned. Suspecting that the husband could very well be involved, the doctor wrote to Mary Jane's brother, suggesting that Mrs. Pritchard should be immediately sent to the hospital for urgent care. After a conversation with Mrs. Taylor, Mary Jane's mother decided that it would be best if she went to Clarence Place, Sauchiehall Street, to nurse her very sick daughter. This was to be a fatal mistake for both mother and daughter.

It did not take long for Mrs. Taylor to begin exhibiting the same symptoms which had taken hold of her now very ill daughter. Mrs. Taylor would last until February 24 or 25, 1865, when she died of "gastric fever," according to the death certificate filled out by her son-in-law Dr. Pritchard. Nevertheless, it would later be fully established that both Mrs.

Pritchard and Mrs. Taylor were poisoned, and that this was the cause of both women's deaths. About a month later Dr. Pritchard was filling out another death certificate stating that his wife had died of "apoplexy." His wife had an attack of severe cramps on March 17 after taking medicine provided by her husband. She would die two days later. It was time to bury his two little problems and move on to other much younger matters. However, there was to be a slight complication or two.

Mrs. Taylor's husband Michael had at first asked Dr. James Paterson who was well known and had been in medical practice for more than 30 years to sign the death certificate for Mary Jane. However, Dr. Paterson was not convinced that it was a fully natural death and subsequently declined the request. Taking up the task, Dr. Pritchard had written, "Primary cause, Paralysis: duration, twelve hours. Secondary cause: Apoplexy: duration, one hour." It was now time to arrange for a funeral at Grange Cemetery in Edinburgh. Before his wife was buried, the coffin was taken to Mr. Taylor's home where Pritchard insisted that it be opened. At that point Pritchard leaned over and kissed his dead wife on the lips with reportedly a "great deal of feeling." In the end Pritchard proved to be a callous criminal even though he always presented a proper and polished front to the world around him. He was a hidden serial killer of the first order and he was acting before an audience.

However, Dr. Pritchard's plans would come to nothing as the procurator-fiscal would receive an anonymous letter written in a slight hand about the good doctor. (The servant girl, perhaps?) The letter suggested that foul play rather than natural death had taken the two women and further that Dr. Pritchard was involved. Before long both women were exhumed. When a post-mortem was performed it was found that both had died from antimony and tincture of aconite poisoning and the only suspect was indeed Dr. Edward William Pritchard. Both women had been taking opium (Battley's Sedative Solution) for pain which was available to Pritchard, and the solution was thought to have been laced with poison.

The End of Days

Before long Pritchard found himself arrested as he left the train on Queen Street Station in Glasgow and charged with two counts of murder. The coroner's jury had easily brought in a verdict of "Willful murder in the case of Edward William Pritchard." His trial, which lasted five days in July 1865 at the High Court of Justiciary in Edinburgh before Lord Inglis, found him guilty mostly on circumstantial evidence since no one had seen the poison or anyone administrating it, but clearly there were no other realistic suspects. Throughout the trial his relatives supported his constant claims of innocence and to some degree the general public's opinion was that he had not killed his wife. The press of course were happy to play on the possibility that an innocent man was on trial. Nevertheless, the jury had spoken. However, there was a very real possibility that young Mary McLeod could have, directed by Pritchard, been the individual who actually administered the poison to both victims as she had a direct and careful hand in their care. The trial would become noteworthy due to the hard-fought battle played out for Pritchard's life and because of the excellent medical evidence brought to it from both the defense and prosecution sides of the case.

His execution on July 28 at 8:15 in the morning would be remembered as a grand affair with estimates of 100,000 on hand to see the last execution to be held where the public would be invited to witness the "Gala Day" in front of the South Prison at the Green in Glasgow. Always up to the task was executioner William Calcraft, ready to give the killer his due at the end of a short drop of the rope. In front of the crowd at Jail Square they got their money's worth. Pritchard was reported by the press to have been "launched into eternity" at the appropriate time and in the appropriate manner. The show would end an hour later as he was cut down. At that point the crowds made their way to the local pubs which reported a good business on that "Gala Day."

Before he took his well-earned drop Pritchard would state, "I acknowledge the justice of my sentence."

There was now no doubt in anyone's mind that he had murdered both women so his sentence was indeed a just one. However, no mention was made about the first servant girl in 1863. Nevertheless, he could only be hanged once, and justice would take its eventual course.

The Reverend Norman MacLeod Barony Church recorded in a letter to his wife the final moments of double murderer Dr. Pritchard.

> Please do not excite yourself when you see by the papers that I have been with Pritchard to the last. I thought it rather cowardly to let Oldham of St. Mary's Episcopal Church do this work alone when we had shared the previous portion of it. So I offered to go, and I am glad I did. I saw it all from first

to last; was with him in his cell, and walked at his back till he reached the scaffold. As to his behaviour, strange to say, no patriot dying for his country, no martyr dying for his faith, could have behaved with greater calmness, dignity, and solemnity! He was kind and courteous (as he always was) to all; prayed with us with apparent deep earnestness; told Oldham to tell his sister that he repented of a life of transgression; was glad the second confession was suppressed, etc. He said before the magistrates, with a low bow and a most solemn voice:

"I acknowledge the justice of my sentence." He had told those about him on leaving his cell: "I want no one to support me," and so he marched to the scaffold with a deadly pale face but erect head, as if he marched to the sound of music. He stood upright as a bronze statue, with the cap over his face and the rope round his neck. When the drop fell, all was quiet. Marvelous and complex character. Think of a man so firm as to say to Oldham:

"I am glad you have come with your gown and bands."

Strange to say, I felt no excitement whatever, but calm and solemn. I gazed at him while praying for his poor soul till the last. But I won't indulge in sensation sketches. May God forgive all my poor sinful services, and accept of me and mine as lost sinners redeemed through Jesus Christ!

I am forever set against all public executions. They brutalize the people, and have no more meaning to them than bull-baiting or a gladiatorial combat. And then the fuss, the babble and foam of gossip, the reporting for the press, etc., over that black sea of crime and death!

As perhaps a final statement on how much Dr. Pritchard was despised by his fellows one may view the Honors Board at the Filey Royal Masonic Lodge. On the board there now stands a place which will forever remain blank. Pritchard's name has been completely expunged from that most memorable list of Masons by the very men who had at one time honored his name. Needless to say, Pritchard's name is no longer mentioned at the lodge.

Christiana Edmunds, the Chocolate Cream Poisoner (1870–1872)

"A long history of insanity."

To some who knew Christiana Edmunds (c. 1835–1907), she was a kind, soft-spoken and educated lady who simply loved chocolate creams. It has been said that she was quite charming to speak to. To others she was an ill-tempered spinster quick to pass judgment upon those who displeased her. No matter what the overall personal opinion was, all could agree that upon reflection she was also quite insane!

Christiana lived in a lodging house at 16 Gloucester Place, Brighton, with her elderly mother who had been widowed some years earlier. Later, during her murder trial, her mother would inform the court that there had been "a long history of insanity" in her family. She hoped this would help save her daughter's life. In fact, her widowed mother would claim that both sides of the family had been affected with insanity. It would appear that Christiana had not escaped that fate as she came to see chocolate creams and other foods as weapons for serial murder. At least, she would *try* to kill more than one, but would be stopped short of her goal. This method would not prove to be a very effective one as only one would-be victim would fail to recover—but one was certainly enough. She would use her weapon first upon a rival for the affections of a gentleman and then for a series of attacks which seem even today to have no real motive other than in the disturbed mind of a young woman who had been hurt in some way.

Dr. Thomas Beard was a married man who held offices very near the lodgings of Christiana Edmunds at 64 Grand Parade, Brighton. From his surgery, whose rooms are now long gone and are now the property of Brighton University, it would be a short walk to his secret love's rooms. Before long he and Christiana were exchanging affectionate letters and perhaps more than that. The doctor would not confirm his affections as he still had his wife to think of and in Victorian times scandal was not good for business. Christiana soon convinced herself that the doctor was only in love with her and no longer wished to be married to his wife. It is unclear as to whether or not Dr. Beard encouraged that point of view. It did not take long for the unstable Christiana to decide that her rival Mrs. Beard was in the way of her advances upon the good doctor so a visit was planned to his wife. It was September 1870 and it was time to act decisively if she was to gain the upper hand. A gift of some fine chocolate was soon personally delivered to Mrs. Beard by Christiana. The note accompanying the chocolate read, "Those done up are flavoured on purpose for you to enjoy."

So over a cup of English tea and a bit of pleasant conversation the gift was enjoyed—at least for a while. Early the next day Mrs. Beard fell violently ill and was taken to the hospital. Some accounts also speak of her servants also partaking of the gift and as such were also said to have

Christiana Edmunds was a Brighton spinster who used chocolate creams to poison unsuspecting, and mostly random, victims in the early 1870s. Only one succumbed, a four-year-old boy who was taking a holiday with his family in the resort town.

needed hospitalization. At first these illnesses were thought to be some type of general food poisoning which was not uncommon at the time. Food preparation in Victorian England certainly lacked many of the sanitary measures we rely on today. Mrs. Beard would soon recover, as would the servants, but if later accounts by Dr. Beard are true, he became suspicious of the chocolates and the woman he was seeing. In fact, it was probably just a bit more than simple suspicion that crossed his mind despite the fact that it may easily have been an accident of the times. He did not, however, see fit to inform the police of his suspicions, nor did he test the chocolates. It is possible that he did confront Christiana and accuse her of poisoning his wife, but if he did the little chat did not work. The good doctor's reputation was on the line and he could not afford the scandal. Best to let this situation fade away and forget about it, but that was not what Christiana had in mind. Dr. Beard would not be able to break away from Christiana Edmunds without someone paying the price of his decision. She had been harmed and she was not to be so easily dismissed.

Poison Upon Delivery

The die had been cast, as then Christiana began her poison murder attempts on the unsuspecting population of the resort town of Brighton. For the next few months Christiana went about purchasing chocolate and peppermint creams from confectioners in Brighton and returning or exchanging them, having added her special ingredient—strychnine. At the time she did not seem to be focusing on anyone in particular. It was attempted murder for murder's sake as her rage continued to grow. Later theories would focus on the possibility that she did this to cover up her first murder attempt on Mrs. Beard.

Isaac Garret was a dentist and a chemist whose office was located at 10 Queens Road in Brighton. It was at Mr. Garret's shop where Christiana obtained her first supplies of strychnine, informing Mr. Garret that she needed to poison some bothersome stray cats. Even though the proper Mr. Garret admonished her that to kill the cats was cruel, he nevertheless sold Christiana the poison. Business was, after all, just business and he had no reason to suspect any other motive in the purchase. When she tried to buy more of the powder, however, Mr. Garret would balk at the sale. This forced her to use a local milliner (someone who makes and sells hats for women) to purchase the poison for her and of course, sign the poison book. What charms she may have used to persuade the gentleman to do her bidding are not clear. Nevertheless, she would now have enough of the poison to continue her work on the unsuspecting people of Brighton.

Christiana then began using young boys from the neighborhood to purchase chocolate creams from a local confectioner located at 39–41 West Street in Brighton. J.G. Maynards, Confectioners, was doing a good business in chocolate creams that year as these boys purchased and then at times exchanged them for boxes with no poison in them. This was the shop where Christiana had purchased her first chocolates. Before long the poison-injected chocolates made their way to the general public. No one knew that an attempted serial killer was about to begin her main work in their seaside town!

The Murder of the Innocent

On June 12, 1871, one of her poisoned boxes of chocolate creams was purchased by the Barker family, who had come to Brighton for a holiday.

After eating the chocolates, which had been purchased from J.G. Maynards, four-year-old Sidney Albert Barker became violently ill and died a short time later. Because of the unexpected nature of the death of the otherwise healthy young boy a coroner's inquest was held. The coroner for Brighton at the time was solicitor David Black who had an office at 58 Ship Street. It would not take long for the jury to return a verdict of "accidental death." The powers to be were as yet unaware that a killer was stalking the popular seaside town of Brighton. They really had no reason to believe that anyone would poison a child.

Despite the attention given to the young boy's death Christiana would intensify her attempts to kill using her poison chocolates. This behavior alone seems to show that she was not in her right mind, as she began to send chocolate creams and other foods such as fruit and cakes to well-known or prominent people who called Brighton home. Her notes would read, "You know who these are from." It would not be long before several individuals became sick from food they had eaten, food which had been delivered in the mails. The residents of Brighton realized that they were being targeted by a serial poisoner. The questions were, when would this person strike again and who among them was doing the work? To cover her tracks Christiana went to the extent of mailing herself some poison food, later declaring to authorities that she had become ill from the delivery.

With these efforts becoming public knowledge, including the poison death of Sidney Barker who it became clear had passed away from strychnine poisoning, Dr. Beard finally stepped forward. He informed the police about his wife's illness months earlier from what he suspected was poisoned chocolate creams, and he pointed to Christiana Edmunds as the probable source of the deadly poison. Before long Edmunds was under arrest and charged with the attempted murder of Mrs. Beard and the murder of little Sidney Barker. Both the police court and coroner's jury were clear that Edmunds was to stand trial for murder. There were no other suspects and with Edmunds in jail no one had recently received any poisoned foods. The police knew that this case was solved and let the public know that once again they were safe to enjoy chocolate treats.

The Trial and Beyond

In January of 1872 Edmunds was found guilty of the murder of Sidney Barker in a trial held in the Old Bailey in London. Soon after the guilty verdict was announced in court she was sentenced to death by hanging. Her attempt to forestall her execution by claiming that she was pregnant was soon disposed of by court appointed doctors and her death sentence was allowed to stand. However, the sentence was not allowed to stand for long. During her trial, Christiana's mother had taken the stand in defense of her daughter with self-serving testimony that not only was there insanity on both sides of the family, but that her daughter had always been less than stable of mind and that she was clearly insane. It was later discovered that at least four close family members had died as a result of some kind of insanity. There was, as one may say, a clear trail of mental illness in her family. The defense had also pointed out during her trial and her appeal that her actions were not of a sane individual. Even the newspapers reported that she was "a poor mad creature" in a campaign to remove Christiana from the death cell and the nearby gallows. Just before she was to be executed, Edmunds' sentence of death was commuted to life in prison.

She was "to be confined during her majesty's pleasure." She would spend the rest of her life in prison and die in 1907 at around the age of 72, still held in Broadmoor Asylum for the Criminally Insane. The asylum in Crowthorne, Berkshire, had been in operation since 1863. Designed by Sir Joshua Jebb, the 53-acre facility was built to house 284 inmates within its secure perimeter. It is now known as Broadmoor Hospital, part of the West London Mental Health Trust.

Reporting on confinement in Broadmoor a year before Christiana's death the *Washington Post* of January 4, 1906, would enlighten their readership on the institution and some of their workings.

> "To be confined during his majesty's pleasure" is the sentence pronounced by the English courts upon those who, indicted and tried for felony in the shape of arson, murderous assault, or homicide, are declared by the jury to be devoid of responsibility for their actions. Criminal convicts of this kind are imprisoned in this great asylum for the criminal insane at Broadmoor, situated within a motor drive of Windsor Castle and about a mile from Wellington College.

The paper further explained that if one is released from Broadmoor the authorities do not keep track of the former inmates. Perhaps this is one reason why Edmunds was never released. They could not be certain that she would not kill again, as the "poor mad creature" would never be cured of her personal demons.

The ex-chief of London's detective police [Chief Inspector John Conquest of Scotland Yard] declares that the former ex-criminal insane are set free at Broadmoor without notification to the authorities. The police hear no more of them after they have left the court, and the ordinary precautions which are followed when a convict is released on license are not observed.

Christiana would never explain why, after attempting to murder Mrs. Beard, she continued to send out poisons to kill strangers. It could have been to simply cover her early attempts at murder, but perhaps she never really understood the reasons herself as to why she did it. The residents of Brighton however, were quite satisfied that she would never again have the opportunity to send anyone else chocolate creams filled with strychnine. That seemed to be the best way to handle "a poor mad creature" and her poisoned chocolate creams.

Mary Ann Robson (Cotton), the Dressmaking Serial Killer of Durham (1873)

"I won't be troubled long."

Not to be outdone by the men, history records that the ladies have at times stepped to the fore of the criminal class and expressed themselves in the ways of serial murder such as the dressmaking serial killer of Durham. She would most definitely top the list in Victorian England.

Mary Ann Robson (Cotton) (1832–1873) did not have a happy childhood by any measure. She would later tell of severe religious nightmares during her childhood. This of course is no excuse for serial murder, but her background does show how intense religious discipline and continued personal frustration can at times lead to criminal activity of a most alarming nature. The question is: Was she insane? Mary Ann was born in 1832 in the typically small English countryside village of Low Moorsley, now known as Tyne. Her parents were in their teens when they married but they were not prepared for their new lives with the coming of a family. Her father Michael was barely able to keep food on the table with the wages he pulled in working as a miner. This however was not an unusual situation at the time. Times were very tough for most working people in Victorian England.

Her father was a Methodist and said to have been extremely religious and as such became a tyrannical disciplinarian to Mary Ann and her younger brother Robert on matters of church law. Religion would become a daily and nearly crushing part of their lives. It would not be unfair to state that an extreme devotion to religion was the mainstay of their lives, and one they could not escape.

In 1840 when Mary Ann was eight the family moved to the town of Murton where her father had found new work in the mines. She was, however, unable to make friends at her new school so discipline problems soon developed. She could not relate very well to other people. It was shortly after moving to the new town that her father was killed in a mining accident. He fell down a 150-foot mine shaft to his death at the Murton Colliery Mine. She was now in a new and strange town without friends and with a poor widowed mother trying to make ends meet. It was a psychological blow she would never really recover from as the small family continued to struggle to survive.

Six years later, when Mary Ann was 14, her mother married Robert Stott. Mary Ann made it clear that she did not like her new stepfather or the brand of rigid discipline he brought to the home. However, she was pleased that his much better wages brought for the first time new things to her life. Nevertheless, after two years she could take the discipline no more so at age 16 she moved out of her mother's home to become a nurse in training at Edward Potter's home in South Helton. Helton was a nearby village, but was far enough away to satisfy her needs for at least minimum freedom. She would stay at the job, which she seems to have done well at, for three years before returning to her mother's home in Murton. By this time Mary Ann had met a man named William Mowbray and had begun training as a dressmaker. According to local village gossip Mowbray was certainly not the first to "be with" Mary Ann as she was known by then for having many male visitors.

When she was 20 Mary Ann decided to marry Mowbray in Newcastle upon Tyne. She had made her final escape from her mother's home, moving to Plymouth, Devon, with her new husband. She was now Mrs. Mowbray, with a fresh start. Over time the marriage produced five children, but tragically four would die from stomach pains and gastric fever. With the remaining child, Isabella, the family moved back to the North East and continued with their lives. Luck, however, did not seem to be with them as the next three children who came died not long after their births.

From Dr. Ian Burney of the History of Medicine Unit at University of Manchester we may read of the changes in criminal life brought on by the recent availability of insurance to a wider range of individuals in Victorian England. It became a commercial transaction of life and death for those with the will to cash in on loved ones' deaths, and Mary Ann it would seem had a good deal of will!

> Every life came to have a monetary value. This was a major change from the courts of, say, the Borgias or Elizabeth I, where the only people at risk were those who were highly placed. With life insurance, everyone, whatever their station, had value for someone else.

Eventually, husband William would become the foreman at South Hetton Colliery before moving on to a job as a fireman aboard one of the new steam-powered ships. This of course allowed Mary Ann to develop new "friends" during the times that he was away. William would also find work in the mines as well as on the railroads to support what remained of his family. His end would eventually come from the now familiar "intestinal disorder" in January of 1865. It would be a small but welcome payday of £35 upon his death as he was thoughtfully insured by the British and Prudential Insurance Company. The 33-year-old widow was now quite prepared to put her past well behind her.

It did not take long for Mary Ann to move on to bigger and better things. She moved to Seaham Harbour in County Durham and was soon going out with one Joseph Nattrass. Unfortunately for Mary Ann he was already engaged to another woman, which did not sit well with her, so soon after his wedding she moved away from Seaham Harbour. This of course does not mean that her murderous ways had been left behind. During her time at Seaham Harbour she took the time to murder her three-and-a-half-year-old girl, which left only one child still alive, Isabella, out of nine she had given birth to. It was time to cash in once again as money was needed to continue her lifestyle, even as simple as it was.

From Seaham Harbour she moved to Sunderland, obtaining a position as a nurse in the Sunderland Infirmary. She worked in the area known as the House of Recovery for the Cure of Contagious Fever, Dispensary and Humane Society. Isabella was soon sent off to live with her grandmother at Seaham Harbour. For a while she was safe.

While working at the infirmary Mary Ann met George Ward. Ward was a patient and an engineer who was recovering at the infirmary. An affair soon developed and in August 1865 the pair married in Monkwearmouth. She was now the newly minted Mrs. Ward. The marriage would last a bit longer than a year as Ward's health continued to decline. His illness was characterized by the usual intestinal problems, accompanied by paralysis. Despite the "nursing" given by Mary Ann, George Ward breathed his last in October of 1866. Even though his doctor was somewhat surprised at the sudden loss of his patient, Ward was not a healthy man and Mary Ann was still able to collect the insurance money due the widow upon his death. Mrs. Ward was now free to continue on as she always had. No one at the time suspected her of any criminal activity, at least not officially. She had successfully disposed of an extra husband or two and things were looking good, but there was more work to be done.

November 1866 found Mary Ann working for Mr. James Robinson, a shipwright at Pallion, Sunderland. Mr. Robinson's wife had recently died and he needed a housekeeper. Within a month Robinson's baby was dead from gastric fever, which seems to have pushed Mr. Robinson into the arms of his new housekeeper, who before long was pregnant. Word then arrived that Mary Ann's mother, who was still living in Seaham Harbour, had become ill, so naturally she went to help. Nine days later her 54-year-old mother was dead. Naturally, Mary Ann took possession of her mother's property and any funds that were left lying around. It had been a good visit for Mary Ann.

With nowhere else to go Mary Ann's surviving daughter Isabella went with her mother back to Mr. Robinson's home. It was not a good move. Within two weeks of the move both of Robinson's remaining children were dead, as was Isabella. By the end of April 1867 all three were buried and out of the way. It was only four months later that the proper Mr. Robinson married his former housekeeper. She was now Mrs. Robinson and living in a very nice home with a caring husband. In November, Mary Isabella Robinson was born. Five months later, in March of 1868, she died from symptoms similar to those that had taken many of Mary Ann's children.

As the bodies kept dropping, James, husband number three, was becoming more than a little suspicious of his wife. He was not the first husband to become concerned when his wife insisted that he take out a generous life insurance policy and he certainly would not be the last. However, his concerns rose even more when he found out that his new wife had stolen at least £50 that he had given her to deposit in the bank and that she had run up debts totaling £60 without his knowledge. What turned out to be the last straw for Robinson was the discovery that Mary Ann had used his children to pawn some of the family's household valuables, the funds from which she retained. That ended his relationship with Mary Ann as he tossed her out. Robinson probably saved his own life by that action!

A New Life with Mr. Cotton

Lacking money and now living on the streets, Mary Ann was desperate. A chance meeting with her friend Margaret Cotton would upgrade her situation considerably. It would, however, become a deadly situation for the Cotton family. Margaret introduced Mary Ann to her recently widowed brother, Frederick, who was living in Walbottle, Northumberland. Frederick, a pitman, had also lost two of his four children. Margaret had been helping him care for his other two young boys, Charles and Frederick, Jr. Mary Ann soon took over the duties of caring for Frederick's children and it was not long before Margaret became ill. She died in late March of 1870 from what was described an "undetermined stomach ailment." While consoling Frederick, Mary Ann once again became pregnant. It would be her eleventh child.

In September 1870 Frederick married Mary Ann even though she had not been divorced from James Robinson. She was now known as Mrs. Cotton. Robert was born in early 1871, but Mary Ann was not about to settle down to any kind of normal home life. Not long after her "marriage" she learned that her old lover Joseph Nathrass was living nearby and was no longer married. They were soon rekindling the relationship where Joseph lived in the nearby village of West Auckland. It was not, however, convenient for Mary Ann to have a "husband" in one town and a lover in the next no matter how close in proximity they were. She soon convinced Frederick to move to West Auckland with his three young sons. It would prove to be a short stay, as 39-year-old Frederick would succumb to "gastric fever" in December of 1871. The "widow" was consoled by Joseph as well as the insurance money she received from the death of her "husband." Mary Ann was also comforted by the knowledge that she had also insured Frederick's three sons.

With no man in the house Joseph soon became a lodger in Mary Ann's home, but he proved not to be up to her standards. In order to keep bread on the table Mary Ann found a job nursing a man named John Quick-Manning who had contracted smallpox, a frequent problem in the 19th century. As he began to recover, the nursing became much more and Mary Ann was soon pregnant by Quick-Manning with her twelfth child. It was time to once again clean house.

In March of 1872 Frederick, Jr., died, shortly followed by Mary Ann's infant son Robert. Somehow all of these deaths do not seem to have made much of an impression on Joseph Nattrass. He paid for that error dearly, dying soon after revising his will to include Mary Ann. Once again the death stemmed from the familiar "gastric fever." However, she still had young Charles Cotton to deal with and so a new insurance policy was drawn on the young man's life. Mary Ann was not wasting any time and as such was about to attract some very unwanted attention.

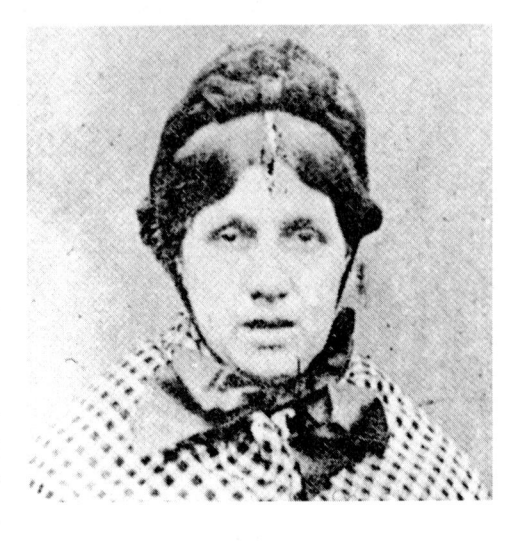

Mary Ann Robson (Cotton) used arsenic to kill twelve of her thirteen children as well as three husbands and probably other friends and family members, profiting through insurance payouts. She was tried and hanged for killing her stepson in 1873.

Before Mary Ann could act upon her next murder she was approached by Thomas Riley, a parish official, who also happened to be West Auckland's assistant coroner. Riley asked "nurse" Cotton if she would help a woman who had also contracted smallpox. Mary Ann was quick to accept the work and the fee which would follow, but complained to Riley that her stepson Charles would be in the way of any work. Mary Ann suggested that young Charles be sent to the workhouse, thus freeing up Mary Ann to do other work. Riley would not approve the workhouse plan and told Mary Ann that Charles could accompany her to the work or she could accompany Charles to the workhouse. It was at this point that Mary Ann informed Riley that the boy was sickly and weak and was not expected to live much longer. "I won't be troubled long. He'll go like all the rest of the Cottons." Riley could see no reason why the boy would not survive and told Mary Ann that the young man would surely recover from any illness. "No, nothing of the kind. He is a fine healthy boy."

Five days later Riley learned that young Charles Cotton had died. Mary Ann had once again moved with great speed, probably starting the poisoning process the same evening she had first spoken to Riley. This was too much for Riley who, upon learning of the death, went directly to the village police station. He was able to easily convince the attending doctor to delay writing the death certificate until a proper investigation could determine the cause of death. It would prove to be the beginning of the end for the dressmaking serial killer of Durham.

After Charles' death Mary Ann's first visit was to the insurance office and not the doctor's. At the office the insurance investigator informed her that no payment would be forthcoming until a proper death certificate had been issued. An inquest was soon held which returned a verdict of death by natural causes. At the hearing Mary Ann had testified that she had used arrowroot to help nurse young Charles. She also told the jury that Thomas Riley had made sexual advances towards her and the fact that she had rejected him was the reason why he had made "false accusations" against her. The story was good enough for the jury at the time, but the press saw this as a possibly good tale of corruption and murder. Newspaper reporters soon discovered that "Mrs. Cotton" had been very unlucky indeed, having lost 12 children, her mother, three husbands, a close friend and a lover, all it would seem due to stomach fevers. The newspapers were asking some very pointed questions about Mary Ann and her background. Mary Ann would say nothing to the press.

The End at Last!

The story caught the eye of the doctor who had tended Charles, who had for some reason of his own kept samples of his body and waste fluids. He quickly found a good deal of arsenic in the samples. The police were soon notified and Mary Ann was arrested on suspicion of murder. After a brief delay which allowed Mary Ann to deliver her 13th child, a lucky number for the young one it would seem, she was tried for murder. The defense tried to show that Charles had died from inhaling arsenic, which had been present in small traces in a dye used in the green wallpaper in the Cotton home. But it would take only 90 minutes for the jury to dismiss this bit of fantasy. There were far too many bodies in this series to simply ignore. The verdict was a firm guilty. Moments later she was sentenced to death upon the gallows. The "merry widow of County Durham" would kill no more.

The *Times* of London would report:

> After conviction the wretched woman exhibited strong emotion, but this gave place in a few hours to her habitual cold, reserved demeanour and while she harbours a strong conviction that the royal clemency will be extended towards her, she staunchly asserts her innocence of the crime that she has been convicted of.

Although the Home Office received several petitions for clemency, none would remove the condemned from the death cell. On March 24, 1873, Mary Ann Robson, England's most prolific serial killer at that time took her well-earned drop in the yard at Durham County Jail under the practiced hands of Askern Thomas of York who delivered a short drop. The classic short drop produced a slow twitching and quite painful death to the convicted dressmaking serial killer of Durham. Reports come down to us that she took a full three minutes of continued struggling, as some body fluids drained, to finally end her murderous days on earth. Some of the press would report that the hangman had not done his job very well as the condemned was allowed to suffer greatly before the end came. That conclusion of course greatly depends on one's point of view. Nevertheless, the corpse was allowed to hang for the full hour while the hangman had his morning tea with prison officials. No matter what the job there was always time during a working man's day for a hot cup of tea.

From Martin Fido's *The Chronicle of Crime* we may read:

> Fourteen murders are confidently ascribed to this woman; a 15th is probable. So single-handedly she has committed as many murders as William Burke and William Hare [serial killing body-snatchers working out of Edinburgh, Scotland] did together some 40 years ago [in 1828], and if but two more of her 21 suddenly-deceased relatives died at her hand, then she exceeds their conjoint total and will become Britain's worst mass [serial] killer, as she is certainly England's.

Bad job or not, the hangman did collect his fee and England was rid of one more brutal serial killer. The final headline would read, "Record-Breaking English Murderess Hanged at Durham."

Kate Webster (Catherine Lawler) and Her Bloody Little Axe (1879)

"But that's not Mrs. Thomas!"

Since her earliest days, she was a common criminal, albeit an incompetent one. By the time Kate Webster (an alias for Catherine Lawler) (1849–1879) was 16 years old she had stolen enough money to purchase a ticket on the ferry. It allowed her to sail away from her home in Kilane, County Wexford, Ireland, across the Irish Sea to England where she would continue to keep herself fed by stealing around town. She was able to keep this activity up for two years before an alert constable caught her with her hand on a young man's wallet with no good reason. Despite her age and good looks the 18-year-old was soon confined to a Liverpool prison where she would reside for the next four years. This would not be the last time she would see the inside of a British prison.

Upon her release Kate decided that she had had enough of Liverpool so off she went to the big city—London. She soon found a position as a charwoman, but scrubbing floors for a living was simply not what she wanted to do. She would also take great care to clean out her employer's possessions while she was at it. Needing even more funds she turned to prostitution to fill her financial needs.

At the same time she moved to Captain Woolbest's home on Notting Hill to work as a housekeeper and cook. She soon found that she had become pregnant. The father of the child was a Mr. Strong with whom she was then living while still working for Captain Woolbest. Her son was born on April 19, 1874, and soon after Mr. Strong abandoned Kate for greener and less complicated pastures. Despite the many problems associated with raising a child out of wedlock in those times she kept her newborn son and took care of him the best she could. After the birth she returned to the streets, moving between prostitution and pickpocketing on the busy streets of London. It would seem that she was simply not a very good pickpocket as she was arrested and jailed on at least 30 separate occasions. One such conviction landed her an 18-month sentence in Wandsworth Prison.

A Very Bloody Murder

Upon her release from Wandsworth in 1877 she found work as a maid. Her first job was with a family named Mitchell in Teddington. It was not a good place for Kate to work, as it turned out the Mitchells, according to Kate, "didn't have anything worth stealing!" She then went from job to job using several aliases, including Webster and even her real last name of Lawler. Her final employer was a rather reclusive 60-year-old widow named Julia Martha Thomas. On January 13, 1879, Kate took the job with Thomas. Mrs. Thomas, a devout Presbyterian who regularly attended church, lived by herself in a small home, Number 2 Vine Cottage, Park Road, Richmond. Her home was a few miles upriver from London near the Thames. She was so taken by Kate Webster that she told friends that she was quite lucky to have hired such a hard-working maid. Mrs. Thomas soon discovered that she had made a grave mistake.

It would take only days for the widow to see that Kate was far from being a good maid. In fact, she was hardly a maid at all, spending a good deal of her time at a local pub called the Hole in the Wall. Kate was soon coming back drunk, which was not what Mrs. Thomas could allow in her home. After warning Kate several times to end her drunkenness Mrs. Thomas decided that she had had enough of Kate Webster. She was after all a proper lady and expected the same from her hired help. Kate was given advance notice of her dismissal, being informed that she was to leave on Friday, February 28. This was a fatal mistake. Mrs. Thomas should have fired Kate immediately. The employer also knew it was a mistake as she asked several of her church friends to stay with her for a while before Kate left. When the 28th came Kate had still not found a new job and Mrs. Thomas allowed her to stay over the final weekend. After a rather heated argument, Webster was told to pack up her things and leave. The argument had so affected Mrs. Thomas' nerves that to calm herself she put on her church clothes and went to church. Her nervous condition and red eyes were seen by many of her fellow churchgoers. She was not one to confront people and her friends at the church did not press her for any details, although many knew of her problem with Kate.

When Mrs. Thomas returned home it appeared that her former maid had left. Feeling relaxed by the fact that she no longer need concern herself with Kate she went up to her bedroom and changed clothes. When she left her room to go downstairs she was immediately attacked by an enraged Kate Webster swinging an axe! Despite the surprise attack on the unarmed woman Kate managed to only hit her with a glancing blow to the side of her head. The blow did not knock Thomas down and soon both were struggling for control of the bloody axe. However, the 60-year-old woman was no match for the fury of Kate Webster. Thomas went crashing down the stairs followed closely by the axe-wielding Webster who, upon reaching Thomas at the base of the stairs, swung the axe and hit the woman directly on the head, planting the weapon deeply into her skull. Death was instantaneous. Mrs. Ives, the next-door neighbor, would later report hearing what she thought was someone falling, but after silence came from the house she quickly forgot about the incident.

Kate would later confess to at least some of the events which passed between herself and Mrs. Thomas.

> We had an argument which ripened into a quarrel, and in the height of my anger and rage I threw her from the top of the stairs to the ground floor. She had a heavy fall. I felt that she was seriously injured and I became agitated at what had happened, lost all control of myself and to prevent her screaming or getting me into trouble, I caught her by the throat and in the struggle choked her.

Chew the Fat!

Now Kate realized it was time to dispose of her mistress and she would do a very good job. She had thought about simply leaving the body but decided that disposal in the river was the best way to proceed. The disposal in fact had been so well organized that it leads one to ask if this was perhaps not the first murder Kate had been involved in. She first grabbed a large copper pot, filled it with water and brought it to a boil on the stove. While the water was heating up she laid out several large knives on the kitchen table along with a large meat cleaver, a razor and a meat saw. She also set out a black leather bag, two glass jars and a medium size wooden box which had been lined with brown paper and sacks of cloth.

First Kate stripped the body of clothes and then she cut off the head, which was placed in the leather bag. From this point it was a matter of which part of the corpse could be chopped up first into conveniently sized portions. Later reports would focus on the meat saw and razor being used to next remove the arms and legs. As the first parts were separated they were deposited in the now boiling water. By this time Kate decided that it was time for a break so naturally she sauntered off to the Hole in the Wall where she would find refreshment for the better part of an hour before returning to the bloody task at hand.

Returning from her refreshment Kate found that the body parts she had placed in the copper pot were sufficiently cooked to be removed and placed into her box. The organs and intestines seemed not to be good candidates for boiling so they were burned as much as possible in the stove. As for the fat? She simply skimmed it off the top and poured it into one of the two jars she had set aside specifically for that purpose. This was a well-planned disposal to say the least! Later reports would focus on the possibility that Kate had actually sold the fat to unsuspecting individuals, but that may simply be another tall tale designed to enhance an already gruesome story. Continuing with the work at hand Kate placed new pieces of the body into the pot, while the bones were placed into the stove to be burned. When all of the parts were cooked or burned she finished placing them in her box, but it seems that it could not hold all of the pieces. Because of this she disposed of one foot in a manure heap. When all was done it was time to clean up and move on to other matters. One of the many factors which would help place Kate's neck into a fine Italian hemp rope was the absolute calmness she displayed while she worked on Mrs. Thomas's body.

Using her skills as a maid she cleaned up the enormous amount of blood and replaced all of the knives and equipment she had used to chop up Mrs. Thomas. The clean-up effort is said to have taken two days as the mess had been substantial. The only tense moment during her clean-up came when a coal salesman visited the home for payment of a coal bill. Kate informed the man that Mrs. Thomas was not home at the time. He would need to come back later. She would learn later that Mrs. Ives had noticed a strange smell coming from the house during the time Mrs. Thomas was being cooked.

It was then time to receive some pay for all of her work. Mrs. Thomas's gold bridgework which had been not so carefully extracted would fetch six shillings. Now re-enforced with more funds Kate naturally returned to the Hole in the Wall for some good times and straight whiskey. Once again she returned to the house for some very nice clothing which included some fine silk dresses. Dressing rather well now she went off to look up an old friend named Henry Porter from Hammersmith. Naturally, Kate would need to take along her black leather bag complete with Mrs. Thomas's head! A girl does need her accessories.

Out on the Town

Henry Porter, who had not seen Kate for 15 years, was impressed with how well she was dressed, which included some fine jewelry. Kate of course gave him a tall tale that she had been widowed from Mr. Thomas who nevertheless had been a wealthy, but older gentleman who had left her in circumstances which allowed her to live comfortably. She took the opportunity of their meeting to mention that she wanted to sell the furniture in "her home." It seemed that not only was Henry Porter in the business of selling estate furniture, but he had just such a client in mind. With thoughts of a nice commission he contacted his friend who owned the nearby Rising Sun Tavern, one Mr. John Church.

After her meeting in Porter's office Kate stopped off for a few drinks with friends, which included Henry Porter. She was still toting her black bag, which seemed to hold something the size of a football, according to witnesses. As they went from pub to pub Henry carried the bag, noting its weight. During the evening Kate excused herself, stating that she had to meet someone. She left with black bag in hand but when she returned all noticed that the bag was nowhere to be seen. After a long day of meeting and drinks it was time for Kate to be off home, but her friends would not allow a "lady" to walk home alone and the son of one of her friends (possibly Robert Porter) was asked to accompany her to her home. At her home the young man was asked if he would be so kind as to help carry a large trunk to Richmond Bridge (some reports mention Hammersmith Bridge over the Thames), which he was happy to do. With the heavy work done Kate thanked the young man and insisted that she was fine now and that he should be off. She told the young man that she was going to meet someone and they were to take away the trunk. Walking away into the darkness and fog of a cool English night he heard the distinct and loud splash of something heavy being tossed into the water. It was time to go home; a job well finished.

The next day a local fisherman spotted something unusual in the mud along the riverbank near Barnes Bridge. He was soon pulling the box on to his small boat and with a natural curiosity opened it up to see what he may. At the sight of the cooked pieces of Julia Thomas he recoiled as he could barely accept what he had before him. At first he did not know what he was looking at. He was soon on to the police station with the disturbing news of his discovery. Inspector Harber, posted to the Barnes Police Station, received the trunk of body parts and immediately called in a local doctor to examine the remains. It would not be long before the doctor declared that the remains were those of a woman and further that the pieces appeared to "show signs of having been boiled." He also informed the inspector that without the head positive identification would be almost impossible. With no identification the find was reported in the papers as the "Barnes Mystery." No one had yet reported Mrs. Thomas as missing. In the meantime, Kate Webster and publican John Church spent the next two days together at his house. They had gone out several times for drinks and became close with a good deal of speed. The local papers would later report that Church's actions had placed Kate's "reputation at risk!" In the meantime, Robert Porter told his father that the box he had carried for Kate seemed to be the same type which was being reported in the newspapers in the Barnes Mystery case.

The time had come to make the final sale and collect the final take for the murder of Mrs. Thomas. The day after the discovery of the trunk in the river found Henry Porter and John Church loading Mrs. Thomas' furniture on to his van. When Mrs. Ives, who owned the cottage and had rented it to Mrs. Thomas, saw what was going on she stopped Mr. Church for a bit of conversation. They both soon realized that the Mrs. Thomas that he was purchasing the furniture from was not the Mrs. Thomas who lived in the cottage. When Webster was called to the front for what the two men thought would be an easy identification the neighbor stated, "But that's not Mrs. Thomas!" It was time for Kate to run,

Kate Webster and Her Bloody Little Axe   77

and run she did. The police were shortly called into the case, which was at first thought to be a simple case of fraud. Henry Porter and John Church had taken a close look at the property and found a letter from a Mr. Menhennick. They soon visited the man who had known the real Mrs. Thomas.

It did not take long for the men to decide that the body in the box and Mrs. Thomas were one and the same. All three men, along with Mr. Menhennick's attorney, went to the Richmond Police Station and made statements on what they had concluded. The police soon found evidence of a murder after a search of Number 2 Vine Cottages where they found the razor, axe and knives as well as some charred bones which had not been removed. They also found a handle from a box which matched the one remaining on the box the fisherman had found. The coroner agreed that there was only one suspect—Kate Webster—but she was nowhere to be found.

Kate had somehow found out that the murder had been discovered and she was off. The police would easily track Kate to Ireland, the first place they looked. There she was living with an uncle, though the police were soon able to show that he had no idea what Kate had been involved in. When taken into custody she was still wearing the old woman's jewelry and clothing. It was more than enough to arrest her and she was quickly returned to England for trial, escorted by two Scotland Yard detectives. Upon her return to England on March 30 she made a long statement in which she accused John Church of being the killer of Mrs. Thomas. She claimed to only have been part of the cover-up. Church was arrested and charged with murder. However, at his committed hearing he was able to not only show a strong alibi for the time of the murder but also show that he had been instrumental in helping to uncover the crime. He would soon be released with all charges dropped while Kate remained in custody at Her Majesty's pleasure.

The Trial

The trial began on July 2, 1879, and it was considered to be so important for a conviction to be won that Solicitor General Sir Harding Gifford himself would stand in court for the Crown. On the bench was Mr. Justice Denman at the Old Bailey. Webster was defended by Mr.

Warner Sleigh. Critical evidence would come from a hat maker named Mary Durden. Called by the prosecution, Durden related that on February 25 the accused had told her that she was traveling to Birmingham to receive some jewelry and other property from a deceased aunt. The problem was that Mrs. Thomas was very much alive at the time. The prosecution saw this as premeditation for murder and pressed the point in court that it was only six days before the deed. The prosecution had one major problem with their presentation. Without a head they had no way of proving that the remains found by the police actually were those of Mrs. Thomas. They would only have circumstantial evidence to show that a murder had occurred and that Mrs. Thomas had been the victim. Doctors could only state for certain that the body parts had come from the same body and that the body had probably come from a woman in her 50s.

The defense would press the possibility that due to Mrs. Thomas's demonstrated agitated state when she last visited her church that she could very well have died of natural causes. It was suggested that she had some type of stroke or other attack and simply fell down the stairs. The defense additionally suggested that either John Church or Henry Porter or possibly both had reason to murder Mrs. Thomas in order to profit from the sale of her personal property. This point was to be later dismissed by the judge as he summed up the case making it clear that there was nothing to show this possibility in the trial testimony and further, that both men had good reputations.

It would be late in the evening of July 8 that the jury would take the case and a little over an hour later the verdict was read. She was found guilty of murder and sentenced to death.

The Execution

The night before she met the hangman she confessed to the murder before the prison warden and prison chaplain Father McEnreg. She told him that she had almost felt that being executed was preferable to the "life of misery and deception" she had lived.

On July 29 at Wandsworth Prison she took her well-earned drop on the gallows by the very skilled hands of Chief Executioner William Marwood, who gave her his customary long drop and quick snap of the neck. Kate would become the only woman to be hanged at the prison and only the second person to be hanged at the facility in the execution shed which had been called "The Cold Meat Shed." Her last words were, "Lord, have mercy upon me." As the black flag was raised the execution team closed the door to the execution shed to allow the corpse to cool for the usual hour. Later, Kate's corpse was cut down and buried in an unmarked grave near one of the exercise yards at Wandsworth. On the handwritten prison record she is listed as "Catherine Webster, interred 29/07/1879." Unmarked or not, she was tossed into grave number 3. With her execution she took with her knowledge of what she had done with the little black bag, which still might have held the head of Mrs. Julia Thomas. After all, a girl has to keep some secrets to herself!

Charles Frederick Peace and the Banner Cross Murders (1879)

"For that I don[e] but never intended."

Charles Frederick Peace (1832–1879), better known to criminal history as simply Charlie Peace, was a small man, of both body and as far as culture was concerned, of mind, even by Victorian standards. He stood at his best at only 5'4", but was nevertheless strong and very quick. He would be reported by the press to be very agile, which would serve him well during his criminal efforts, and it would keep him alive during some very desperate struggles he would encounter as he worked his crimes. His size would also help him squeeze into some very tight spots. He would eventually claim fame as "The King of the Cat Burglars." In his *A Book of Scoundrels* Charles Whibley wrote, "Not only had he reduced house-breaking to a science, but, being ostensibly nothing better than a picture-frame maker, he had invented an incomparable set of tools where with to enter and invade his neighbour's house."

Peace was born in Sheffield, in the north of England, on May 14, 1832. His father was a humble shoemaker. During his early teens he was apprenticed to a rolling-mill, but an injury to his leg while on the job crippled him and soon put him out of work. The accident involved a piece of searing hot steel which had flown off and hit Peace's leg just below the knee. The injury kept him in the hospital for the better part of two years. This early injury left him wandering from place to place collecting and selling musical instruments and anything he could find. He had also acquired a goodly talent playing the violin, well enough we are told to have played at times in small local concert halls and pubs. He was also a prolific burglar by night, even while seeming to ply his musician's trade as his real work. He planned his crimes very well, spending time to check out his targets, always dressed in the clothes of a gentleman out on the town. Some press reports would refer to him as the Gentleman Burglar. Police would also find that he was much the master of disguise. Charlie moved to Dornall, a suburb of Sheffield, in 1875 and began to use the alias John Ward.

The Early Days

Peace's earliest crime may have been the theft of an old man's gold watch. From there he soon moved on to home burglary. On October 26, 1851, he broke into a lady's home in Sheffield and made off with property which was later found in his possession. After his arrest he would come into a piece of good luck. At his trial his former employer spoke highly of the young man and due to his employer's reputation Peace would only spend a month in jail.

By 1854 Peace was hard at work breaking into several upper-class homes in Sheffield but his luck would not hold. He was arrested for the break-ins, along with a woman he was living with as well as his sister, Mary Ann Neil. On trial at the Doncaster Sessions his convictions on October 20, 1854, would result in a sentence of four years' penal servitude. The women were convicted of being in the possession of stolen property and both were sentenced to six months at Her Majesty's pleasure. It was not long after that Mary Ann Neil died.

Peace was released in 1858 to once again pick up his violin as well as his burglary kit, going back to his more lucrative work. In 1859 he married a widow named Hannah Ward but she could not change his ways. On August 11, 1859, he broke into a home in Manchester, leaving with a rather generous booty for the night's work. However, there was so much loot that Peace decided to bury it in a nearby field. It did not end up being a very good hiding place, as it was soon discovered by the police. They left it in place to try to trap the thieves. Peace and another man were caught digging up the booty and during the arrest Peace attempted to kill one of the officers who had trapped him. His reward for this failure would be six more years of penal service.

He was released early in 1864. Only two years later he was caught in the act of burglarizing a well-to-do home in Lower Broughton, Manchester. He would blame his capture on being less than up to his full capability due to having taken too much whisky before the job. On December 3, 1866, once again standing before the Manchester Assizes, he received a sentence of eight years of penal service. During his time in Wakefield Prison he was able to smuggle a small work ladder into his cell along with a homemade saw made of tin. With these items he made it to the roof through a hole he had cut in his cell but he was spotted by one of the guards. They fought, with Peace besting the man and then running along the prison wall. However, the loose bricks were literally his downfall as he subsequently fell to the ground. Not seriously hurt, he was soon hiding in the prison governors' house on the grounds where he managed to change his clothes. For an hour and a half he was relatively free until he was discovered in the governors' bedroom. He would then see time in Chatham, Gibraltar and Millbank prisons before he once again gained his freedom in 1872. He was 40 years old, having spent the better part of 15 years in various prisons.

He looked up his wife and then joined her and his children in Sheffield where he seems, on the surface at least, to have been involved in honest work, mainly making picture frames. Though he could very well have kept up his work in other people's homes he does not seem to have been discovered for the next two or three years.

The Crimes Continue

As far as anyone knew in 1876, Charlie Peace was a rogue and a burglar (known as a portico thief), but no one knew at the time that he was also a killer, having taken the life of a police constable during one of his many burglaries in Manchester. It would be a few years before a prison confession would clear up that matter and only when he faced the gallows and had nothing else to lose would Peace come clean. He confessed to the Reverend Littlewood as he waited in the condemned cell that he had murdered Police Constable Nicholas Cock in Whalley Range, Manchester. It was his first known murder. The officer had surprised him in the course of his work, Cock having entered a gentleman's home around midnight on the evening of August 1 where he was subsequently killed by Peace. Peace's first gunshot went wide, perhaps deliberately so, but the determined officer continued to close in on Peace, drawing his truncheon. Peace's second shot was fatal. An 18-year-old gypsy named William Habron who lived near the scene of the crime was soon in police custody for that murder. In a trial that Peace actually attended, Habron was convicted and sentenced for the death of the officer. His brother John Habron, also arrested for the murder, was acquitted. He was very lucky to have been spared the walk to the gallows and the fine work of William Marwood. Needless to say, when all of the facts of Peace's confession were verified, young Mr. Habron was released, having learned a very sharp lesson on being in the wrong place at the wrong time as he quietly faded into history.

Peace in 1876 was living next to a Mr. and Mrs. Dyson. Mrs. Dyson succumbed to Peace's charms and Peace was soon using their home as his own. For Mrs. Dyson's part she would deny his claim of the nature of their relationship, strenuously calling Peace a demon who was "beyond the power of even a Shakespeare to paint." Her letters to Peace which would become part of the court record would prove otherwise. She was "very familiar" with Charlie Peace. To escape this now most unwanted guest, the Dysons moved to Banner Cross. It was evidently not far enough away, for as the Dysons arrived at their new home with the moving van they found that Peace had beaten them to it. As they came out of the van Peace came out of their new front door! He told the couple, "You see, I've come to plague you, and I'll plague you wherever you go." He meant every word of it. Near the end of June 1876 Mr. Dyson wrote a note to Peace and threw it over the wall into Peace's garden. "Charles Peace is requested not to interfere with my family."

It did not take long for Peace to make good on his promise as he began slandering the Dysons around the new neighborhood. On July 1 Peace and Mrs. Dyson met on the street and he attempted to trip her. Later that evening, while Mrs. Dyson was with friends, he came up and threatened to kill her and her husband.

Having had enough of his continuing slander, Mr. Dyson eventually swore out a warrant against Peace. Peace learned about the warrant for his arrest and decided to do something about it before he was served. On October 29 Peace waited outside the home for his chance to attack in the dark. When he saw Mrs. Dyson come out of the communal toilet located at the far end of a small terrace he made his presence known. "Speak, or I'll fire!" When Mrs. Dyson saw Peace she screamed and ran towards the house. At the same time her husband, upon hearing the scream, ran out of the house. Peace showed his gun and shot him to death on the porch. The shot passed through his temple. Peace then fled into the night. Rushing to her dying husband's side Mrs. Dyson screamed, "Murder! You villain! You have shot my husband!"

After the murder of Arthur Dyson, Peace knew he had no choice but to run. He had clearly been seen by Mrs. Dyson and he knew that if he was captured his end would come on the gallows. He climbed a back wall and walked to Sheffield. Continuing on he went to Attercliffe Railway Station and fled to York. From there he made his way to Cottingham and Hull. The police were hot on his trail but he was able to evade capture even though while detectives were searching his home he was hiding behind a chimney stack! Moving around the country he ended up in East Terrace, Peckham, in London. He took the name Mr. Thompson and began working during the day as an organizer of musical events around town. He would play his violin at these events. His performances included renditions of several well-known hymns. For an amateur he was considered quite skilled. At night, however, "Mr. Thompson" went around town driving his pony and cart throughout South East London looking for places to burglarize. He carried his burglary tools in his ever-ready violin case, sans violin. He was also well-armed. This was very rare for any burglar in England at the time.

Capture

There was soon a reward offered at £100 for his capture as the police began to circulate his description to all station houses.

**Charles Peace wanted for murder
on the night of the 29th inst.**
He is thin and slightly built, from fifty-five to sixty years of age. Five feet four inches or five feet high; gray (nearly white) hair, beard and whiskers. He

lacks use of three fingers of left hand, walks with his legs rather wide apart, speaks somewhat peculiarly as though his tongue were too large for his mouth, and is a great boaster. He is a picture-frame maker. He occasionally cleans and repairs clocks and watches and sometimes deals in oleographs, engravings and pictures. He has been in penal servitude for burglary in Manchester. He has lived in Manchester, Salford, and Liverpool and Hull.

    The police were under a great deal of pressure to solve what had become a long series of burglaries reported as being quite daring by the

An 1878 newspaper graphic of Charlie Peace, a long-time burglar and two-time killer, being apprehended by Police Constable Edward Robinson, who was wounded five times during the struggle.

press. Peace's work would finally come to an end at 2 a.m. on October 10, 1878. Police Constable Edward Robinson, along with a second officer, were patrolling the Blackheath area of southeast London when they spotted a small flickering light coming from the rooms at 2 St. John's Park. The rest of the house was dark and clearly this was not a resident moving about in the dark. Calling for backup, the two men were soon joined by a police sergeant who ordered the men to stand watch until the suspected burglar exited the home. Peace eventually came out of a window with stolen property in a bag and jumped to the ground only to be surprised by Police Constable Robinson who was hiding nearby. Seeing the officer, Peace yelled, "Keep back or by god I'll shoot you!" A short chase ended in the garden. At that point Peace turned and fired two shots at the officers. Peace was in the habit of tying a pistol to his wrist so that it could not be knocked out of his hand and it was now time to test that theory.

The officer was only momentarily stunned by the gunfire, but he soon recovered and grabbed hold of Peace. As the two men struggled, Peace yelled, "I'll settle you this time." Peace fired off three more rounds which struck Police Constable Robinson in the head and arm (or came very close to his head depending on the source). Nevertheless, the now very determined officer would not let go of his suspect and was soon aided by the other two officers. The police now had their man, but they did not know who he really was. Police Constable Robinson would recover from the *five* wounds inflicted by Peace and once again would be back on patrol.

The First Big Trial—Attempted Murder

On November 19, 1878, Peace, still using the alias of John Ward, the name he had given to the arresting officers, was put on trial. He had earlier stood before the magistrates of Greenwich Police Court and was remanded for a week. At the time he had refused to give any name and was therefore described as "a half-caste about sixty years of age, of repellent aspect." Peace was actually only forty-six but looked much older. Before Justice Hawkins he was tried on charges of burglary and attempted murder of P.C. Robinson. It did not take long for the jury to convict "Ward" of attempted murder of a police officer. It was noted in the press that upon conviction the prisoner "groveled" for his life, which seems to have helped him avoid the gallows. The judge, Sir Henry Hawkins, sentenced the prisoner to life in prison for the attempted murder of a police officer. Peace had told the court that he had fired his pistol simply to frighten the officer. However, evidence showed that the officer had covered his head with his arm, that being the only reason he was not fatally wounded. Clearly Peace had intended to murder the officer. Police Constable Edward Robinson was, at the recommendation of the jury, awarded £25 for his courageous service. He was also presented with an inscribed gold watch from the people of Blackheath who naturally saw him as a hero. His gold watch is now on display in the Metropolitan Police Museum.

Escape Out the Window

> "It was now established beyond doubt that the burglar captured by Police Constable Robinson was one and the same as the Banner Cross murderer."—A London daily newspaper report

It did not take long for the authorities to discover the real name of the man now serving a life sentence. Susan Grey, who had been living with Peace in Peckham as Mrs. Thompson, was confronted by the police. She knew of course that he was a wanted killer whose real name was Charlie Peace. Police confronted "Mrs. Thompson" who knew that if she did not admit the truth of the matter that she could very well be held as an accomplice after the fact in a murder. Seeing that there was no way out, it did not take long for Mrs. Grey to spill the beans on her "husband."

With this new information the police knew they had at last discovered the fugitive they had been hunting for the murder of Arthur Dyson. Peace soon found himself on a train wearing prison clothing and being escorted from Pentonville Prison to Sheffield in Yorkshire where he was to stand trial for the last time. On January 17, 1879, Peace was taken to the town hall where he was charged with murder. On January 22, he was being taken from his holding cell in London back to his second hearing in Sheffield. He knew full well that he would not escape the gallows so while on the train he convinced his escorts that he urgently needed to go to the lavatory. They kept his handcuffs on but removed the chains that had connected him to one of his police escorts. This was his last chance at freedom and he took it. Peace threw himself out of the lavatory window, which nearly killed him as his body bounced along the track. It was a close shave, as one of the warders had caught him by his left foot. Peace, however, was able to kick himself free with his right foot. He fell to the track. After the train came to a stop a quick search along the rails found Peace "apparently unconscious and bleeding from a severe wound in the scalp." His injuries had been great enough to put him in the hospital. He was very lucky to not have been bounced under the train as it was moving. Nevertheless, he was successfully delivered to the courtroom in Yorkshire just a bit the worse for wear, and his final trial for murder commenced.

The Murder Trial

On February 4, 1879, Peace, now well enough to stand trial, stood before Leeds Assizes. His examination before the magistrate had been a hurried and very strange affair. It was held in a cold hallway at town hall lit by a series of candles. It was described by the press as cold, dark, dismal and cheerless. It would seem a rush to try Peace at the earliest possible moment. The examination was very much a clandestine operation and Peace soon found himself on trial for murder. His trial for the murder of Arthur Dyson would last for only one day.

The presiding judge was Justice Lopes. Mr. Campbell Foster, Q.C., would stand for the people and Mr. Frank Lockwood was to defend Peace. Fifteen years later Mr. Lockwood would be found working as solicitor-general. Both men commented about and protested against the press coverage of the Peace murder trial and hearings. Lockwood complained that "for the sake of snatching paltry pence from the public, these persons had wickedly sought to prejudice the prisoner's life." Not since the Rugeley Poisoner William Palmer in 1856 had the general public been so excited by a criminal case as more and more facts about Peace's criminal career were examined in the pages of the daily press.

Much of the defense work would focus on the letters and notes which had passed between Peace and Mrs. Dyson. Clearly these two people were much more than friends. The prosecution would focus on the facts that witnesses had seen the murder and Peace's hand had held the gun as he took Arthur Dyson's life. Five witnesses had seen Peace in the neighborhood and had heard the shots.

The jury would take only 12 minutes to convict him of murdering Arthur Dyson. Moments later he was condemned to death.

On the Gallows

As soon as it was legal, the powers-that-be would place Charles Peace on the gallows. There would be no time wasted on this killer and lifetime criminal. Before he died on the gallows on February 25, 1879, he wrote out his own memorial card while he waited in the death cell. The last line would be his final lie.

> In Memory of Charles Peace who was executed in
> Armley Prison Tuesday, February 25th 1879. Aged 47.
> For that I don but never intended.

Mr. William Marwood, chief executioner for London, was not impressed with the reputation of the man who became known as the "King of the Cat Burglars," and gave him his proper drop at Armley Prison to a well-snapped neck. The press would report that "Charley Peace at Last Goes to the Gallows." As was tradition he was cut down within the hour, found to have been properly and legally hanged and dumped into an unmarked hole in the ground within the walls of the prison. Whatever is left of Mr. Charles Peace is still in residence rotting within those stone walls. It is a sure sign that even the best of criminals cannot escape the dedicated efforts of Scotland Yard.

Percy LeFroy Mapleton and Murder on the Brighton Line (1881)

"Man found dead this afternoon in tunnel here."

Percy LeFroy Mapleton (1860–1881), a journalist by profession and the godson of Sir John LeFroy, governor of Tasmania, can claim the dubious honor of being the first wanted man in British criminal history

Percy LeFroy Mapleton and Murder on the Brighton Line 89

to have his description, including a line drawing of his profile, in the daily papers to help facilitate his capture. He would also be the first suspect appearing on a Scotland Yard wanted poster. The public was fascinated with the prospect of being included in the nationwide hunt for a possible killer. That new test of criminal investigation would be remembered in years to come as other famous crimes were publicized. This was only a small taste of things to come, and it was a very good test as daily paper sales increased considerably. This was an area of sales which had perhaps been overlooked. A rival newspaper would report, "*The Daily Telegraph* has made history by publishing the picture of a man wanted for murder today."

The director of the Criminal Investigation Department (CID) at the Yard, C.E. Howard Vincent, was the man who decided to make his appeal directly to the press as investigators were having very little success in locating their suspect. The newspapers were more than happy to participate. This was welcome news for the police who were not always on good terms with the boys in the press rooms. On July 1, 1881, the *Daily Telegraph* published this first police description of murder suspect Percy LeFroy Mapleton: "Age 22, middle height, very thin, sickly appearance, scratches on throat, wounds on head, probably clean shaved, low felt hat, black coat, teeth much discoloured."

The editors of the *Daily Telegraph* were so taken with the new task at hand that they went well beyond the simple few lines posted by the police. The paper would closely follow the hunt and later the case carefully and detailed a much greater description of the suspect. For the first time they included a

Percy LeFroy Mapleton was the first wanted man in British criminal history to have his description, including this line drawing of his profile, published in newspapers to help police facilitate his capture. He was also the first suspect to appear on a Scotland Yard wanted poster.

line drawing of the accused, which had not been part of the original request.

> He is very round shouldered, and his thin overcoat hangs in awkward folds about his spare figure. His forehead and chin are both receding. He has a slight moustache, and very small dark whiskers. His jawbones are prominent, his cheeks sunken and sallow, and his teeth are fully exposed when laughing. His upper lip is thin and drawn inwards. His eyes are gray and large. His gait is singular; he is inclined to slouch and when not carrying a bag, his left hand is usually in his pocket. He generally carries a crutch stick.

Not surprisingly one could find this description and drawing posted in places frequented by the public, such as the many local pubs and coffee houses.

Murder on the Brighton Line

The victim was simply a target of opportunity for a desperate man. Sixty-four-year-old Isaac Frederick Gold was a regular passenger on the two o'clock express train from London Bridge Station to his home in Brighton. Mr. Gold was a coin dealer by profession whose work frequently brought him to London. This was business as usual. Monday afternoon, June 27, 1881, found Mr. Gold once again on the London express seated comfortably in the third carriage of the train in a first-class smoking compartment. A sickly looking young man named Percy LeFroy Mapleton would soon join him. They would be alone for the entire run. There would be no outside witness to the events which would soon unfold—only the bloody carriage would stand as mute testimony to the vicious attack. Nevertheless, the carriage would hold enough evidence to allow the authorities to come to the only logical conclusion possible—murder! Some of the other passengers would later recall that they thought they may have "heard the sound of gunshots as the train entered a tunnel."

When the train arrived at Preston Park Station just outside of Brighton, Richard Gibson, a ticket collector on duty at the platform that day, saw what he thought was a passenger who had been attacked. The man had stepped unsteadily off the train from a first-class carriage, hatless with no collar or tie and seemingly covered with blood. Moving at once to assist the stricken man, Gibson was told by the confused young man that he had been attacked on the train just before it entered the tunnel at Merstham. He stated that he had heard a shot, but lost consciousness he supposed due to a blow to the head. Sitting down on the platform and continuing the story, he further described two men he said had been traveling in the same compartment, but as he had taken a blow to the head he was unable to remember anything else until he exited the train at the Preston Park Station. To be sure, the man was indeed a bit confused and very unsteady, but even at this early point the story did not seem to ring true.

The ticket collector would later recall that to his knowledge no one else had exited the carriage. He was quite clear on that very important point. He did notice that a gold chain was hanging out of the man's boot and pointed this out to the confused man. The passenger informed the ticket collector that he had placed the chain in his boot for safekeeping. Feeling that there was a great deal more to the story and noticing that the battered passenger still seemed to be confused and unsteady, Gibson brought the man to the office of the station master, Henry Anscombe. After a short conference with the platform police, Anscombe had the platform police inspector bring the man to the police station. At the same time the ticket collector was sent to inform the Railway Police that an assault had occurred on one of their trains.

At the stationmaster's office Mapleton stated that he had been shot while he occupied the first-class carriage. Neither Anscombe nor the police inspector believed that the man had been attacked since no one had been seen to leave the closed carriage except Mapleton. He also did not seem to have been shot. A search of his clothing soon located two rare German Hanoverian medals. Mapleton had no explanation for these medals. These would later prove to be counterfeit, but they matched coins found in the bloody carriage. The police soon came to the conclusion that the young man had attempted to commit suicide. Since this was a criminal offense he was taken to the local police station for a further interview. They had also concluded that the young man was mentally unstable and perhaps not responsible enough to take care of himself. Mapleton went quietly along with them and made no effort to escape, clearly believing that his story would hold together.

At the station he was interviewed by Detective Constable Howland. Howland took down the particulars of the alleged assailants, after which Mapleton was taken to the county hospital to get his wounds patched up. Mapleton was so bold with his tale of being attacked he even offered a reward for the capture of his reported attackers. He was becoming calmer and less confused but the story of his attack did not seem to make any sense to the officers. They knew he was not telling them all that he knew. It was soon discovered that his wounds were for the most part superficial and not anywhere near what would be expected, considering the amount of blood on Mapleton, not to mention what was still in the carriage. It was beginning to look like some kind of murder had occurred, but where was the victim? There was certainly no body anywhere on the train which had been searched from one end to the other! The doctor who examined Mapleton informed authorities at the hospital that the wounds were superficial and felt that the "victim" should be held. Learning of this, Mapleton "suddenly remembered" that he had an important appointment to get to, but not in Brighton—he needed to be in London. Kept under police escort, he was soon purchasing a new collar and tie as he prepared to leave for the capital.

Escape!

At that point Detective Sergeant George Holmes was detailed to take the "victim" to his home on Cathcart Road, Wallington, Surry. In more politically correct times Mapleton would perhaps have been referred to as "a person of interest" at this early stage of the investigation. While they were making the run to Surry, detectives had organized a search of the tracks in the event anything tangible could be discovered. The search soon brought results, as a body, which had clearly been dumped along the track, was discovered. Upon closer examination, it was found that the dead man had been shot as well as being stabbed in the neck. A blood-stained knife was found near the body. It had obviously been used in the murder, which made the discovery of critical interest in the case. The bloody body was located near the tracks in the Balcombe Tunnel and a report was soon flashed down the line. The telegram from the station master at Balcombe put a whole new twist on the case of the bloodied young man.

> Man found dead this afternoon in tunnel here.
> Name on papers 'I Gold.' He is now lying here.
> Reply quick.

In a telegraphic flash, Percy LeFroy Mapleton went from possible assault victim to attempted suicide to prime suspect in a particularly bloody murder. The carriage he had ridden in was pulled into a siding and once again closely examined. There was blood everywhere, showing that a great struggle had occurred. Blood was found staining the door handle, the footboard, the mat and the walls. Suggestively, there was blood on the windowsill of the car. The police also found three marks made by bullets, a blood-stained newspaper, a blood-stained handkerchief and some gold coins similar to the two which had been found on Mapleton. This was no suicide attempt. This had been a brutal attack and a cold-blooded murder and the prime suspect was still out and about. It is interesting to note that despite the great struggle for life in the small car, including several pistol shots, no one on the train seems to have heard any of the struggle.

Detective Holmes arrived at Mapleton's Surry home at 9:30 that evening. It turned out to be a boarding house owned by the young man's relatives. The detective had been instructed by telegram, due to the discovery of the body, not to let the man out of his sight. As Holmes waited outside for Mapleton to change clothes and clean himself up, the "victim," out of the detective's sight, slipped away out the back door. The prime suspect in a brutal murder had disappeared and a nationwide search soon began, using the many resources of the British press. There was also a substantial reward for information, which hopefully would lead to his arrest, published in the papers. The newspapers were going to wring this story for as much as they could get out of it. The public were not only being taken along for the investigation, they could also acquire a nice reward for the work. Needless to say, many were keeping their eyes open for the killer of the Brighton Line.

The inquest into the death of Isaac Gold began on June 29, 1881. The inquest was held by Coroner Wynne Edwin Baxter. This inquest, which was held for several days, was a nightmare for the police, especially Detective Sergeant Holmes and other officers who had charge of the early portions of the investigation. They were mauled at the inquest and in the press for perceived "inefficiency" which led to the suspect's escape even though Mapleton was not an official suspect at the time he had slipped away. The inquest jury would easily return a verdict of "willful murder against Percy LeFroy Mapleton." After the inquest verdict was announced, the company who ran the train upon which the murder had occurred offered a rather large reward for information which would lead to Mapleton's arrest. The new reward was soon reported by the press. Newspaper sales continued to climb.

The Capture and Endgame

On July 8, Mapleton was located in a house at 32 Smith Street, Stepney, where he had paid for his lodgings under the name of "Park." The fact that he went out only at night and had kept the shades drawn during the day had not kept him safe from capture. The capture was not made due to great skill on the part of detectives or efforts by the public, however. Nor would it be the many wanted posters or news reports. Mapleton had foolishly telegraphed his former employer, requesting that his wages be forwarded to his new address in Stepney. The officers of Scotland Yard were soon knocking on his door. When he was arrested he said very little to the officer who nevertheless did write down whatever particulars he had to say for possible use in a trial: "I am not obliged to say anything and I think it better not to make any answer. I will qualify that by saying I am not guilty."

The arresting officer was none other than Scotland Yard's Detective Inspector Donald Swanson. Swanson would in seven short years also find himself involved with one of the most difficult cases of his career. Along with brother officers he would do his best to track down Jack the Ripper! A search of Mapleton's rooms located the blood-stained clothes he had worn on the train. He would be later identified by a pawn shop clerk as the man who had sold a revolver and some counterfeit coins to the shop owner.

A Fast Trial and a Good Rope

Mapleton was tried before Lord Chief Justice Coleridge at Maidstone Assizes. He was dressed in full evening wear because the very vain prisoner thought this would impress the jury. It did not. Evidence showed that Mapleton was in great need of money and had gone to London Bridge Station in the cowardly hopes of robbing a lone female passenger. When none presented themselves he settled on an old man

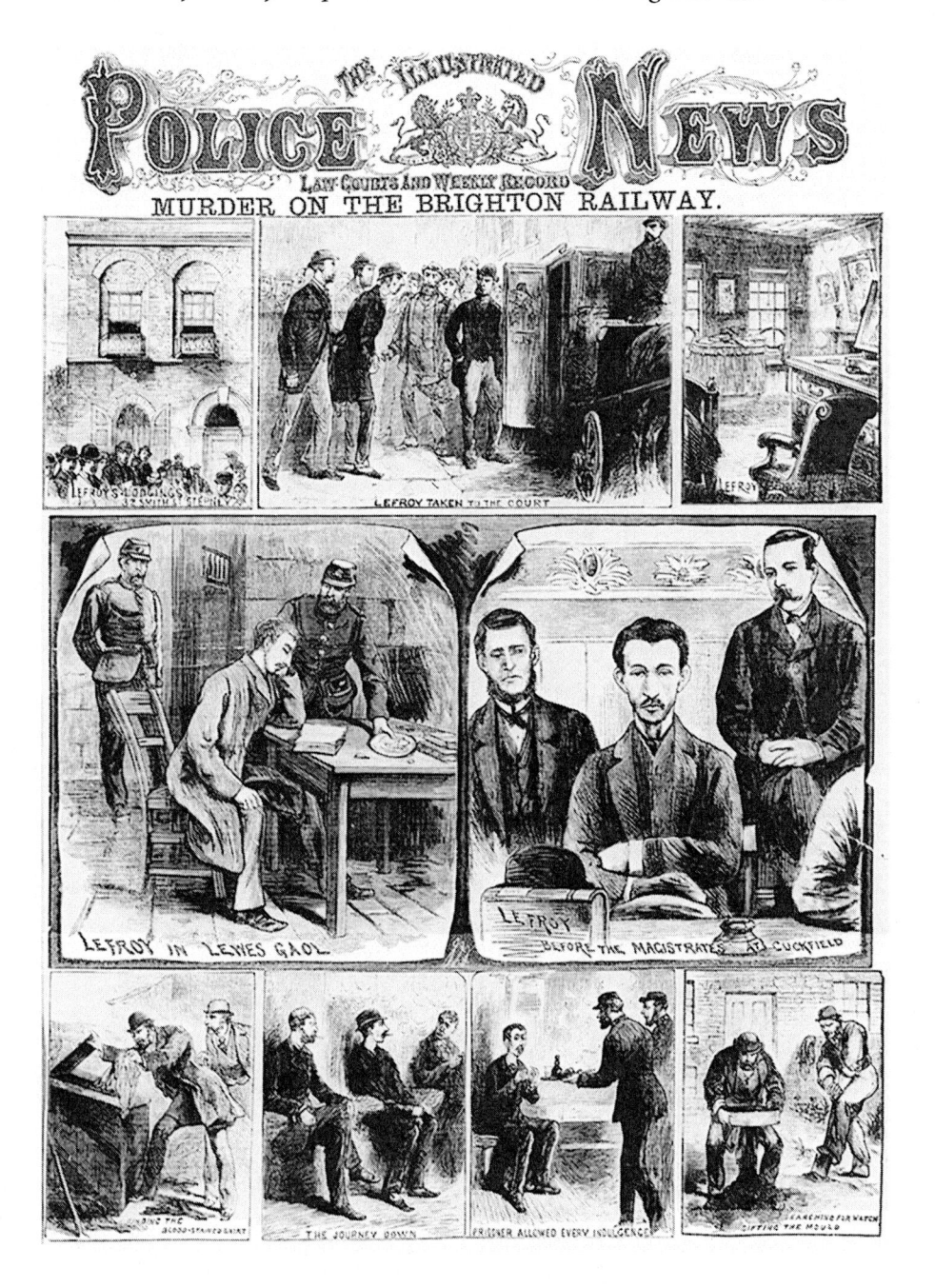

Percy LeFroy Mapleton and Murder on the Brighton Line 95

The Illustrated Police News had thorough coverage of the 1881 trial of Percy LeFroy Mapleton.

he thought he could overcome without too much trouble. He was after all carrying a pistol and a knife. Mr. Gold, however, did not go down without a valiant struggle. It was soon quite clear by the overwhelming amount of evidence against him that the verdict was never in doubt. The jury took only ten minutes to find Mapleton guilty of murdering Mr. Gold on the Brighton Line.

Before he was executed Mapleton made a full confession to the priest who stayed with him before he was buckled and placed on the gallows. He also confessed to the unsolved murder of Lt. Percy Roper of the Royal Engineers. Roper had been shot in his quarters at the army's Brompton Barracks, which was near Chatham Dockyard, earlier in 1881. However, later Mapleton recanted that part of his confession and the case remains officially unsolved. On November 29, 1881, Mapleton, looking quite calm, but not very well dressed, took his well-earned drop on the gallows due to the fine work and long drop of executioner William Marwood at Lewes. It was, as they say, "a clean kill!" After the prescribed time he was cut down with his then room-temperature corpse tossed in a hole on the grounds of the prison. The newspapers of the day would report that it was once again safe to travel on the Brighton Line.

As for the press and Scotland Yard they now had a most effective new tool which would help both pursue their individual goals. The men of the press could sell more newspapers and Scotland Yard could get the word out on wanted criminals and involve a very large number of citizens in their work of bringing these criminals to the bar of justice. They could also review this case in the files set aside for the Black Museum.

John Henry George Lee, the Man They Could Not Hang (1885)

"It was the Lord's hand which would not let the law take away my life."

John Henry George Lee, Jr. (1864–1945), stood on the gallows on February 23, 1885. He had been placed there for the brutal axe murder of his employer, Miss Emma Keyse, and the arson of her seaside home.

This was meant to be the end of Lee's criminal career and the end of his life. However, as fate would have it, this day turned out to be the start of his new lease on life and one which would forever tag him with the title of "the man they could not hang." On this sunny day the executioner would not collect his fee and the black flag would not be raised over the prison. It would become one of the most well remembered events to come out of Victorian England and the talk of all the pubs.

Lee was born on the 15th of August in 1864 in Abbotskerswell, Devon, England, to John Lee, Sr., and Mary Lee (nee Harris). There is nothing of particular interest during his childhood which could point to his career as a criminal and rogue. He left school in 1879 to join the Navy. Indeed, the 1881 census for England finds young John working as a "2nd Class Boy" on Her Majesty's Ship *Implacable*. The then 17-year-old was serving in the Royal Navy on a ship which had served at Trafalgar in 1805, but on the side of the French. The three-gun decked ship, built in 1800, had been originally christened the *Dugay-Trouin*, but having been captured by the British was refitted and renamed the HMS *Implacable*. Lee's ship would still be afloat in 1949, but by then an offer was made to return the ship to France. The honor was graciously declined as neither France nor England had any use for a leaking 149-year-old warship. It seems that the ship was not old enough or famous enough to have been of any interest to either nation so she was simply towed to a deep spot in the English Channel and sunk. As for Lee, an injury would see him invalided out of the Navy and he was soon back on the familiar streets of Torquay, working as a footman.

John Henry George Lee was tried and condemned to hang for the 1884 murder of his employer, Miss Emma Keyse. In a history-making turn, the hangman was unsuccessful—three times!

Lee did not do well in the civilian world, as he soon turned to things criminal. It was not a good choice of occupation. The year 1883 found John Lee on trial for theft from his employer. He was still working as a footman, and he was duly convicted of the theft. Sentenced to one year at hard labor he would spend his time at Exeter Prison and was released in 1884. It would not be the last time Mr. Lee would see the inside of that dark stone-walled Victorian prison. The fact that he had a record would be one reason why authorities would take a close look at Mr. Lee for other criminal matters.

The Murder on the Shore

News reports informed the nation that a brutal murder had been committed and then a well-known home had been destroyed to cover the crime. Little attention would be paid to the details of the murder; after all, there was much to do and life was hard in Victorian England. Nevertheless, much of England would soon be transfixed on the story of the man who was suspected of being the killer. He was not famous yet, but he was about to become one of the best-known men in Europe.

THE MURDER AT BABBICOMBE

The village of Babbicombe, situated on the shore of a small bay on the South Devon coast, between Teignmouth and Torquay, was the scene of a cruel murder perpetrated on Saturday, the 15th inst. An elderly maiden lady, Miss Emma Keyse, sixty-eight years of age, resided in a pretty marine villa at the foot of the cliff, surrounded by wooded pleasure-grounds, which is called "The Glen." She is said to have dwelt there more than forty years.

The authorities were first called to the Keyse home in the early morning hours of November 15, 1884, because of the fire which would eventually raze the entire cottage. The Glen was a low-thatched house which had been the home of elderly spinster Miss Emma Keyse for many years. After the fire had been put out it would not take long to discover her body in the burned-out remains of the seaside home. It would take no time at all to discover that the fire had not taken the life of Miss Emma Ann Whitehead Keyse—she had been hacked to death and the fire had been set in an attempt to cover up her brutal murder. The victim's throat had been cut and the body would also show three blunt force trauma wounds to her head. The body had been set on fire to disguise the injuries, but it did not do the job very well. There was not enough time to dispose of most of the corpse or enough heat to reduce it to a fine ash. Due to the vicious nature of the murder, Scotland Yard detectives were called in.

It did not take long for authorities to focus on Miss Keyse's employee—one John Henry George Lee. Lee lived in nearby Abbotskerswell and had only worked for Miss Keyse for a short time. Evidence presented at his later trial, held in the Old Bailey, was seen at the time as being very weak indeed and completely circumstantial. The press was not impressed with the evidence against Lee. "Convicted on thin circumstantial evidence" would cry the headlines, as Lee came closer to the gallows. Focus was made on an unexplained cut on Lee's arm and the possibility that he was the only male thought to have frequented the home. Miss Keyse was known to have "often entertained visitors," according to press reports, and the possibility of a stranger being involved in her murder was never fully explored. Lee was, however, not the only person who had been in the home.

There were, of course, the servants—cook Elizabeth Harris and sisters Eliza and Jane Neck—who also had full access to the home and the victim. The prosecution was able to show that no property had been taken, so the murder and destruction of the home did not seem to have been a cover-up for robbery. Indeed, the fact that no property was taken is circumstantial evidence that Lee, a convicted thief, was not the killer, as surely a man who had a record of theft would have taken something of value. It must also be said that no one could ever be found who could actually place him at the scene of the crime during the murder and subsequent fire. Some other unspoken motive was in

Elizabeth Harris was a cook for John Henry George Lee's elderly employer, Miss Emma Keyse.

play as the killer silenced and attempted to completely destroy the victim and her home.

As for Mr. Lee, he would claim no knowledge of the murder and would never change his innocent plea—critically even as he stood on the gallows he would declare his innocence. Earlier, he told the judge, "The reason I am so calm is that I trust in the Lord and he knows I am innocent." During his trial, Judge Sir Henry Manist had stated, "You say you are innocent, I wish I could believe you." Even with that and the very weak case he sentenced Lee to death!

The "Hanging"

Monday, February 23, 1885, found a good crowd outside of Exeter Prison anticipating a hanging. While he awaited his execution Lee would state, "They have not told six words of truth—that is, the servants and that lovely step-sister, who carries her character with her." Once again Lee would inform a priest that he had nothing to do with the murder and that the state was killing an innocent man. The evening before the work was to be done hangman James Berry of Heckmondwike in Yorkshire had spent the time preparing the gallows and stretching the rope. This was the usual method. The rope was strong and the platform worked properly. The trap opened each time he tested it the night before. However, when Berry pulled the lever on the day of execution while Lee stood on the platform the drop moved, but did not fall away, which left the condemned man still very much in place and very much alive. Lee was removed to the condemned cell and the trap was again tested. It worked properly. Again Lee was placed over the proper place marked by Berry, the lever was pulled, and Lee was still alive. Berry even took the extreme measure to jump up and down on the trap and it would not budge. Again Lee was taken away and Berry tested all of the mechanisms to perfect result. After a third failed attempt to execute Lee the prison governor stopped the execution and reported to authorities at the Home Office. This had never happened before at his prison and he needed guidance. As for Berry, he was completely unable to discover why the gallows would not work as it had many times before. This was a first for him as well.

The crowd outside the prison, which included several members of the press, was soon informed that the hanging had failed three times.

The crowd was told that the hanging had been halted—at least for that day. The authorities were at a loss at what to do as the story of "The Man They Could Not Hang" was taken up by the press. The execution was officially postponed for an undetermined time while those in government discussed the problem. There were now loud demands for Lee to be removed from the condemned cell and given a prison sentence in place of hanging. More and more the government heard from the press that this was a very weak case and that only Providence had saved Lee's life. It would not take long for the Home Office, in the guise of Home Secretary Sir William Harcourt, to issue a reprieve, which stipulated a life sentence for John Lee. Harcourt would report, "It would shock the feeling of anyone if a man had twice to pay the pangs of imminent death." Lee was now world famous and the talk of London, but he was still very much in prison and that was not to change for a good many years. No loud protests could take him out of prison.

There is much speculation even today as to why the trap did not fall for Lee, but most are hinged on very thin evidence such as the wood swelling on the trap due to damp weather, a constant issue in England no doubt, to the possibility of a fellow prisoner placing a wedge of wood in the way of the opening. The truth of the matter probably lies in the fact that the gallows had been moved only recently to the location for Lee's execution and the long metal hinges were probably not installed correctly when it was rebuilt. This construction error seems not to have mattered when there was no human weight on the trap, but caught on the side of the opening when a man was standing on it in just the correct way. Sounds perfectly logical—but then again there were those tests conducted the night before and during the day of the execution with weighted bags! Why did it always work then? Even the executioner would not claim to have an answer for that one. In the end no one would really know why they could not hang Lee. As for Mr. Berry, he would not be able to collect his fee and he had to walk away with a less than perfect record.

A Postscript from the Gallows

"It proved impossible, yet again, to hurl him to perdition."

As soon as Lee was securely housed in prison he began a series of petitions to successive home secretaries, always claiming that he had not murdered Miss Keyse and in fact that he had not been anywhere near the cottage at the time she had been killed. He would also report that he had no idea who would have wanted to murder the old woman as she seemed to have no enemies that he could think of. It was still quite clear even in his mind that no one really hated the old woman and nothing had been taken. For the next 22 years he would keep up his petitions, and on December 18, 1907, the home secretary finally released him from Portland Prison. Now it was time for John Lee to tell his story and he found that there were still plenty of people in the new Edwardian world willing to pay to hear all about "The Man They Could Not Hang." Lee began to tour the country, supporting himself with lectures on his life in prison, his trial and especially his claims that he was innocent of this particularly brutal murder. What the crowds really wanted to know was what it was like to stare into the abyss and walk away from the gallows three times in a single day. Lee was happy to be able to relate to them what he knew of the matter. But even he could only guess why he was still alive.

On January 22, 1909, 44-year-old Lee married Jessie Augusta Bulled from the Newton Abbot in Deven, which was not far from where the murder had taken place some 24 years earlier. They would have two children—John Aubrey Maurice, born on January 10, 1910, and a daughter born on August 10, 1911. By that time, however, Lee had deserted his pregnant wife and first child to a local workhouse. He would never see his daughter, having left England for the United States on February 28, 1911, with a barmaid named Adelina, never to return. She would claim to be his wife, but a marriage never occurred. Thus it was proved that he may not have been a lady-killer, but he was certainly not much of a husband or father. Lee would eventually settle in Wisconsin with Adelina, and on August 1, 1914, daughter Evelyn was born. However, tragedy would follow his youngest daughter, as she died suddenly at the age of 19 on October 12, 1933.

After living illegally in the United States for many years Lee reportedly died of natural causes at age 80 on March 19, 1945, in Milwaukee, Wisconsin. He had lived 60 years after the rope had been placed around his neck and 32 years after the death of his "executioner." Even at the end of his life he continued to claim that he had not murdered Miss Keyse and that he had no real idea who did. It has been reported that Lee's gravestone may be viewed at Forest Home Cemetery in Milwaukee under the name "James Lee." Further, his story is said to have been put to film during the silent film era. As for his "wife" Adelina—she would die on January 9, 1969. The newspapers would take no notice of her death. There was after all a war raging overseas and the United States was a little more than six months away from landing men on the moon for the first time in human history. By that time "the man they could not hang" had for the most part faded into history.

Who Really Did It?

Did Lee really murder Miss Keyse and get away with murder even though he went to prison for 24 years? Or did someone else—whose name we shall never know—commit this horrible crime, sending an innocent man to prison those many years? It is a bit more than pure speculation, but there is indeed one possible alternate suspect, albeit a circumstantial one. His name was Reginald Gwynne Templar and he happened to be Lee's attorney! Templar had been a regular visitor of Miss Keyse at "The Glen" and was said to be a good friend of both Miss Keyse and Lee. Suspicion comes from the fact that Mr. Templar wrote to Lee while he was in custody, offering his legal services. The letter was written on the morning of the fire, when arguably many knew of the fire and the loss of Miss Keyse, but few knew that a murder had occurred. The investigation was just beginning, and very little information was available to anyone outside of the early investigative team. Lee quickly accepted the offer, but Templar was only able to represent him for a very short time. Templar had evidently become ill, but it may be that in representing Lee early on he had all the information he needed from Lee to cover himself. And he no longer needed to speak to Lee to find out what he really knew about the murder and Templar's possible connection to it.

It would later be reported that Lee had confided to his other solicitor that Templar himself had been in Miss Keyse's home on the very night of the murder. The question of course is: How did Lee know he had been there? Was he told by Templar or had he seen the man there himself? The circumstantial evidence of murder could have been easily used for either or both men. It is possible that both men were somehow involved in some way and could not implicate each other. Not long after the conviction of John Lee, Templar, said to be gravely suffering from insanity, died. On his deathbed Templar allegedly spoke of murder, but there was no clear confession of his being involved with the Keyse case. Was he the killer? We shall probably never know for sure as the record shows that only one man was ever convicted of the crime and served a prison sentence for it and his name was John Henry George Lee and that conviction has never been set aside. Case closed?

Adelaide Blanche Bartlett and the Pimlico Mystery (1886)

"Now that it is all over she should tell us, in the interest of science, how she did it."

Adelaide Blanche Bartlett's trial for murder would go down as one of the most baffling in judicial history. She began her life in mystery, and mystery would follow Adelaide Blanche de la Tremouille (b. 1855) for the rest of her life. Adelaide was born in Orleans, France, reportedly to a young English girl named Clara Chamberlain and Adolphe Collot de la Tremouille, Comte de Thouars d'Escury. Her father was wealthy and well connected. Her mother was obscure with no connections to anyone in power. There was, of course, no marriage. During the trial her father would be referred to as "Somebody Important in France" and the people who paid for her defense as "anonymous wealthy friends." Political power was on full display for this trial.

Adelaide spent her childhood in France before being sent to live with her mother's sister and husband in Kingston-upon-Thames, England. In 1875 the 19-year-old was introduced to a gentleman who owned several grocery stores. Edwin Bartlett was comfortably well-off and immediately took to the young Adelaide. Edwin, eleven years older than Adelaide, became quite infatuated with the beautiful young lady and was soon asking her to marry him. In official Victorian manner Edwin contacted Adelaide's father in France for permission to marry her. This was granted, along with a small dowry.

They were soon married, but Edwin felt that his new bride needed a bit of improvement in the education department. Her new husband sent Adelaide off to a boarding school in Stoke Newington. Arrangements were made for Edwin to visit during school holidays for the two years that his wife spent at the school. Leaving the Stoke Newington school Adelaide was then off to a finishing school in Belgium. After a year in Belgium she was ready to take her place beside her husband and in 1878 she moved in with Edwin in an apartment situated over one of his shops in Herne Hill.

It would not take long for problems to develop. Soon after the couple moved in together Edwin's mother died and his father moved into a room which was part of the upstairs apartment. If reports are correct Edwin's father took an instant dislike to Adelaide. He resented his son's wife coming between him and his son. Before long the older Bartlett was accusing Adelaide of having an affair with Edwin's younger brother Frederick. Adelaide denied the affair with Frederick, and this accusation forced Edwin to defend his wife's honor. He demanded that his father swear out a statement that the allegations were false and to do it before an attorney.

Not long after the move Adelaide became pregnant. Some reports claim that this was the only time the couple had relations, which were conducted solely for the purpose of getting Adelaide pregnant. A month before the expected delivery a nurse named Annie Walker moved into the home. Nurse/midwife Walker soon suspected that this would be a difficult delivery and as such suggested to the couple that they engage a doctor. Walker was most concerned that the child would not survive without close medical assistance. Mr. Bartlett would have none of it, responding that he did not want another man "interfering with his wife." The delivery did indeed turn out to be a difficult one, but only at the last minute did Bartlett finally allow a doctor to be called in. The doctor was barely able to save Adelaide, but it would be far too late to save the child. This dreadful experience pressed hard on Adelaide, who resolved to never again attempt to have a child.

The Preacher Cometh

In 1883 the Bartletts moved to East Dulwich, England, living once again above one of Edwin's stores. It would, however, be a move in 1885 to Merton Abbey near Wimbledon (site of the world-famous tennis matches) where the real trouble began for the couple, with a few strange twists to the usual story. In residence at Wimbledon was 27-year-old George Dyson, a Wesleyan minister, and as would soon be shown, a ladies' man.

What makes this arrangement somewhat unusual was the friendship that developed. Apparently, Edwin Bartlett believed that all people should be able to delight in two spouses. He would explain that one spouse should be for purely platonic comfort and companionship and the other for what he would call "passionate adoration." Dyson became friends with both Mr. and Mrs. Bartlett and an "affectionate relationship" with the minister was openly encouraged by Mr. Bartlett. Edwin in fact made it clear that he was happy to see the minister and his wife kiss while he was present. Later reports would speak of Dyson being encouraged to fondle Adelaide while Edwin watched! To say the least, this was not a normal Victorian relationship. Carrying developments even further, Edwin made out a new will which left his considerable estate to his wife and stated that she was free to marry in the event of his premature death. After finishing his new will Edwin made it clear that he actually expected his wife to marry the minister upon his death. It was a very unique arrangement, but one which was reportedly never to go beyond a purely platonic relationship as long as Edwin was alive. The reverend was soon writing poems to Adelaide.

In August of 1885 Edwin and Adelaide moved into the first floor of 85 Claverton Street, Pimlico, England. The furnished rooms were let in the house of Mr. Frederick Doggett, who was by profession a registrar of births and deaths. After the move Edwin purchased a season ticket on

Adelaide Bartlett was brought to trial in 1886 for the apparent poisoning death of her husband but was found not guilty.

the train for the run from Putney to Waterloo for Dyson. This ticket was said to have been purchased to make it easier for Dyson to travel to see Adelaide for her personal instruction in history, geography, mathematics and Latin. However, Mr. Doggett's maid would later report that she found Dyson and Adelaide in compromising situations on more than one occasion, including finding them both lying on the floor in each other's arms. It would seem that another kind of instruction was on the minds of both student and teacher.

Edwin Becomes Ill

Edwin had been having trouble with his teeth for years, and his decaying teeth were causing much pain and very foul-smelling breath. As such, Adelaide could no longer bear to be near him so while he slept in his drawing room on a small folding bed she slept on a couch. In December 1885 a well-respected dentist removed his rotting teeth and the pain which had come with them. At the same time Dr. Alfred Leach, who knew Edwin had been treating himself for apparent syphilis with mercury, diagnosed his condition as gastritis accompanied by diarrhea. The treatment by the doctor improved Edwin's health, but he remained depressed and at times hysterical. Adelaide would remark, "If Mr. Bartlett does not get better soon his friends and relations will accuse me of poisoning him."

A new doctor named Dudley was called in for a second opinion. He reported that although Edwin's gums were inflamed due to the recent work on his teeth his overall physical condition was sound for a man of his age. The doctor recommended that Mr. Bartlett partake of a daily walk out in the clear air. The walks soon found Edwin feeling a good deal better and before long he began to demand "his marital rights" from Adelaide. With his breath still not fresh enough to suit her, Adelaide was not a willing wife in such matters. There was of course also that very close relationship with the Reverend Dyson to think of.

Some Liquid Chloroform Would Do

It was not unusual at the time for chloroform to be used as a liniment applied to the skin for rheumatic pain and, for that matter, a drop or two in a sugar lump was often used to cure seasickness. Nevertheless, on December 27, 1885, when Adelaide asked her good friend the Reverend Dyson to purchase her some chloroform he had a few questions to ask about its intended use. The young lady informed him that her husband was suffering from an "internal complaint" which had caused paroxysms. Their doctor was unaware of such problems, but Adelaide assured her friend that she had experience with such things and that a bit of chloroform was just the ticket. And so the Reverend Dyson was off to the chemists in Putney as well as over to Wimbledon. On December 29 he was able to present his married love with a four-ounce bottle of chloroform he had combined from his purchases. He could not however, have been totally convinced of Adelaide's reason for needing it—he told the chemists it was to be used to remove some grease stains.

"Mr. Bartlett is dead!"

The night before his death Edwin had another dental treatment. Upon returning home on December 31 Edwin went upstairs for some much-needed rest. At the time Adelaide happened to mention that she would quite regularly give some chloroform to her husband in a form of sleeping drops. Just before four in the morning Adelaide was up and sending the Doggetts' maid out to fetch Dr. Leach. All of this activity woke the Doggetts who were met by Adelaide saying, "Come down, I think Mr. Bartlett is dead!" The Doggetts were then told that Adelaide had gotten up and found Edwin lying face down on the floor. To revive him she had tried to pour "nearly half a pint" of brandy down his throat. Mr. Doggett checked Edwin and found that his body was quite cold. Clearly he had been dead for several hours by the time the doctor arrived. Looking around he saw a wine glass on the mantel near his bed. Brandy was his guess as to what had been in the glass, but he also smelled the glass and ether came to mind. He also saw a tumbler half-filled with Condy's Fluid. Condy's Fluid was used as a disinfectant as well as a deodorant; it contains sodium chloride at a 4% concentration. When the tray containing the tumbler was brought down by the maid Mr. Doggett spotted a one-ounce bottle upside down in the tumbler as if something had been added to the tumbler. Needless to say, the unlabeled bottle was passed along to the coroner. There was also a bottle of chlorodyne (tincture of morphine and chlorine) to be found. What was not found was the small bottle of chloroform.

The Coroner's Inquest

The autopsy was conducted on January 2, 1886, by five doctors out of Charing Cross Hospital headed up by a Dr. Green. Their work showed that there was no evidence of death by natural causes. What they did find was a distinct smell of chloroform when the stomach was opened. In fact, the team found liquid chloroform in the stomach which appeared to be fresh out of a bottle. There was no doubt that Edwin had died by chloroform poisoning. The only question was how it got to the man's stomach. When examined at the inquest Adelaide admitted that she had acquired chloroform but explained that even though she had intended to use it on her husband if he demanded sexual relations with her the opportunity never appeared. She further explained that she declined the sexual advances not only because of Edwin's continued bad breath, but also because she was betrothed to the Reverend Dyson. Finally, she reported that she had confessed the betrothal to her husband on New Year's Eve, leaving the bottle on the mantelpiece. When she awoke early the next day, Edwin was dead.

As the coroner's inquest wound up its work in February the Reverend Dyson confirmed that he had purchased the chloroform, but he refused to take any blame for the murder. It would not take long for the coroner's jury to give a verdict of "willful murder against Adelaide Blanche Bartlett in the death of Edwin Bartlett" as well as charging the Reverend Dyson with being an accessory before the fact. They were convinced that he had not been involved in the actual murder.

A Trial at the Old Bailey

On April 13, 1886, the trial was opened at the Old Bailey before Mr. Justice Wills. In the dock stood 30-year-old Adelaide and 28-year-old George Dyson. For the prosecution stood Attorney General Sir Charles Russell. For the defense Adelaide's father had hired Edward Clarke, one of the best in the business at the time. However, before the trial began the prosecution withdrew its case against the preacher and he was duly discharged with a directed verdict of not guilty.

The prosecution proposed three possible ways the chloroform could have been introduced into Edwin's stomach. Suicide was mentioned for the jury to hear, but that was dismissed as "highly improbable." There was simply no evidence of such behavior. Accidental poisoning was then to be considered, but because of the great pain which would have accompanied such accidental consumption the victim would surely have discovered the supposed error well before a fatal dose was introduced. Also, a victim in that kind of pain would certainly have cried out for help. That left only one possible solution to the death—"deliberate administration by a third party." In other words—murder! The prosecution then went on to state that Adelaide had used the chloroform to render her husband unconscious, then poured the rest of the chloroform down his throat. The only problem was, how did she do it without damaging his throat as she administered the poison? Down a small tube perhaps?

The defense then called forth their series of questions for the witnesses, and these questions and answers were able to show at least some reasonable doubt. The reverend himself was called for the prosecution, but he was no help to them. He testified that suicide could very well have been on Mr. Bartlett's mind, as his illness had convinced him that he was terminally ill. He further testified that Adelaide had not instructed him to throw out the bottles (he did it anyway) and that she had not asked him to conceal the fact that he had purchased the chloroform. He stuck to the story that the chloroform had been acquired to remove grease stains off a suit. No one could really prove otherwise.

Dr. Leach, who had doctored to Edwin, testified that Adelaide had cared for her husband throughout his illness and showed the man nothing but kindness. He further reported that Edwin had been hysterical towards the end and the doctor felt that he was becoming unbalanced. Finally, the doctor testified that if Edwin had been forced to ingest the chloroform he would have involuntarily vomited up at least some of the liquid which would have burned the throat. No vomit was found.

Dr. Thomas Stevenson, who worked at Guy's Hospital in London as professor of medical jurisprudence, was also a senior analyst to the Home Office on medical matters. He testified that to his knowledge there had never been a case of murder by liquid chloroform in British legal history. He further testified to the difficulty of pouring chloroform down the throat of someone who had been rendered unconscious. It was likely that it would have just as easily been poured down the victim's windpipe. However, the autopsy had shown no burning in the throat or windpipe. Finally, it was shown that there was a trace of chloroform in the victim's intestinal tract, indicating that it had been in his system for a good period of time. That was a complete surprise to the doctors.

The Verdict and the Aftermath

The foreman of the jury made it very clear where they stood on the matter: "Although we think grave suspicion is attached to the prisoner, we do not think there is sufficient evidence to show how or by whom the chloroform was administered." Therefore the only possible verdict would be one of not guilty. The people in attendance broke into loud and victorious applause.

After the verdict and release of Adelaide, Sir James Paget of St. Bartholomew's Hospital stepped forward to pose a request to the young woman. "Now that it is all over Mrs. Bartlett should tell us in the interests of science how she did it." Adelaide, continually professing her innocence, would never comment on how it could have happened. As for Adelaide and the now much wiser Reverend Dyson, the records show that there was never a marriage between the two. Dyson faded from the stage and Adelaide Bartlett returned to the place of her birth in Orleans, France. In her wake she left behind one of the true mysteries in criminal history from the late 19th century. Just how did she kill her husband? Even the newspapers would report, "And science still wonders how she did it." It is difficult to call this case an unsolved murder as no one really believed that she was innocent and no other person was ever brought to the bar of justice for the murder of Edwin Bartlett.

Florence Maybrick and a Little Arsenic with Breakfast (1889)

"Because I have sinned once must I be misjudged always?"

James Maybrick (1847–1889) was very different than he seemed to be in the proper Victorian world he helped create and lived in. To all outward appearances, the 42-year-old Maybrick was a very successful middle-class businessman who dealt in cotton futures, was in fine health, and lived in a well-run home with a 24-year-old American wife. James's world was nothing more than a thin veneer for an over-extended lifestyle, which only came to the fore whenever guests left his 20-room home in the suburb of Aigburth near Liverpool, England. Maybrick was so low on ready cash that he demanded his wife run his household of five servants on a mere £7 a week, including obligatory business dinners. From this sum Florence was to pay bills, purchase food and pay for the servants. Despite the shortage of funds James managed to maintain a mistress at £100 a year for twenty years and keep his cabinets filled with every conceivable medicine for his hypochondriac view of his health. So bad was his hypochondria that he was diagnosed as suffering from a "severe psychological disturbance." He had convinced himself that he could die at any moment and thus used the most drastic of Victorian cures—he took a dose of arsenic on an almost daily basis. In point of fact, he had become a very rare arsenic addict!

Maybrick's habit had begun innocently enough in 1877 when he contracted a bad case of malaria while on a business trip to Norfolk, Virginia. The cotton business had required the trip at a particularly bad time of the year for the disease. Doctors in Virginia treated him with strychnine and arsenic in a desperate gamble to save his life, which after a time worked. However, even though he had been cured, Maybrick continued to take both drugs, with an especial emphasis on the arsenic. He would confirm his habit to one of his friends around 1883. "You would be horrified, I dare say, if you knew what this (powder) is. It is arsenic.... We all take some poison more or less; for instance, I am now taking arsenic enough to kill you. I take this arsenic once in a while because I find it strengthens me." He would continue his habit until his death in 1889. All a friend would say was, "Maybrick's got a dozen drug stores in his stomach."

The unlikely couple had met in March 1880 on the R.M.S. *Ballic*, a British White Star liner (of R.M.S. *Titanic* fame). Florence Elizabeth Chandler was the daughter of a well-heeled Mobile, Alabama, banker and acted the true Southern belle. From that point on they became a couple, marrying on July 27, 1881, in the famous church at Piccadilly, London—St. James. For the next three years they lived half the year in Liverpool, while the other half, the cotton season, was spent in Virginia. They finally settled in 1888 in their 20-room home known as Battlecrease House in Liverpool. Along the way James Chandler was born to the

Florence Chandler and James Maybrick met in March 1880 on the R.M.S. *Ballic*, a British White Star liner. Florence, a Southern belle from Alabama, was the daughter of a banker and 28 years younger than her soon-to-be husband.

couple in 1882 with Gladys Evelyn arriving in 1886. The Maybricks would become known for throwing lavish parties, which placed Florence more often than not at the center of attention.

As would be expected with the arsenic use, along with other drugs, the situation became more than Florence could tolerate. She knew of course about the lack of money, having in 1887 been put on a strict budget, but she only discovered her husband's mistress after the birth of her second child. She would write to her mother about some of the problems she was having at the time.

> I am utterly worn out, and in such a state of overstrained nervousness I am hardly fit for anything. Whenever the doorbell rings I feel ready to faint for fear it is someone coming to have an account paid, and when Jim comes home at night it is with fear and trembling that I look into his face to see whether anyone has been to the office about my bills.... My life is a continual state of fear of something or somebody.... Is life worth living? I would gladly give up the house tomorrow and move somewhere else but Jim says it would ruin him outright.

The drug use seemed to have added much to her distress over the situation. She consulted the family doctor, one Dr. Richard Humphreys, reportedly telling him, "James is taking some very strong medicine, which has had a bad influence on him." Dr. Humphreys replied, "Well, if he should ever die suddenly, call me and I can say that you had some conversation with me about it." It did not seem to dawn on Dr. Humphreys that he should have a talk with James about his unusual habit. Perhaps he had a suspicion that young Florence would deal with the situation herself.

A New Friend

Almost as if on cue, young Alfred Brierley, a cotton broker, appears on the scene at a dinner and dance given at the Maybrick home. It did not take long for the depressed Florence to spot the six-foot Brierley with his broad shoulders and pointed beard. Indeed, she was immediately drawn to him and made plans to see him again despite Alfred's reluctance to get involved with a married woman. He did, however, notice her charm and beauty, not to mention her youth. On March 22, 1889, Florence reserved a suite of rooms at the Flatman Hotel in London in the name of Mr. and Mrs. Thomas Maybrick. It was a hotel well known to the men of Liverpool involved in the cotton business, so this use of her real last name would later astonish the authorities, who wondered why she would take such a chance. Nevertheless, Florence gave James the story that she needed to visit a sick aunt and she was off to spend two days with a now less than reluctant Alfred. It would be a short-lived affair however, as Florence would later explain, "Before we parted he gave me to understand that he cared for somebody else and could not marry me and that rather than face the disgrace of discovery he would blow his brains out. I then had such a revulsion of feeling I said we must end our intimacy at once."

It would be only days before James became aware of his wife's secret tryst. At the races in Liverpool Alfred Brierley was seen talking to Florence in such a way as to suggest something more than friendship. James, who had been tipped off to his wife's earlier encounter with Brierley, did not ignore the situation. That evening a violent fight occurred over the tryst at the hotel, which was overheard and later recalled by Alice Yapp, who was employed by Mrs. Maybrick as nanny to the two children.

Florence Maybrick and a Little Arsenic with Breakfast

As James tore Florence's dress and blackened her eye he shouted, "This scandal will be all over town tomorrow." For a man who had done much to secure the false impression of wealth and control the event had been devastating. For Florence it meant a beating, which gave her a black eye and other bruises. The servants soon pulled him away from his wife.

With her beating still fresh in her mind, Florence purchased a box of 12 flypapers. Two days later at a different store she bought 24 more and began soaking them in water. The resulting solution contained arsenic, which had been part of the chemical solution placed on the strips. Florence was not overly secret in her work as a maid who found the papers was told that the solution was intended as a face cream.

It did not take long for James to come down with something. On April 27, he awoke to vomit and discovered that his arms and legs were numb and cold. Nevertheless, business had to be conducted so he decided to keep an appointment in Cheshire. It was not a good decision. The weather had been bad all day but a severe rainstorm caught him in the open and he became soaked and chilled to the bone. When he became worse the next day Dr. Humphreys was called in to diagnose a case of chronic dyspepsia. In point of fact, the doctor did not have a clue as to what was wrong with James; the symptoms did not readily match any illness he was familiar with. Florence did her best to point in the proper direction by reminding

Florence Maybrick likely killed her husband, James, a hypochondriac and arsenic addict, in 1889. She was, in fact, convicted of the charge, but upon public outcry the sentence was commuted to life. She served 15 years before being released.

the doctor of her husband's use of "strong medicine." To this James informed his doctor, "I can't stand strychnine or nux vomica at all."

On April 29, with James now in his bed but feeling better, Florence went out to purchase more flypaper. She seemed to have run out of face cream, and it would take a day or so for the new 24 sheets of flypaper to leach the arsenic into the water. The next day James left his bed to continue his business affairs having gotten over his "chronic dyspepsia." On May 1, Florence decided to prepare the evening meal for her husband, which was unusual because a maid usually prepared it. After the meal James again became sick and vomited. Arsenic would later be found in the unwashed container that had held the meal.

Her Final Days of Freedom

For the next few days, as James Maybrick's health continued to deteriorate, Florence made plans to once again see Alfred Brierley. On May 8, she wrote "Dearest Alfred" in hopes of seeing him very soon. In that letter she informed her lover about the state of affairs.

> Dearest,
>
> Your letter under cover to John K. came to hand just after I had written to you on Monday. I did not expect to hear from you so soon, and had delayed in giving him the necessary instructions. Since my return I have been nursing M. day and night. He is sick unto death. The doctors held a consultation yesterday, and now all depends upon how long his strength will hold out. Both my brothers-in-law are here, and we are terribly anxious. I cannot answer your letter fully today, my darling, but relieve your mind of all fear of discovery now and in the future. M. has been delirious since Sunday, and I know now that he is perfectly ignorant of everything, even of the name of the street, and also that he has not been making any inquiries whatever. The tale he told me was a pure fabrication, and only intended to frighten the truth out of me. In fact he believes my statement, although he will not admit it. You need not therefore go abroad on that account, dearest; but, in any case, please don't leave England until I have seen you once again. You must feel that those two letters of mine were written under circumstances, which must even excuse their injustice in your eyes. Do you suppose that I could act as I am doing if I really felt and meant what I inferred then? If you wish to write to me about anything do so now, as all the letters pass through my hands at present. Excuse this scrawl, my own darling, but I dare not leave the room for a moment, and I do not know when I shall be able to write to you again. In haste, yours ever.
>
> Florie

However, Florence decided not to mail the letter herself, rather entrusting that vital task to maid Alice Yapp. It was a grave error, as Miss Yapp decided to open and read the letter. When she finished spying on her mistress she gave the indiscreet letter to James's brother Edwin Maybrick. Edwin soon informed his other brother Michael that some type of foul play was afoot and that he needed to come to London at once. Upon Michael's arrival it was decided to call a family friend, Dr. William Carter, into the case for a detailed medical opinion of their brother's worsening condition. Carter would soon report, "God forbid that I should unjustly suspect anyone. But do you not think, if I have serious grounds for fearing that all may not be right, that it is my duty to say so to you?" James had less than 48 hours to live, and during that time the whole Maybrick household plotted to watch every move Florence made. On May 9 those watching over James took samples of food and water which had been given to him, along with samples of urine and feces to test for arsenic. The doctors would find none. Later that evening Nurse Gore would observe Florence enter James's room and remove a bottle of meat juice into the washroom. She returned a short time later and placed the bottle back on the nightstand "surreptitiously," as reported by Nurse Gore. The doctors would later find half a gram of arsenic had been in the juice. What they could not say was when it had been placed in the bottle.

James, even though he moved from consciousness to delirium, seemed to notice that something was decidedly wrong. "There are some strange things knocking about this house." As Florence gave some medicine to her ill husband he complained, "You have given me the wrong medicine again!" All Florence could say was, "What are you talking [about]? You have never had any wrong medicine." By the morning of May 11, Maybrick was clearly losing his hold on life. All in the household knew that it would not be long before he was dead. Sensing the inevitable, Florence wrote a quick letter to Dr. Hopper, who at the time was Maybrick's doctor, attempting to explain the present situation.

> My misery is great and my position such a painful one that when I tell you that both my brothers-in-law are here and have taken the nursing of Jim and management of my home completely out of my hands, you will understand how powerless I am to assert myself. I am in great need of a friend. Because I have sinned once must I be misjudged always?

It would be at this point that a grand twist to the adventure came to the fore. After writing the letter to Dr. Hopper Florence reportedly fell into a coma for a period of 24 hours. It would later be ascribed to exhaustion brought on while caring for her dying husband. It was during her coma that James Maybrick would breathe his last at 8:30 p.m. on May 11, 1889. Having lost control of her household and certainly control of her husband's care, Florence became the only person, in a crowded house, who could not have administered any poisons to James—she was unconscious at the time!

For two more days Florence was held against her will in her own home as the Maybrick brothers and staff searched for any evidence in James's supposed unexpected death. It was reported in newspapers that the finding of her letter and some "'Arsenic Poison for Cats' was enough for the family members to call the authorities." Maid Alice Yapp seems to have been the one who found an envelope of arsenic, as well as five other bottles, some meat juice, a glass, rag and a handkerchief. All of the items had trace amounts of arsenic and of course the envelope was saturated with it. The next day Police Superintendent Isaac Bryning arrived to place Florence under arrest for the murder of her husband. "Mrs. Maybrick, I am about to say something to you. After I have said what I intend to say, if you reply be careful how you reply because whatever you say may be used in evidence against you. Mrs. Maybrick, you are in custody on suspicion of causing the death of your late husband, James Maybrick, on the 11th instant."

An inquest would be held from May 14 to 28 and based upon the May 13 post-mortem a verdict was issued that death was "due to inflammation of the stomach and bowels set up by some irritant poison." The inquest would hold Mrs. Maybrick for her trial on murder charges. Alfred Brierley was nowhere to be seen.

A Trial in Liverpool

The trial began on July 31, 1889, in St. George's Hall, Liverpool. Evidence was presented that James Maybrick's body at death contained ½ grain of arsenic—more than enough to kill anyone if administered at one time. It was shown that arsenic was found in a bottle of meat juice which had been prepared by his nurse but was never taken by James. It was also disclosed that Maybrick's arsenic habit had progressed to taking ⅓ grain of arsenic every day for at least the preceding 18 months. Finding

Florence Maybrick and a Little Arsenic with Breakfast

½ grain in his system would have been little surprise. In fact, if he had not had the poison in his system that would have been very unusual. Nevertheless, Florence Maybrick was convicted on August 7, 1889, of murdering her husband after the jury of 12 deliberated for only 38 minutes. Within a few more minutes the judge sentenced her to death. It would not be long, however, before the British public as well as the people of the United States began to voice their views that the conviction had been less than satisfactory. Even the venerable *Times* of London chimed in: "It is useless to disguise the fact that the public are not thoroughly convinced of the prisoner's guilt."

On August 23 at 1:30 a.m., three days before her scheduled execution by hanging, Home Secretary Henry Matthews commuted her sentence to life in prison. In his ruling Matthews stated that although he felt Mrs. Maybrick had attempted to kill her husband, there was in fact no evidence that he died of arsenic poisoning. Therefore, she would serve her sentence on attempted murder even though she had not been convicted of that charge! Her defense attorney, Sir Charles Russell, would state: "She is to suffer imprisonment on the assumption of Mr. Matthews that she has committed an offense for which she was never tried and of which she has never been adjudged guilty,—i.e. attempt at murder. Reasonable doubt means acquitted in law!" The words of the law in this case seem to have made no difference, as the government arbitrarily decided they wanted their pound of flesh.

Lost Years and Final Release

Despite the many problems with her case Mrs. Maybrick would spend the next 15 years in prison, first at Woking Prison in Surrey and then at Aylesbury Prison in Buckinghamshire, as prisoner LP29 (Life Prisoner). She spent the first nine months at Woking Prison in solitary confinement. It was reported that she was fed gruel and bread and that her cell was only seven by four feet and contained only a hammock and three small shelves. Her cause was not forgotten, as American presidents Grover Cleveland and William McKinley both sent appeals on her behalf to the English authorities. But with such British noteworthies as Queen Victoria opposing her release, it could only occur when a new ruler would come to the throne before Florence could see freedom. On January 25, 1904, at 6:45 a.m., Florence Maybrick was finally released from prison. From the prison she was escorted by the American ambassador across the channel from Southampton to Le Havre, France. After a visit with her aging mother she sailed to New York on the *Vaderland* using the assumed name of Rose Ingraham. It was the first time she had seen America in 20 years.

She spent the next few years giving lectures and newspaper interviews. Florence even wrote a book about her life entitled *My Fifteen Lost Years*. In 1917 she began using her maiden name, Florence Chandler. After her brief celebrity status ended she faded into obscurity, living in the outskirts of South Kent, a small town in Connecticut, in what has been reported as "a wooden shack." She died there at the age of 76, on October 23, 1941, surrounded, it is said, by her many cats. Her death was not noticed by many newspapers as war news was starting to take center stage. She is buried in a small cemetery in South Kent under a simple cross, which bears the initials F.E.C.M. (Florence Elizabeth Chandler Maybrick).

Mary Eleanor Wheeler Pearcey, a Woman Scorned (1890)

"The law must take its course."

On November 29, 1880, 14-year-old Mary Eleanor Wheeler's father, Thomas Wheeler, was executed at St. Albans Prison in Hertfordshire for the murder of Edward Anstee, a local farmer. It was a clear case and, indeed, before he was hanged Thomas Wheeler wrote to the farmer's widow, asking for her forgiveness. He also apologized for the murder. It was a hard lesson to learn for his daughter, to whom he wrote that he hoped his "sins" would not be visited upon her or her mother. Thomas's wife managed to move on, but his daughter found her way to the gallows a little more than 10 years later.

Other than the fact of Mary Eleanor Wheeler's birth in 1866, there is little one can learn of her early childhood. Certainly her father's death by execution when she was 14 would have greatly affected her, but to what extent would be mostly speculation. The death, after all, did not

Mary Eleanor Wheeler Pearcey, a Woman Scorned

push her older sister to murder. In her late teens she began a relationship with John Charles Pearcey, but this relationship, similar to her others, did not last. She did, however, begin to use his last name. It is suggested that this was a way of distancing herself from the shame attached to her father's execution.

Not one to stand still, she was soon seeing other men and never seemed to need work to support herself. (Was she perhaps a prostitute?) She was said to have had "shapely hands" and "lovely russet hair and fine blue eyes." Wealthy men always seemed to be around as "gentleman friends." In fact, one of her married admirers, one Charles Creighton, had rented rooms for Mary at 2 Priory Street, Kentish Town in North London, in the event-filled year of 1888. It was noted that Mary drank quite heavily at this point but was said not to be an alcoholic though she did suffer from bouts of depression. Creighton was a weekly visitor, which left plenty of time for Mary to entertain other men. A light placed in the window would alert another friend, furniture remover Mr. Frank Samuel Hogg, that Mary did not have other guests and the coast was clear. Entry into her rooms was no problem—Frank had a key. He also had a wife and daughter, both named Phoebe. Even though Mary and Phoebe were said to be friends, Mary apparently decided that she wanted to be with Frank on a more permanent basis, which put his wife and daughter decidedly in the way. Mr. Creighton was not party to her plan.

Mrs. Phoebe Hogg had taken ill in February 1890 and was not yet fully recovered when she was invited to afternoon tea by Mary Pearcey. Mary had given a few pennies to a young man named Willie Holmes to deliver the invitation to Mrs. Hogg on the morning of October 24, 1890. A neighbor named Charlotte Priddington would later recall that around 4 p.m. on the day in question she heard what sounded like breaking glass coming from inside Mary's home. Charlotte called to her neighbor over the fence, but received no reply. Three hours later at around 7 p.m. the body of a woman was found on the pavement (or on a rubbish heap depending on the source) in Crossfield Road, Hampstead. Clearly it had been dumped where it was found as there was no evidence of a local struggle.

The body had its head wrapped in a cardigan, which was removed by officers at the scene. The bloodstained cardigan had been covering the face of Phoebe Hogg, as well as the deep gash in her throat—so deep it had nearly severed her head. She had clearly been beaten and had a fractured skull. It was also noted that she had several bruises on her arms and head, probably inflicted as she was trying in vain to defend herself. There had clearly been a relentless and determined attack on the woman.

That evening a very bloodstained black pram was discovered in Hamilton Terrace. This being about a mile from where the body of Mrs. Hogg had been dumped, the police did not yet connect the two. The next morning a small child's body was found in Finchley near where the pram had been discovered. The doctors determined that the child had suffocated, but were not ready to focus on murder as the instrument of the child's death. It was later suggested that little Phoebe had been put into the pram alive, with her mother's body placed on top allowing both to be transported. During this transportation the child could have suffocated due to the weight of her mother. It might have been simply an accident.

Phoebe Hogg and her child were soon missed, and when the discovery of a body was reported in the local papers Frank Hogg and his sister Clara went to the local police station to report them missing. From there Clara went to visit Mary to ask whether or not she had seen her sister-in-law, but Mary reported that she had not. However, Mary did agree to accompany Clara to the morgue to see if the woman who had been found was indeed Phoebe Hogg. The visit to the morgue proved to be quite controversial as Mary's behavior was so strange that it was noted by the attendants. Even though Mary had agreed to go to the morgue with Clara she seemed to be more interested in preventing Clara from identifying the body than helping. When the body was displayed under a cover it was clear that the injuries had been extensive at which point Mary became nearly hysterical when it was uncovered. Clearly it was Phoebe Hogg, or at least what remained of her.

The women were then asked to take a look at a baby pram which had been found with bloodstains on it. Clara was able to identify it as belonging to little Phoebe. Police would later discover that a neighbor of Mary's had seen her pushing the pram the night of the murder. She had also seen a large object being carried in the pram, but the object could not be identified by the witness. Clearly, it had been the wrapped corpse of Mrs. Hogg.

With his wife's body positively identified police immediately began to suspect her husband Frank Hogg of committing the crime. He was soon searched as was his home, which is where the authorities found the key to Mary's house. With this evidence Frank was forced to admit that he was having an affair with Mary Pearcey, an affair which had begun before he married Phoebe.

The police soon found their way to Mary Pearcey's door on Priory Street. At the home they conducted the usual "thorough search" and were rewarded with a good deal of evidence. The kitchen was found to have substantial bloodstains and blood spatters in several areas including on the walls and ceiling. Clearly they had located the murder room. Blood was also found on a fire poker and a large carving knife as well as on an apron and skirt. The struggle for life surely must have been made in the kitchen where there were two broken windows and other clear signs of a violent struggle. There was also a rug, which had been cleaned with paraffin, but not well enough to remove all of the bloodstains. As the search for clues continued, Mary's behavior became bizarre as she sat at her piano. She began to sing and whistle loudly. She attempted to explain the bloodstains away, saying they were from her "killing mice, killing mice, killing mice."

The detectives had seen and heard enough. They arrested Mary and Detective Inspector Banister charged her with the murder of Mrs. Hogg and her little girl Phoebe. A search of Mary soon revealed bloodstains on her clothes and scratches on her hands as if she had been involved in some type of struggle. They also found that she was wearing two wedding rings. One of those rings would be later identified as belonging to Mrs. Hogg.

Trial at the Old Bailey

Mary Pearcey's police court hearing in Marylebone proved to be most complete, as all of the evidence was displayed for evaluation. However, the most interesting piece of evidence came from Mary herself, but not from the witness stand. Sarah Sawhill had been assigned to look after Mary during the police court hearings. During a casual conversation with Sawhill, Mary admitted that Mrs. Hogg had indeed come to her home for tea. Mary also stated that a problem had developed when Mrs. Hogg allegedly made a remark that offended her, leading to an argument. At this point in the off-the-cuff conversation, Mary realized that she may have said too much and was possibly incriminating herself. She would say no more on the matter. Nevertheless, she was held over for trial at the Central Criminal Court of the Old Bailey.

Mr. Justice Denman held court that December 1st morning as he had eleven years earlier for Kate Webster and her little axe of murder. It would be a three-day trial for the "woman scorned" as she was brought under the prosecution of Mr. Forrest Fulton, assisted by Mr. C.F. Gill. Her defense team was led by young Mr. Arthur Hutton. Hutton would later gain fame as counsel for "George Chapman," the Borough Poisoner, but that was in 1903, 13 years in the future. This was December of 1890 and Pearcey would plead not guilty to the charges.

The prosecution had a very strong case and the verdict was never really in doubt. Jealousy was of course the cause of the murder since before he married Phoebe, Mary had Frank all to herself. When he married Phoebe and kept up his affair with Mary she had only a share of his affections. The bloody cardigan was found to have been one that Frank had given to Mary. And a witness came forward to state that the window shades had been drawn the afternoon of the murder, apparently to keep out any prying eyes. Another witness came forward to testify that she had seen Mary pushing a heavily laden pram near where the body of Mrs. Hogg had been dumped. The pieces were falling into place.

Although Mary did not testify, her attorney Arthur Hutton attacked the circumstantial evidence, such as he could. He postulated that it would have been impossible for someone as slight as Mary to have been capable of inflicting so much damage to Mrs. Hogg. He could not, however, work his way around the massive amount of blood evidence nor the fact that victim and suspect were together behind closed doors at the time the murder was thought to have been committed!

It was noted by the press that throughout the trial Mary was calm and in fact quite impassive to her surroundings. Just before noon on the third day of the trial the case went to the jury, which took 52 minutes to convict her of murder. Before the judge donned the black cap he asked Mary if she had anything to say as to "why the Court should not give her judgment of death in accordance with the law?" Calmly she replied, "I say I am innocent of this charge."

Having spoken her piece, which was believed by no one in the courtroom, Mr. Justice Denman placed the black cap on his head and sentenced her to death. At the time there was no automatic appeal. The Court of Criminal Appeal would be established in 1907 for such matters. Nevertheless, her solicitor Mr. Hutton made a strong effort to have the death sentence reduced, claiming that Mary had committed the murder in an epileptic fit and was therefore not totally responsible for her actions. The facts themselves would indeed show that she was certainly not in her right mind. Upon review, the Home Office decided that there were no reasons for any delay and the paperwork was marked with a final statement that "the law must take its course."

The night before she was to be executed, Mary asked her attorney Mr. Freke Palmer to place a personal ad in the Madrid, Spain, newspapers. The cryptic ad read: "MECP last wish of MEW. Have not betrayed. MEW." She would not explain what the message meant nor who MECP was. She also steadfastly refused to admit that she had killed anyone. Was she covering up for another killer or was this just one last attempt to stave off her execution? It is possible that the only meaning of the note was to add to the confusion and possibly delay her execution.

Execution Day

> "I have never seen a woman of stronger physique ... her nerves were as iron cast as her body."—Sir Melville Macnaughten

When Mary arrived back at Newgate Prison she was given a bath (mandatory) and issued a prison gray shift dress. She was then escorted to the condemned cell. By this time she would be constantly under watch by three wardresses taking shifts around the clock. For this execution Sir James Whitehead, sheriff of London, had made the decision to exclude newspaper reporters from the hanging. His reasons were said to be her age and sex. What he really wanted was the execution to go off with as little publicity as possible. This was not a popular hanging.

On the Tuesday morning of December 23, 1890, executioner James Berry entered the condemned cell at just before 8 a.m. Always the gentleman, as he entered he said, "Good morning, madam." He shook her hand and then continued, "If you're ready, madam, I will get these straps round you." Mary replied that she was quite ready to end this all. Sheriff Whitehead then asked her if she had any final statement to make. From her executioner we learn that she replied,

"My sentence is a just one, but a good deal of the evidence against me is false." With that said two of the wardresses took up positions on each side and prepared to escort her to the gallows. Mary who felt she did not need escort only replied, "Oh well, if you don't mind going with me I am pleased."

A single noose hung loosely from the wooden beam. From it Berry had set the drop at nine feet. As she was positioned for her execution she was held by two warders and Berry placed the white cotton hood over her head and adjusted the rope. Berry then checked to see that the fall was clear and quickly pulled the lever. Mary disappeared from view, leaving only the rope in sight, which snapped tight as it caught the falling woman by the neck. As the rope creaked and swung back and forth she would make no struggle; Berry had done his work well, snapping her neck instantly. Her still and cooling corpse was allowed to hang for the customary hour before being cut down and buried in an unmarked grave within the stone walls of Newgate Prison.

However, despite her execution, that was not the last that London would "see" of Mary Eleanor Wheeler Pearcey in more ways than one. Her wax figure was soon on display at Madame Tussaud's in an appropriate place of honor in the Chamber of Horrors. An estimated crowd of 30,000 came to see her upon the exhibit opening. London, it would seem, could not get enough of Mary. The museum also purchased the pram from Frank Hogg as well as other articles closely related to the case that had been found in the bloody kitchen. One may wonder how often Frank visited the figure of his former lover in the Chamber of Horrors and what he may have thought of the strange display? We may also ask if he knew more about this case than he would ever speak about.

Needless to say, she has a well-earned place behind the doors of Scotland Yard's Black Museum, which happens to be where one may find the noose that was used to snap the neck of Mary Eleanor Pearcey.

A Ghost of a Chance

As if the East End London residents in the 1880s needed any more strange and terrifying tales coming to the fore concerning their patch of ground, there comes one more which focuses on the infamous section known the world over as Whitechapel—home to Jack the Ripper. This time, however, we come face to face, so to speak, with the ghost of Mary

Pearcey, who has been reported over the years by local residents walking along the often fogged-over streets of Whitechapel. Those who report their encounters with the spectral Pearcey report that when she is seen she is invariably dressed in bloody clothes and at times she is even seen pushing the black baby carriage, blood-soaked of course. Some who have gone for help, thinking she is real and in some sort of trouble, also report that she would simply vanish into the night as they attempted to aid her. There are also the many times that those who drive find themselves "almost" running into her when she pushes the pram in front of their cars as they pass along the streets of Whitechapel. As always when they get out to see any possible victim or damage that may have been done, Mary and the bloody pram are nowhere to be seen. The question is why would her spirit walk the streets of Whitechapel and not those of Hamilton Terrace where she committed her only *known* murder? Does she have one more secret to tell?

Dr. Thomas Neill Cream, the Lambeth Poisoner (1891–1892)

"I am Jack the..."

As Dr. Thomas Neill Cream (1850–1892) was about to be executed for the poison murders of several London prostitutes, he is said to have uttered words which would forever place his name on the list of Ripper suspects, even though he could not have possibly committed the murders. As he was about to take his drop into the void of death, he was reportedly heard by the hangman James Billington to state, "I am Jack the...." It was a final game to be played on his executioner and perhaps he felt they would not hang him, at least not then and there, if he was "Jack." He was wrong, as his neck was cleanly snapped before he could finish his final lie. In point of fact, the doctor was in the State Penitentiary at Joliet, Illinois, from November 1881 to July 1891, far from where the Ripper was doing his work.

Joliet Prison operated from 1858 to 2002. It was built by the labor of convicts, who mined the local limestone for its construction. During the American Civil War both convicts and Confederate prisoners of war were housed within its walls. At its completion it was the largest prison in the United States. Joliet would become famous internationally in the early 1920s when Richard Loeb and Nathan Leopold were given life sentences to be served at Joliet for the kidnapping and thrill murder of little Robert Franks in 1924. The prison finally ended its run in 2002 when authorities decided that the costs to maintain the facility were too great. They also cited the obsolete nature of the structures and the dangerous conditions they afforded not only to the prisoners, but also to the correction officers who worked there.

Despite all evidence that he could not have been guilty of the Ripper murders but because he was a suspect for a very short time as he waited in the death cell at Newgate, just to make certain of this, Dr. Cream's solicitor sent a petition to the Home Secretary. Among other documents the file included a sworn affidavit from Mr. Thomas Davidson. Mr. Davidson worked for Messrs. John Rose & Co. of Quebec, and had, as part of his accounting and bookkeeping duties, investigated the whereabouts and situation of Dr. Cream upon the death of Cream's father, William, in 1887. Mr. Davidson assured the Home Secretary that the man now being held for the murder of four London women could not have been implicated in the Ripper murders. "Dr. Thomas Neill Cream, a life prisoner [was held at the time] in Joliet Prison, State of Illinois, U.S.A. for complicity in murder," therefore he could not have been the Ripper. Sadly for Cream the petition had little effect. Even though he was not "Jack" he was still a brutal killer who had been convicted of murdering at least one of his patients using his favorite poison—strychnine.

Just for Starters

Cream was born in Glasgow, Scotland, in May 1850. He was the first of eight brothers and sisters in a family who moved to an area just outside of Quebec City, Montreal, Canada, in 1854. By the time he was 13 he showed all the signs of being a very troubled young man. From November 12, 1872, until March 31, 1876, he would study medicine at McGill College in Montreal where he would graduate with honors.

It would not take long for Dr. Cream to begin practicing his new skills on a woman he met named Flora Elizabeth Brooks. Miss Brooks became pregnant, most likely by Cream, and the newly minted doctor used his not so skillful hands to perform an abortion, which nearly cost Miss Brooks her life. Nevertheless, Brooks's father, an influential hotel owner in Waterloo, forced a marriage, which occurred on September 11, 1876. The next day Cream fled to England. He did, however, leave her a note! Upon his return to Canada his wife died under mysterious circumstances, which caused him to flee to Scotland. Only much later would he be suspected of her murder. He was soon registered as a graduate student at St. Thomas's Hospital in London as well as becoming qualified as a surgeon from the Royal College of Physicians and Surgeons in Edinburgh, Scotland. Once again, a pregnant woman he was alleged to be having an affair with was found dead. She had been poisoned by chloroform and discovered in a back alleyway in August 1879. Dr. Cream soon ran off to America, once again escaping a trial.

A few years later found Dr. Cream in Canada working as an abortionist. Things went well for a while until the body of Kate Gardener, a young chambermaid whom it was said he "knew well," was found in Cream's office. There was a bottle of chloroform next to her. Cream was very lucky not to have been charged with Miss Gardener's murder.

In August 1880, having moved to safer grounds in Chicago, he was again found to have been involved with the mysterious death of a woman, Julia Faulkner. Cream had set himself up in a small medical clinic in Chicago near a known red-light district to be close to prostitutes who could use his illegal services as an abortionist. This time he was arrested on murder charges, but again he escaped justice because investigators could not find enough evidence to go to trial. The year 1881 found Cream marketing a concoction of his own, said to combat epilepsy. One of his patients was a 61-year-old railway agent named Daniel Stott who sent his lovely wife Julia Abbey Stott to the good doctor to pick up his "medicine." Mrs. Stott was soon picking up more than just medicine from Dr. Cream and before long her husband became suspicious of the affair. At that point Cream added a bit of strychnine to the mix, which was administered by his loving wife, and by June 14, 1881, there was no more Mr. Stott of Boone County, Illinois.

It was then that the personality and excessive ego of Dr. Cream comes through. Stott's death had been attributed to epilepsy until Dr. Cream demanded, in writing, that an exhumation and an autopsy be conducted. When strychnine was discovered in Daniel Stott's stomach, the only suspect was Dr. Cream, who was arrested along with Mrs. Stott, who quickly turned state's evidence to avoid imprisonment. Dr. Cream found himself imprisoned at the Illinois State Penitentiary at Joliet. It was a life sentence.

At a later date, rumored to have been erected in the dark of night, unknown individuals erected a tombstone over Mr. Stott's grave. It left little to the imagination:

> DANIEL STOTT
> DIED JUNE 12, 1881
> AGED 61 YEARS
> POISONED BY HIS WIFE
> &
> DR. CREAM

Despite his life sentence, Cream would serve only 10 years. He was free to murder once again, thus proving the value of a true life sentence. After Cream's release in 1891, which is said to have been aided by a bribe from his brother, he went to Quebec, Canada, for a brief stay with his family. The primary reason for the visit, however, was to pick up his $16,000 share of an inheritance from his father. It was a short stay, as he sailed for England in September of that year. Arriving in Liverpool on October 1, 1891, he began a short career as a poisoner in the London boroughs of Lambeth and Walworth. He had also been an abortionist, a blackmailer and an arsonist, but murder was his main work. It was his use of strychnine in Lambeth which would cause the newspapers to later name him the Lambeth Poisoner. He was in a filthy and dangerous Victorian ghetto racked with desperate poverty, filth, disease, crime and prostitutes. He was truly home at last!

The East End of London

Cream began his "work" soon after arriving in England. The first of his four victims was a well-known prostitute named Ellen "Nellie" Donworth. On the evening of October 13, Donworth had gone out with Cream for some drinks at the local pub and perhaps a few other activities. Nineteen-year-old Ellen made the mistake of accepting some medicine from her new "doctor customer" and paid the price with her young life on October 16 from strychnine poisoning. A man had been seen leaving her rooms at Duke Street but could not be identified at the time. Ellen would make it out of her room only to collapse on the street on nearby Waterloo Road. Her client, "Fred," was long gone. It was later reported that Cream once told a prostitute that "he lived only to indulge in women." This seemed to include killing them whenever he fancied.

A letter to the police from "H.W. Bayners, barrister" (a pseudonym Cream used) gave information that the heir to the W.H. Smith fortune had been involved in the murder. It was to be the first in a series of letters from the killer to the police. Less than one week later another local prostitute named Matilda Clover accepted a pill from the doctor. The 26-year-old died on the morning of October 20 of strychnine poisoning, thus alerting the police to a new serial killer in the south of London. Yet she was originally thought to have died from "delirium tremens" (a result of alcoholism) before a second letter arrived stating that Dr. William Broadbent and Lord Russell had poisoned Clover. With a second look at the victim the authorities soon agreed that a murder had indeed occurred, but the suspects were not Broadbent or Russell.

After Donworth's murder, Cream wrote the first of a series of blackmail notes to people of prominence that he felt he could acquire some form of payment from to keep quiet about murders that they had nothing to do with. The first known blackmail note was sent to Frederick Smith, the son of William Henry Smith, a member of the House of Commons and a former First Lord of the Treasury. The note demanded that the writer be hired as his attorney to prevent evidence of Mr. Smith's involvement in murder being discovered and sent to the authorities. Being innocent, Smith sent the letter to Scotland Yard. No money would exchange hands. When a similar attempt at bribery arrived in Dr. William Broadbent's hands, he passed his letter on to Scotland Yard.

For Cream it was time for a short vacation back in Canada. So far as can be ascertained, no women died in Canada at his hand while the serial killer was on vacation. He was back in London by April 2, and apparently looking for more ready victims. He soon found Louisa Harris, who used the alias Lou Harvey. Harris was a prostitute like the other victims, but she became suspicious of the doctor's insistence that she take some pills that he offered. She pretended to swallow them but palmed the pills, later throwing them into the Thames River from a bridge.

On May 6, 1892, *New York Times* readers were treated to an interesting report of murder coming once again from London. Under a banner headline "Mysterious London Crime," the report detailed the poison murders of two young women.

> A case that, from the mysterious circumstances connected with it has thus far baffled the police is attracting considerable attention in this city.... On the 12th of April a report was circulated in South London that two young girls had been poisoned at a house in Stamford Street, Waterloo Road, Lambeth. A police constable went to the house, where he found a young girl named Alice Marsh, aged twenty-one years, lying in the passage in her nightdress. She was apparently in a dying state, suffering from the effects of poison, which had been delivered to both women by way of the Guinness they had drunk. In another part of the house the police discovered another young girl, fully dressed, named Emma Shrivell. [The 18-year-old] also appeared to have been poisoned.

What the report failed to state was that the killer himself had called the police to the house, but in that he had made a fatal mistake. The killer sent a note to the police informing them where to find "two dead girls," but the strychnine he had given the two women had not worked as fast as he planned. It was a poorly executed murder plot. The victims would live long enough to supply a very good description of their killer!

The women were taken to St. Thomas' Hospital, but before the cab could make it to the hospital Marsh died. Shrivell made it alive but died in great agony a few hours later. Despite the letter informing the police that poison was the cause of the deaths, spoiled canned salmon was initially suspected. Dr. Cuthbert Wyman was first to see the women and would later describe what he had seen. He was quick to dispel the salmon theory. "On her admission to the hospital the Shrivell girl was unconscious and suffering from attacks of convulsion, which became more severe every ten minutes. She was kept under the influence of chloroform for three hours, and directly it was taken from her she died. From the general appearance of the body the cause of death was quite consistent with strychnine poisoning." Dr. Wyman would also conduct the post-mortem, which showed that the poison had "caused death by asphyxia."

The coroner's inquest was held the next day as the hunt began for the Lambeth Poisoner. One of the first to testify was the constable who had gone to the home and found the two stricken women. The officer testified, "Emma Shrivell had told me on the way to the hospital that she and Alice Marsh had met a man known to them as 'Fred,' and that he had given them some globules, which they had swallowed. He afterward accompanied them to their home, where he remained until 2 o'clock the next morning."

As the reports came into the police station from the hospital, an inspector was sent to the home at 118 Stamford Street, a well-known house of prostitution. At the home he found "on a sideboard in the rooms occupied by the girls a letter from some man accepting the girl's invitation to tea. There was no envelope, but the letter was addressed from some hotel in Chatham."

Due to the doctor's initial investigation the coroner ordered the contents of the women's stomachs be analyzed. "There was no sign of any disease and the symptoms were not consistent with canned or putrefied meat poisoning." The report came back clearly "showing that strychnine in large quantities had been administered to them, but by whom or for what motive is a mystery." It would not take long for the coroner's jury to render a verdict in the cases of Alice Marsh and Emma Shrivell. It was "death by person or persons unknown." The hunt would now be in full swing for the mysterious visitor named "Fred." Unlike the Ripper, this serial killer was writing to the police to brag about his accomplishments. He was even able to leave a few clues for the officers to follow. The poisoner had also accused two local doctors, accusations which

The execution of Dr. Cream, as seen on the cover of the November 19, 1892, edition of *The Illustrated Police News*.

Scotland Yard detectives quickly and easily disproved. One of the notes, however, did have one vital clue. It mentioned that Matilda Clover had been murdered, yet up to that point the authorities were convinced that her death had been by natural causes. The writer of the note, who had to be the serial killer, was then first referred to as the Lambeth Poisoner by the London press.

The undoing of Dr. Cream came at the hands of his fifth intended victim, Lou Harvey, who had foiled his plot to kill her. As before, and after, the doctor had written to the police, informing them where to find his latest victim. However, this young prostitute had become suspicious of her new companion and had thrown his gift of pills into the River Thames. She was able to provide a very detailed description which included his "cross-eyes" and thick glasses and she would eventually point Dr. Cream out at his murder trial for the death of Matilda Clover.

Fate then stepped in as Cream's ego took hold of him. The doctor had met an American police officer from New York and was more than happy to lead the visiting officer on a tour of where the poisoner's victims had lived. Thinking that the good doctor had much too much interest and much too much information about these murders, the American officer shared his suspicions with Scotland Yard. The Scotland Yard detectives agreed that Cream had too much knowledge and interest in the case so they soon placed Cream under surveillance. While keeping him under watch as he frequented prostitutes in the Lambeth area, the authorities learned through their contacts in America that Cream was suspected of poison murders in the United States, specifically the one in 1881.

Arrest, Trial and Execution

On June 3, 1892, the Lambeth Poisoner was arrested. Cream insisted that they had the wrong man, stating that his name was Dr. Thomas Neill. This partial name was picked up by the press, which began using it. Despite the name change, he was charged with the single count of murder in the death of Matilda Clover. The five-day trial began on October 17 and it would prove to be an open and shut case. He was easily identified by Lou Harvey, still very much alive, no thanks to Dr. Cream!

Dr. Thomas Neill Cream, the Lambeth Poisoner 135

"The Poisoning Mysteries" of Dr. Thomas Neill Cream, who killed an unknown number of persons using strychnine. He taunted the police with false tips in the form of letters accusing other people of the murders.

The expected guilty verdict was rendered by the jury of twelve, followed shortly thereafter by the death sentence being announced.

Dr. Thomas Neill Cream took his drop on the Queen's gallows on November 15, 1892, but as stated before, was unable to finish his final sentence in his little game of death. "I am Jack the...." Needless to say, he was not the infamous Jack the Ripper despite his rather theatrical final statement! The reported comment by Cream remains nothing more than a repeated rumor, as there were police and other witnesses to the execution close enough to have heard such a comment, but they never reported it. The source of the rumor that Cream spoke those words must therefore be suspect. James Billington, Cream's executioner, was noted for being a bit of a practical joker and this would have been a typical joke for him. If he did mean it to only be a practical joke it must also be said that he never recanted his statement that Cream did indeed confess if only to his executioner.

His death mask may now be viewed by a select few who are lucky enough to be escorted through Scotland Yard's Black Museum. As one may well expect the Lambeth Poisoner case file, one of the most infamous to ever come out of London, is also featured in the Black Museum.

Amelia Elizabeth Dyer, the Baby Farmer Most Foul (1896)

"You'll know all mine by the tape around their necks."

Insanity and serial killing are not always found in one and the same individual. In this case, however, they most certainly are. For the ten years before she became somewhat of a household name in England, Mrs. Amelia Elizabeth Dyer (1839–1896) had been in and out of asylums, irrefutable evidence that she had been insane for a very long time. These facts were brought forward as part of a vigorous defense during Dyer's two-day trial, but nothing could banish the image of dead babies floating down the Thames River out of the minds of the jury. Despite what might normally have been a convincing defense of mental incapacity, the jury convicted the 57-year-old woman in only five minutes! Even taking into account that British juries were notorious for their fast verdicts, this short period of time must surely be very close to a record. There was no doubt in anyone's mind that the quite hard-faced and matronly looking woman in the black bonnet and old shawl was a most foul serial killer of babies obtained by baby farming. News reports coming in were

Amelia Elizabeth Dyer, the Baby Farmer Most Foul

read by the people of London: "The baby, recently delivered, was found in a box by a Dr. Barton. The child was pinned in a bundle. There was a piece of tape round the child's neck, and it was tied in a knot.... Death was due to strangulation."

From hometown.aol.com we learn some of the background of "baby farmers" and why they came to the fore in Victorian England.

The practice of baby farming grew up in late Victorian times when there was great social stigma attached to having a child out of wedlock. Proper adoption agencies and social services didn't exist in the 1890s so an informal, untrained group of women offered fostering and adoption services to unmarried mothers who would hand over their babies plus, say, ten pounds in cash (quite a large sum of money then) to them in the hope that the child would be re-homed. Most of the babies were, in one way or another. It is probable that some were sold to childless couples and others fostered/adopted for a few pounds. Unmarried mothers were often desperate, so answered the adverts placed in newspapers by seemingly reputable people. Getting rid of a child in this way had obvious advantages to the mother—it was simple, quick and legal with few questions asked. If the baby farmer moved on the baby's mother was often too frightened or ashamed to tell the police so it was very easy for unscrupulous women to kill off unwanted or hard to foster (sell?) babies.

Dyer first came to the attention of the police when a doctor informed them that there were several suspicious deaths of children who had been placed into the care of Mrs. Dyer. It was 1879 and a trial was held, but not for murder. The trial would find her guilty of neglect, ending with a sentence of only six months. It was this trial and conviction which would later be described as "the event" which pushed her over the edge to insanity. After this period in custody Dyer

Amelia Elizabeth Dyer, under the guise of a baby farmer, was a serial killer of children. She was convicted of one of the murders and hanged in 1896.

would spend repeated periods in mental hospitals. She had been diagnosed as having suicidal tendencies and mental instability. She returned to baby farming, but when deaths happened under her watch she did not attempt to have doctors certify those deaths. A doctor, after all, had caused her to come to the notice of the police earlier. From this point on she would simply dispose of the bodies herself. With some parents seeking their children after they had been placed in her care, Dyer began to move around a great deal, using various aliases. The police at this time did not have a good lock on who she was or even that they were looking for one woman to connect to a series of child murders.

Amelia Elizabeth Dyer was not poor by the standards of Victorian England. She was born in a small village near Bristol to a master shoemaker and his wife who made certain that their daughter learned how to read. She would develop early on a love of poetry and literature. Dyer, a devoted member of the Salvation Army, had moved to Kensington Road, Reading, Berkshire, in early 1895 some months after being released from the asylum, for the final time as it turned out.

Helena Fry

Not long after moving to Kensington Road, Dyer began to place advertisements in local papers seeking opportunities to care for babies. Naturally, hard-pressed women seeking help sought out the kindly looking "grandmother" to help care for their little ones. She looked to all the world to be very safe. A Mrs. Fry, having seen one of the ads, needed just such help with 15-month-old Helena Fry and Mrs. Dyer seemed just the ticket. When she left her child with Mrs. Dyer, she did not know it would be the last time she would see little Helena alive.

On March 30, 1896, a bargeman working the Thames River near Reading would spot an unusual object floating in the river. Opening the brown paper parcel, he discovered the remains of Helena Fry. The Thames River Police were soon called into the case, as was Scotland Yard. The killer would soon be easily identified. Detective Constable Anderson made the key discovery. By using a microscope on the paper, he found an address on the brown paper parcel which had held the child! This led police authorities directly to the home of Mrs. Dyer, but she was nowhere to be seen. She was moving on to other babies.

The hunt was now on for a serial killer who targeted babies (the so-called baby farmer), used several aliases and was constantly changing her address. Despite her precautions, on April 4, 1896, inspectors from Scotland Yard caught up with Mrs. Dyer and placed her under arrest. They were, however, too late to save four-month-old Doris Marmon and 13-month-old Harry Simmons.

Doris Marmon and Harry Simmons

Little Doris Marmon had recently been entrusted to Dyer's care by her mother for £10. In the *Bristol Times & Mirror* Dyer had advertised for babies: "Married couple with no family would adopt healthy child, nice country home. Terms, £10." Miss Marmon would answer the ad and received a letter from Dyer as Mrs. Harding.

> I should be glad to have a dear little baby girl; one I could bring up and call my own. We are plain, homely people, in fairly good circumstances. I don't want a child for money's sake, but for company and home comfort. Myself and my husband are dearly fond of children. I have no child of my own. A child with me will have a good home and a mother's love.

Doris Marmon's mother was not married and Dyer came to the conclusion that she did not want to be with her child any longer. She was wrong, as Miss Marmon had decided to keep Doris. Not long after the little one was placed in her care Dyer strangled the child, later said by the press to be a "sweet little poppet," and dumped her remains in the Thames. She had kept the baby's corpse in a brown paper parcel for three weeks until the smell from decomposition became too much. On April 10, while Dyer was in police custody, a carpetbag containing the body of little Doris Marmon was fished out of the Thames. Doris would be the second-to-last victim of baby farmer Amelia Elizabeth Dyer and the one who would help send her to the gallows. But the record would show that little Doris was not alone when she was placed in the river. The wrapped carpetbag, which held the baby's remains, also held the body of 13-month-old Harry Simmons. Both still carried the deadly trademark of Amelia Elizabeth Dyer; both bodies had white tape tied around their necks, tape which had been used to strangle them.

For a while Mrs. Dyer's daughter Polly and her son-in-law Arthur were taken into custody from their home in Willesden in the northwest area of London. It was at their home that Mrs. Dyer had taken custody of little Doris, and the baby's clothes were located by the investigating officers in their house. However, they were soon released after an investigation showed that they were completely unaware of what Mrs. Dyer had been up to. In fact, no one in her family had suspected that she had been a serial killer for those many years.

Under police interrogation it would not take long for Dyer to admit to murder. The police confronted her with the fact that seven small corpses had been recovered from the Thames and all of the babies had the identical white tape drawn around their necks. Dyer then informed the police that they would be able to easily identify any number of her kills. "You'll know all mine by the tape around their necks."

Completely insane and quite proud of her "work," Mrs. Dyer explained to the astonished officers that she felt that she was ridding the Earth of these "shameful bundles." It was her job to pass these "little innocents" from life and "into the arms of the river" and she felt quite justified in her actions on this matter. It must be said, however, that Victorian society must hold at least some of the blame for this situation, as many "proper" Victorians also viewed these children as "shameful bundles." By the time her trial began authorities could count no fewer than seven victims of Mrs. Dyer that had been collected from the river, including Doris Marmon and Harry Simmons, all with tape around their necks. There was much evidence that could lead one to believe that many more babies must have been murdered by this serial killer in the black bonnet.

The Baby Farmer Inquest and Trial

During the inquest the authorities were unable to link Dyer's daughter or son-in-law, Arthur Palmer, to the murders as accomplices. During the inquest Arthur would be discharged as a result of a long confession penned by Amelia Dyer while she sat in Reading Goal.

> Sir will you kindly grant me the favour of presenting this to the magistrates on Saturday the 18th instant I have made this statement out, for I may not have the opportunity then I must relieve my mind I do know and I feel my days are numbered on this earth but I do feel it is an awful thing drawing innocent people into trouble I do know I shall have to answer before my Maker in Heaven for the awful crimes I have committed but as God Almighty

is my judge in Heaven as on Earth neither my daughter Mary Ann Palmer nor her husband Alfred Ernest Palmer I do most solemnly declare neither of them had anything at all to do with it, they never knew I contemplated doing such a wicked thing until it was too late I am speaking the truth and nothing but the truth as I hope to be forgiven, I myself and I alone must stand before my Maker in Heaven to give an answer for it all.
witness my hand Amelia Dyer
April 16, 1896

Trial was held in the Old Bailey on May 21 and 22, 1896. On the 22nd she pled guilty to the murder of Doris Marmon. Strong evidence of insanity was clearly shown not only by her many periods in asylums, but by her calm assurance that she was somehow doing "good works" by murdering these children. The prosecution argued that her "exhibition of mental instability" had only been an act used to avoid suspicion and throw the authority off track, as they happened during periods of time when she was suspected of other murders. She was still very proud of her work on the "shameful bundles."

The jury agreed with the prosecution, and she was soon found guilty and sentenced to death by hanging by Justice Hawkins, who thanked the jury for their work. Dyer's daughter escaped conviction even though she had given graphic description of disposing of some bodies. The newspapers reported the case to the British public and it cannot be said that the reports were favorable to Mrs. Dyer despite newspaper coverage that the woman was not quite of "right mind." It may be said, however, that more than a few in England at the time felt that perhaps Dyer's work was not completely as evil as the papers were reporting it. The tip of the scales of justice could very well have moved in other directions.

The End of Days

Deciding not to appeal her sentence of death, Dyer spent her last few days in the death cell writing out her "last true and only confession" into five English exercise books. The night before her execution the prison chaplain asked her if she had anything to confess. With this question Dyer handed the priest the five standard exercise books with the report, "Isn't this enough?"

The next morning, on Wednesday, June 10, 1896, Dyer was prepared for the gallows by James Billington, the first in a long line of family executioners, who had spent the previous night at Newgate Prison in preparation for the scheduled execution. At her drop on the gallows serial killer Amelia Elizabeth Dyer became the oldest woman executed in England since 1843.

With her execution comes a mystery or perhaps best described as only a partial story. Authorities were able to show that she had been active in baby farming for at least fifteen and perhaps as long as twenty-five years. Partial records, her many moves, and river tides being what they were during that period indicate that we will never really know how many young victims died by her insane mind and well-practiced hands. The only fact we can state with any certainty is that her known body count of seven must surely be far too low for this kindly looking yet completely insane serial killer. What is certain is that an unknown number of future "shameful bundles" would be able to live out their lives because this baby farmer had met the hangman at Newgate Prison.

After Days

It did not take long for a popular penny ballad to make its way to the streets of Victorian London. Inspired by the crimes of Amelia Elizabeth Dyer, who had by then been dubbed the "Ogress of Reading," the ballad would become well known to the children of London.

> The old baby farmer, the wretched Miss Dyer
> At the Old Bailey her wages is paid.
> In times long ago, we'd 'a' made a big fy-er
> And roasted so nicely that wicked old jade.

In a twist worthy of Hollywood, two years after Dyer took her well-earned drop on the gallows, railway workers made a disturbing discovery while inspecting train carriages at Neuton Abbot, Devon. The men found a small parcel which contained a three-week-old baby. The baby girl was cold and wet but very much alive. The little girl was the daughter of Mrs. Jane Hill who had been recently widowed. As she could not care for the child she had given her up to Mrs. Stewart for £12. Mrs. Stewart had picked up the child at Plymouth Station and authorities found that she had dumped the child on the next train stop. Scotland Yard would soon discover that "Mrs. Stewart" was actually Mary Ann Palmer, the daughter of Amelia Dyer!

Samuel Herbert Dougal and the Moat Farm Murder (1899)

> "...did feloniously, willfully, and of his malice aforethought, kill and murder Camille Cecile..."

Samuel Herbert Dougal (1846–1903) was certainly a womanizer—it was what kept him in funds. It was only later in his life that he would turn to murder. It was not a wise move, but there is the possibility that murder had always been part of the mix, but evidence of this possibility simply does not exist. At this point criminal history records "only" a single murder.

Dougal had served by all accounts a successful career in the British Army. Most of his military career was spent in the Royal Engineers where he rose to the rank of chief clerk. Much of his time in the army was spent overseas; at one point he spent nine years in Halifax, Nova Scotia, Canada. It was while in Canada that he met, married and lost two wives. His first wife died after what was reported to be a "sudden illness" in 1885. It did not take long for the unit's chief clerk to move on, marrying his second wife only two months after putting his first wife in the grave. As fate—or perhaps other forces—would have it, his new bride would also die some three months after they were married. Luck, if that was what it was, was not on his side when it came to marriage. By 1887 Dougal had had enough of army life and it was time to move on to other things back in Great Britain.

A New Career

His many years in the army had not prepared Dougal for a good job in the civilian world. As such he spent the next few years going from job to job. He also went from one woman to another seeking, it would seem, some form of financial support. He finally landed a job as a civilian working in the office of the commander of the British Forces in Dublin, Ireland. This work was not to last, as Dougal's true nature was discovered. He was busy forging monetary documents, which after his conviction earned him a 12-month sentence at hard labor. However, only two months into his sentence Dougal attempted to kill himself. Failing in this, he spent the next 10 months (the remaining time on his sentence) in an asylum. Perhaps that was the real reason for the "attempted" suicide.

In the autumn of 1898 Dougal met 55-year-old Camille Cecile Holland. Holland was single, well off, and living alone in Elgin Crescent, London. In the verbiage of her time she would have been called a woman of "independent means." She had resources of around £6,000 to £7,000 in the form of stocks and company shares which in 1898 was a goodly sum. To be sure, Samuel Dougal took careful note of her resources and made plans to acquire some, if not all, of them. News reports would state that he "cultivated her acquaintance." It must be said, however, that Miss Holland never completely trusted Mr. Dougal. There was a reason why she was independent and well off. She had been very careful in money matters.

Nevertheless, by January of 1899 Samuel and his "new wife" Camille could be found in their new home, Coldhams Farm, having moved to Saffron Walden near Clavering. It was a quiet, out of the way farmhouse that some may have even called lonely. Even though the farm property had been selected by Dougal and despite his insistence that it be registered in both of their names, Camille made certain that only her name would be found on the paperwork. She was a care-

Samuel Herbert Dougal was convicted and hanged for the murder of his common-law wife, Camille Holland, in 1899. His motive was purely financial.

ful woman. The property needed some work to really make it a home so the couple took lodging with Mrs. Wisken at Market Row, Saffron Waldon. Mrs. Wisken would know them as Mr. and Mrs. Dougal, even though no formal marriage had been performed.

The Moat Farm

Coldhams Farm became home to "Mr. and Mrs." Dougal on April 22, 1899, and was renamed the Moat Farm. On May 13 they hired a maid, Florence Havies, who promptly moved in. It did not take long for Dougal to decide that Florence was just what he was looking for in an upgrade. It was time to "seduce" the housemaid. In fact, he made inappropriate advances on Florence the very next day while he was alone with her in the kitchen. When that failed, on the evening of May 16 he attempted to enter her room. Her screams soon alerted Camille who rushed to the maid's room and promptly sent her "husband" to bed. That night and the next two nights found Florence and Camille sleeping in the same room. Both women realized that this situation was not going to work out and something needed to be done. Miss Holland would have to tell him to leave, as she now knew that she had made a grave error "marrying" Dougal. Dougal had other plans.

Despite the argument about the maid Dougal had not left yet. In fact, he was able to convince his wife to go for an evening ride. On May 19 Samuel and Camille went out at around 6:30 p.m. for a ride on the "pony and trap." When he returned to the farmhouse at 8:30 p.m. Camille was not with him. Naturally Florence wanted to know where she was, finding that she was now alone in the house with Mr. Dougal. He told her that Camille had gone off to London and that he expected her to return later that evening. From that time to around 12:45 that next morning Dougal made a succession of trips in and out of the house. Upon his final return that morning he told Florence that his wife had not returned from London and off she went to bed. Samuel did not attempt to enter her room. Perhaps he was too tired from all the work he had been doing that night to mess around with Florence. As for Florence she had made her own plans.

Florence was up early and by 7 a.m. was ready for her chores. She was surprised to see that Dougal was already up and in fact was already eating breakfast. He told Florence that he had received a letter from Camille in London to the effect that she had decided to extend her London stay for an impromptu holiday. The fact that she would be alone for an extended time with Samuel was of no consequence to Florence as her mother soon arrived to take her away from the Moat Farm. With her wages in hand, Florence left the Moat Farm, never to return.

Dougal soon hired a new maid, Miss Emma Burgess. Later news reports would inform their readership that Mr. Dougal and his series of "maids" had taken up the practice of bicycling in the nude! Burgess was followed by a new "Mrs. Dougal" who became his official third wife. (He did not count Camille.) For the next four years a number of women would visit the farm as Mr. Dougal entertained several liaisons with some of the village ladies, covered as "strange women" by the late Victorian press. It would become a scandal, but one which did not go well beyond the local area. He had good cover for his activities, becoming a regular at the local church to which he became known for his rather generous contributions to the redecoration of the church interior and the expansion of the churchyard and renovation of an old graveyard. This cover of community involvement, allowing him contact with many local women, was about to come to an end. Dougal realized that his efforts to diminish his "missing" wife's accounts had drawn attention to himself, so he fled the farm for London. It was not far enough to escape the police, however. In March of 1903 he was arrested and charged with "forging and uttering a cheque value £28 15s. payable to J. Heath, dated 28th August 1902, purporting to be drawn by Camille C. Holland at Clavering."

A Forgery Trial and a Belated Search for Camille

At his trial for forgery the prosecution showed that Dougal had been moving money from Camille's account over an extended period of time into his own accounts. He had also sold off her shares and company stocks and had eventually transferred the Moat Farm to his name, removing Camille from the title. He had taken nearly everything by this point, forcing the authorities to ask what had really happened to Camille since none of the checks and transfers had been done by her. It was time to take a close look at the Moat Farm, so on March 19, 1903, the police took possession of the property.

The local *Essex County Chronicle* would report on the police occupation of the farm as they made their search for any signs of the missing woman. "The police officers engaged in searching at the Farm occupy the farmhouse, preparing their meals and making their beds for themselves. Detective-Sergeant Scott acts as chef." On April 27, in front of a crowd including locals, curious visitors from far away, and local and national newspapers, a body was discovered on the Moat Farm. Once again the *Essex County Chronicle* would report on the incident:

> Throughout the week, people have flocked to the Moat Farm in crowds, the majority of the visitors being ladies. Oranges and nuts were sold as at a village fair, and the raucous voices of the vendors were heard on every side. Souvenir postcards of the Moat House and of the grounds, showing many of the holes made by the police and the tent-like awning which conceals the grave, commanded an enormous sale. A number of the sightseers brought Kodaks with them in search of effective snapshots and a still larger contingent were relic-hunters.

Of the Body

The body had been in the ground in a semi-open grave for four years and naturally identification was going to be difficult. The moldering corpse had been placed in a sack and dumped in a drainage ditch. Once removed from the grave it was taken to the conservatory on the Moat Farm and laid out for close examination. There were, however, still clues to be found. With the help of her former landlady Mrs. Wisken and aided by Miss Holland's nephew, Ernest Legrand Holland, they were able to identify pieces of the clothing found in the grave and the authorities were certain that they had found the remains of Camille Holland. They were also able to identify some of the jewelry found on the corpse. Finally, the shoes found in the grave were taken by the police to cobbler Mr. Mold who was able to testify that it was indeed his name on the shoes and that he had made the shoes for Miss Holland. The body itself would give little to aid in the identification. The method of murder was another thing entirely.

Soon after it was removed from the ground an expert from the Home Office, Professor Pepper, along with divisional police surgeons Dr. Spraque and Dr. Storrs, examined the corpse. Their examination showed that Camille had been shot in the head at close range. Summing up, Professor Pepper would write that the shot "must have caused immediate insensibility, which would have continued until death." There would be no doubt that whoever the victim was she had been murdered and intentionally dumped into a crude grave. Since no other missing person could possibly match the remains, the identity was clear.

The Trial for His Life

"On the 19th May 1899, [Samuel Herbert Dougal], did feloniously willfully, and of his malice aforethought, kill and murder Camille Cecile Holland at Clavering." It was June 22, 1903, a sunny day at Chelmsford and the hall was filled. In Shire Hall, Dougal was indicted for murder by the police court and he would be held over for trial.

Before a crowded courtroom, prosecutor Mr. Gill KC opened with the argument that on May 19, 1899, Samuel Herbert Dougal had persuaded Camille Holland to go out for a pleasant ride in their pony and trap. That he then drove her to a pre-prepared grave far enough away from anyone who might hear a shot and then took out his pistol and like the coward he was shot her in the back of the head. After the murder Mr. Gill reported that Dougal had simply dumped her body in the hole, covered her up lightly and calmly drove home.

The defense could show very little other than circumstantial evidence. The jury soon took the case and for 56 minutes debated the fate of Mr. Dougal. When they returned, the guilty verdict did not surprise anyone—least of all Samuel Dougal.

Donning the black cap, the judge passed the required sentence on the convicted killer, sending him to the hangman.

> It is my duty to pass upon you the sentence of the law—that you be taken from hence to the place from when you came, and from there to a place of execution, and that you there be hanged by the neck until you be dead, and that your body be afterwards buried within the precinct of the prison in which you shall have been last confined after your conviction. And may the Lord have mercy on your soul.

Execution

At 8 a.m. on July 14, 1903, Samuel Dougal was executed at Chelmsford Prison. After the required time his corpse was cut down, examined and pronounced to have been properly executed. One news report would end its coverage of the execution with the note that they were "ridding the country of this deceitful felon." The body was soon tossed in an unmarked grave on the grounds of Chelmsford Prison as the black flag of execution was raised over the prison. On a wall near the grave a brick was marked SHD to indicate his place in the ground. Essex County, England, thus removed one of their more notorious citizens, the case was stamped "closed" and Scotland Yard added yet another case file for the Black Museum.

Section III

The 20th Century— A New Era for Murder

The Stratton Brothers and a Thumbprint to the Gallows (1905)

"I am an independent witness."

It was 8:30 in the morning on Monday, March 27, 1905, and Chapman's Oil and Colour Shop on High Street in Deptford should have already been open for business. It was a clear, cool day and nothing seemed out of the ordinary. However, when William Jones went to the paint shop that morning he found the door locked and the shutters closed. It was not like 71-year-old manager Thomas Farrow (1834–1905) to cause the shop to be closed so late on a business day so Jones tried knocking on the door. Receiving no response from Farrow or his 65-year-old wife Ann (1840–1905), who lived with her husband above the store, Mr. Jones became concerned. He was able to look into the store through a window and as his eyes became accustomed to the darkened room he saw signs of a struggle. Chairs had been knocked over and there was general disarray about the place.

Now quite concerned, Jones ran to a nearby shop for help. He soon returned with Louis Kidman, a local resident quite familiar with the shop and Mr. & Mrs. Farrow. They broke into the shop and discovered the corpse of Mr. Farrow in the front of the business. Clearly this was a case of murder and robbery. Continuing their search, they located Mrs. Farrow in her bed upstairs, unconscious and barely alive. Both had been badly beaten. The police were called to the scene and Mrs. Farrow was brought to the hospital. She would never regain consciousness and was therefore not able to identify the attackers. The police now had a brutal double murder on their hands.

It soon became clear that robbery was the motive for the attack, but there had not been any forced entry. It was suspected that Mr. Farrow must have been called to the front of the shop and simply opened the door. The officers discovered that it was general knowledge that Mr. Farrow would collect the week's sales in a small cashbox and upon each Monday visit the bank to make his deposits. The amount estimated to have been taken from the cashbox was £10. The empty cashbox was found on the floor near Mr. Farrow's body, and in fact it was said to be "in the way" of the investigation. In order to give the doctor easier access to Mr. Farrow's body, Sergeant Albert Atkinson pushed the box to the side without putting on gloves. In earlier days the box would not have been a valuable clue to help solve this case. That was about to change.

As the investigation continued, Chief Inspector Frederick Fox and Assistant Commissioner of the Metropolitan Police and head of CID (Criminal Investigation Department) Melville Macnaghten arrived to take over the case. They discovered that Mr. and Mrs. Farrow had been attacked in different locations. They also found two women's stockings that had been left at the scene. Blood was found on both of these. Because the Farrows were both in their nightclothes the police formed the theory that the killer had knocked on the door, which awakened Mr. Farrow who opened the front door. He was probably attacked immediately upon opening the door and even though he was half asleep he fought the two men until he was beaten to unconsciousness. He had several defensive wounds on his body and did not go down easily. From there the killer or killers found Mrs. Farrow upstairs, attacked her and located the money box. The empty box was simply discarded.

A Greasy Smudge

When the empty cashbox was pointed out to Macnaghten, he decided to have a closer look. The outside was covered with smudges of dirt mixed with blood and could not reveal anything of value. However, the underside of the tray in the box did hold a vital clue to the

The Stratton Brothers and a Thumbprint to the Gallows

murders. Macnaghten noticed a "greasy smudge" which to his trained eye appeared to be a fingerprint. Keeping the possible evidence in mind he picked up the cashbox using his handkerchief and handed it to another officer who carefully wrapped it in paper. The small box was soon on its way to Scotland Yard's new Finger Printing Bureau. Although it was not known at the time, the investigators had discovered *the* vital clue to the murders. It was a clue which would eventually add a critical new tool to law enforcement and become a guide to how business would be conducted in future British murder investigations.

At the time, the Finger Printing Bureau was commanded by Detective Inspector Charles Stockley Collins. Collins was regarded as the foremost fingerprint expert in England; if anyone could prove this case based on a single greasy print it was him. However, even if investigators could discover who had left the print, it was not entirely certain that the prosecutors could convince a jury that this new method could be used to identify a single individual exclusive of all others. It was a great risk, but one which needed to be taken at some time and this seemed to be the best case to test the method in a court of law.

Collins was soon at work pulling the print. He was able to state that the print had been made by a right-hand thumb. His first job was to eliminate the officers who were investigating the double murder, as well as the Farrows. Having done that, the Scotland Yard team began the detailed work of matching the print to any of the 80–90,000 sets on file at the time. There was no match, which meant that although the person or persons who had committed the crime might very well be known criminals, they had not yet been fingerprinted. It would now be the job of detectives to utilize the usual methods in the search. On March 31 Mrs. Farrow died without regaining consciousness. There was thus no witness description from either of the victims. Other witnesses would need to be located.

Hardworking detectives soon located several witnesses who could describe individuals who had been around the store near the time the crime was thought to have been committed. One witness described two men, one who wore a dark blue serge suit and bowler hat while the other man had on a cap and was dressed in a dark brown suit. This witness had seen these two men on the morning of March 27, at around 7:30 as they were leaving Mr. Farrow's paint shop. The police also interviewed a young girl named Ellen Stanton as well as a local professional boxer named Henry John Littlefield, both of whom identified Alfred Stratton as the man in the dark brown suit. Now Scotland Yard had a name to work with.

Further investigation led officers to Annie Cromarty, the girlfriend of Alfred Stratton. Under questioning Annie told the police that Alfred had a dark brown coat, but had gotten rid of it along with a pair of shoes the day after the murder had become known from newspaper reports. She also volunteered that he had asked for a pair of her old stockings. When officers checked the description of Alfred's brother Albert they soon realized that he matched the second man seen leaving the paint shop. The two known vagabonds with local criminal ties soon became the prime suspects in a double murder.

On April 2, the brothers were taken into custody and taken to the Finger Printing Bureau for prints. It would not be long before detectives were able to match the greasy print found on the cash box with the right thumbprint of Alfred Stratton. Scotland Yard detectives had their men—now they had to convince a jury that the new science of fingerprinting was absolute proof of a single suspect being linked to a single print at the crime scene. It was, after all, the only tangible evidence they had linking these men to the crime other than the sighting of two men leaving the shop.

The Fingerprint Trial

During the trial it soon became evident that the use of a new type of evidence would be an uphill battle. None other than Dr. Henry Faulds, a pioneer in the new field of fingerprinting and the man who had introduced the western world to this new science, was scheduled to take the stand. At this time, Dr. Faulds mistakenly believed that an individual match to a single print was unreliable and certainly not enough to condemn a man to death. As would be expected, the defense made much of his thoughts on the matter. Dr. John George Garson was also called. He testified that anthropometrics was much more reliable as a means of identification than fingerprints. (Anthropometrics, or the "Bertillon System," developed by Alphonse Bertillon [1853–1914], was a method of human body measurement thought to be able to identify an individual as a criminal in a specific crime.) In 1900 Garson had

The Stratton Brothers and a Thumbprint to the Gallows 155

testified before the Beplar Committee against using fingerprints as a form of identification in criminal cases. Politics and professional rivalry was being played out in this trial as both of these men were professional rivals of Edward Henry, then commissioner of the Metropolitan Police and the man who had established the Finger Printing Bureau. Henry attended the trial; a fact which was not missed by the popular press at the time.

Nevertheless, the prosecution continued and formed a very strong case, calling more than 40 witnesses. This case would not be allowed to stand on one fingerprint alone, even though the print would continue to stand as the prime piece of evidence. The pathologist who did the post-mortem on the Farrows for the Home Office testified that the wounds inflicted on the victims were consistent with tools owned by the Stratton brothers and would have easily have killed them. Henry Littlefield and Ellen Stanton were both called to the stand and were both firm in their identification of Alfred Stratton. Albert Stratton's girlfriend, Kate Wade, not wanting to be considered "an accessory after the fact" in a murder, testified that Albert usually stayed with her, but was not with her the night of the murder. Alfred's girlfriend Annie testified that he had come back to her place on the morning of the murder with a good deal of money, but he had refused to tell her where he had gotten it. He of course was also not with his girlfriend that night. As he was tossing out his clothes he had told her to tell anyone who asked that he had been with her that night. This was only after he saw reports of the murders in the local paper. He knew the police were closing in.

It was time for defense attorneys Curtis Bennett, Harold Morris and H.G. Rooth to press their case. They were able to cast some doubts on the testimony of some of the prosecution's witnesses. They were so confident in their work that they even allowed Alfred to take the stand. As it turned out, he had an interesting and very false tale to tell. He told the court that he had been asleep in his rooms early on the 27th when his brother Albert tapped on his window. Albert, it would seem, needed money to pay for a night's lodging. As the story continued, a quick check revealed that he had no money to lend, but when he returned to the window his brother was gone. Being the good brother that he was, he went out looking for Albert and found him on Regent Street. (This part of the story was necessary because both brothers had been recognized by several very reliable witnesses on Regent Street.) This point in the now very tall tale finds Alfred relating that he invited his brother to sleep on his floor and conveniently both were together until well after the murders, parting each other's company at around 9 a.m. that morning, well after the bodies were discovered.

The story, which was not very convincing to begin with, was about to fall apart. While the brothers were held in jail, one of the jail workers, William Gillings, had a short but very telling conversation with Albert Stratton. Stratton was reported as saying: "I reckon he [Alfred] will get strung up and I shall get about ten years.... He has led me into this." Prosecutor Richard Muir (1857–1920) used Albert's words as a confession to at least being at the scene of the crime, but in order to get a conviction he would need more. At the time, the science of fingerprinting was not considered admissible in British courts so Muir would need to not only understand as much as he could of this new science he would also need to explain the evidence very carefully to the all-male jury.

Inspector Collins was brought to the witness box as an expert in fingerprints. Collins was able to explain to the jury in layman's terms how the newly developed system of fingerprinting had developed and how it could he used to identify a single individual, who in this case had left behind a single greasy print. The inspector then showed the jury of 12 the cashbox which had been taken from the scene of the crime and explained how the print had been copied by the officers for comparison. At this point in the questioning by prosecutor Muir, Inspector Collins carefully showed the jury how the single print recovered from the murder scene exactly matched the right thumbprint of Alfred Stratton. He showed that there were 12 points of agreement from his print taken while in custody at Scotland Yard to the one from the box.

In order to put some type of reasonable doubt on the evidence put forward by Inspector Collins, it was time for the defense to put Dr. John Garson on the stand. There were two problems with Dr. Garson's testimony; first, even though he had studied the new science of fingerprinting, he was not an expert and in fact he felt the science was unreliable. Second, he had written letters to both sides of the trial soliciting payment for expert testimony, which could go for or against fingerprint evidence. In short, for a fee he would be happy to testify for either side depending only on who would pay the highest price! Mr. Muir knew he had his man when he confronted Dr. Garson on the stand.

Mr. Muir: How can you reconcile the writing of these two letters in the same day?
Dr. Garson: I am an independent witness.

Mr. Justice Channell, the trial judge, had heard enough, stating that the writing of these two letters to both the prosecution and defense showed that Dr. Garson was an "absolutely untrustworthy" witness and that the jury should not take his testimony as evidence of anything.

Dr. Henry Faulds had been scheduled to testify, but with the discrediting of Dr. Garson the defense team decided to withhold testimony from Dr. Faulds fearing that the prosecution may have something on Dr. Faulds which could call into question his testimony as well. The defense simply could not take the chance of another surprise.

When the jury received the case it would take a full two hours before they found both Stratton brothers guilty of murder. On May 23, 1905, both killers faced the gallows and were hanged for the most part on the value of a single greasy fingerprint. Due to the efforts of Richard Muir and Inspector Collins, criminal investigators now had a powerful new weapon with which to fight crime and which had been severely tested in a court of law.

Dr. Peter Hawley Harvey Crippen and Miss Ethel Clara Le Neve (1910)

"Good morning, Mr. Dew."

Hawley and Cora Crippen could never be mistaken for a happy couple, although the union did at least seem to work while they lived in New York City. Dr. Crippen, born in Michigan, qualified as a doctor in 1885, had a going practice in the city and enjoyed the work. Cora was born Kunigunda Mackamotzki, and went by the stage names Belle Elmore when she played in music halls and Cora Motzki when she worked operettas. Yet in 1900 the couple left New York and moved to North London into a home at 39 Hilldrop Cresent, Camden Town.

In London, Dr. Crippen gave up medical practice and became the London manager of an American patent medicine company. The 38-year-old man was small, described as "5 feet 4 inches, sandy moustache, balding hair, gold-rimmed glasses and false teeth," and had his office in London's Shaftesburg Avenue. As for Cora, his second wife, she was described as "boisterous, full-bosomed, and lacking in feminine charm." She had also been described as "vulgar, domineering and promiscuous." It was not a good match for the quiet, polite and somewhat shy Dr. Crippen.

During their stay in London the good doctor decided he had had enough of his very demanding wife. The demands, which most grated Dr. Crippen, were Cora's desire to become an opera star, said to be obviously well beyond her abilities, and her continuingly increasing sexual demands on her husband. When her husband was unable or unwilling to meet her demands, Cora would simply go elsewhere, but she did not go far. It would seem that her work in the world of theatre afforded her many opportunities of an amorous nature. Her singing career was a failure, so she found her place as the treasurer of the Music Hall Ladies Guild, a charity office on New Oxford Street, guaranteeing that she would still have close contact with people in the theatre, including many well-known stars of the day.

Cora began to take boarders into their three-story home. In fact, these were little more than low-level individuals in the theatrical world who paid little, if anything, for their lodging. In short order, Cora settled her affections on an American actor named Bruce Miller, who soon openly took Dr. Crippen's place at night. By 1907 Dr. Crippen had been reduced to little more than a servant in his own home as he cared for Cora's many lodgers.

Mrs. Cora Crippen had aspirations to a life in the theatre, but failing that, she surrounded herself with entertainment types, even offering some of them room and board for little to no money.

Dr. Crippen and Miss Le Neve

Dr. Peter Hawley Harvey Crippen killed his wife, Cora, in 1910. He was the first fugitive to be captured through the use of wireless radio technology. He was fleeing to Canada with girlfriend Ethel Clara Le Neve and was recognized by the captain of the ship on which they were traveling.

The situation may very well have remained that way for a much longer time had it not been for Miss Ethel Clara Le Neve.

After his domestic chores were done, which included cleaning the boots of Clara's boarders, the early rising Dr. Crippen would move on to work in his office, which had become his escape and only pleasure. Crippen's work included duties as an anesthetist for a dentist as well as selling patent medicines. His training as a homeopathic specialist in America did not allow him to become a licensed physician under the rules set forward by the BMA (British Medical Association). He would need to find other work. That was until he hired Ethel Clara Le Neve as his secretary and bookkeeper. Ethel was everything his wife was not. She was an understanding 24-year-old who paid attention to the doctor and did not attempt to put him down. He soon told her of his marital problems. Before long the doctor and Miss Le Neve were meeting in London hotels. For three years the doctor went from the love of Miss Le Neve to the ever-expanding demands of his overbearing wife. He knew he had to do something, but the proper Dr. Crippen never seemed to have simply allowed himself to walk away. Instead, he decided to slowly poison his wife and then when the work was done cut her into easy-to-dispose-of pieces. It seemed best at the time.

One Less Wife, If You Please

Dr. Crippen had taken to giving Cora doses of a nerve-depressant called hyoscine whenever her sexual demands were more than he could bear. The drug was also a hypnotic, which could, if used to excess, become a dangerous poison. On January 17, 1910, Crippen purchased the last five grains he would need to finish off his overbearing wife. A few days later, on January 21, Cora had her final dinner party with her entertainment friends. It was suspected that Dr. Crippen gave Cora the fatal and probably full dose later that night. Most likely Cora was fully disassembled by the next morning.

Dr. Crippen went about the disposal of his wife in a systematic manner, as he separated her considerable flesh from her bones and buried them in the cellar. Detectives would use the term "filleted" as they discussed the method used to slice up his wife. The bones he broke up and burned in the cellar grate. The flesh had been covered with quicklime and reportedly wrapped in his pajama top before being buried. In short order what had been Cora was completely gone, at least for the time being.

On February 20, 1910, a ball had been given for the Music Hall Ladies Guild Benevolent Fund. Two of those in attendance were Mr. and Mrs. Nash who knew Dr. Crippen, but were better friends of Crippen's wife. Also in attendance were Dr. Crippen and his typist Miss Le Neve. This alone caused a few tongues to wag, but what caught the eye of the Nashes was the expensive diamond brooch worn by Miss Le Neve that they knew belonged to Mrs. Crippen. Doing nothing for the time being, the Nashes went about their business until other facts came forward. The following March the Nashes took a trip to New York during which time a friend of theirs gave them the news that Mrs. Crippen was dead. They would, upon their return to England, ask about their friend Mrs. Crippen, at which time the good doctor informed them that his wife was not only alive, but that she had in fact left him and gone to California to visit a sick friend. "Some little town near San Francisco with a Spanish name I think."

Before long Ethel moved into his 39 Hilldrop Crescent home and the lodgers were told that they were no longer welcome. Gossip continued as friends made inquiries to California, seeking information on the whereabouts of Cora "Belle" Crippen. No one seemed to have heard anything about the woman. For extra cash Dr. Crippen pawned some of his wife's jewelry, but other pieces he gave to Ethel. He had also given his new lady some of Cora's furs and other clothing. That, and the fact that Ethel could be seen about town wearing Cora's well-known diamond clip, came to the attention of Scotland Yard, by way of Mr. and Mrs. Nash, who promptly sent Chief Inspector Walter Dew (1863–1947) to investigate. Dew was promoted to chief inspector of CID at the start of the 20th century and was well respected.

Inspector Dew wrote in his report:

> It will be gathered from the forgoing that there are more extraordinary contradictions in the story told by Crippen, who is an American citizen, as is Mrs. Crippen, otherwise known as Belle Elmore. Without adopting the suggestion made by her friends as to foul play, I do think that the time has now arrived when "Doctor"' Crippen should be seen by us and asked to give an explanation as to when, and how, Mrs. Crippen left this country, and the circumstances under which she died.

When Inspector Dew began looking into the case he did not have evidence of foul play, but he knew something was not quite right. Earlier in March, Crippen had reported that his wife had "passed on of pneumonia up in the high mountains of California." It was now July and the inspector wanted more details. At this point the easygoing Crippen changed his story and told the Scotland Yard inspector that his wife was very much alive but had run off with her old sleeping companion Bruce Miller. They were said to be living somewhere in America, and the doctor had not wanted the public humiliation brought on by Cora running off. "I suppose I had better tell the truth; all my stories about her illness and death are untrue, so far as I know she is not dead at all."

To Inspector Dew this seemed a reasonable explanation, but he checked the whole house, top to bottom, just to be sure. The inspector also included the cellar during his search where he unknowingly walked over the decomposing flesh of a murder victim. The inspector found nothing suspicious at the time and left, but when he returned on July 11 for some clarification on when his wife had left him he found that Dr. Crippen had left the house and was not expected to return. Ethel, who was still passing as Dr. Crippen's housekeeper and aide, was also gone. They had left no forwarding address.

The Atlantic Ocean Chase

It became clear at this point that some type of crime had been committed and the inspector began a very close and detailed two-day search of Dr. Crippen's home, including the new coal cellar floor. Before long, a team of men from Scotland Yard found the decomposing fleshy remains of a body. Even though the remains had not been in the ground for very long, the quicklime had done a fairly good job. Pieces of "filleted" flesh, to include the chest, stomach, muscle, and buttock were found in a *man's* pajama top, but there was not enough remaining to show if the rotting pieces of corpse had been a man or a woman. The coroners, Dr. Augustus Joseph Pepper (1849–1935) and Dr. Bernard Henry Spilsbury (1877–1947), would need to use abdominal scars on the flesh to indicate the cellar grave contained some of the final pieces of Cora Crippen. He also found hyoscine poison in the body parts. On July 16, 1910, a warrant was sworn out at the Bow Street Police Court for the arrest of Dr. Crippen and his "housekeeper." The well-publicized nationwide manhunt was on.

The doctor was on the run, but he was unaware that Inspector Dew was already after him. In fact, Dr. Crippen thought that he had gotten away clean, but in an abundance of caution he traveled with Ethel in disguise. On July 20, the couple left Antwerp, Holland, on the S.S. *Montrose*, sailing for Canada. They had been in Rotterdam and were traveling as father and son! Ethel was disguised as a young man, and the couple was registered as Mr. John Philo and Master Robinson. It was, however, not a very good disguise.

During the voyage, Captain Henry George Kendall became suspicious of the pair, as they appeared to be just a bit too affectionate for a father and his reportedly 16-year-old son. The captain would tell reporters, "The younger one squeezed the other's hand immoderately. It seemed to me unnatural for two males, so I suspected them at once." As it turned out, the captain enjoyed reading the newspapers of the day and he knew of the £100 reward for a "Doctor Crippen and his mistress." The newspapers were well into reporting the story of the "London Cellar Murder." Except for the name, he felt this pair seemed to match, despite the disguise. When he was sure, he went to the ship's wireless room and sent a Marconi telegraph to London—attention Dew of Scotland Yard. The message was sent to the owners of the ship who promptly informed Scotland Yard—and the press!

> Have reason to believe Dr. Crippen and Miss Le Neve are traveling as passengers on my ship. They are posing as father and son and should reach Quebec on July 31.
> Await instructions. Kendall.

Captain Kendall may not have realized it at the time, but this was the first time the new ship-to-shore wireless system had been used to help catch a wanted fugitive who was on the run. The press soon published accounts of the daring escape and the case conducted by the Yard. They were also informed that during Captain Kendall's personal investigation he had found ladies underwear in the cabin occupied by the pair in question.

It did not take long for Inspector Dew to spring into action. The detective soon booked passage on the White Star liner S.S. *Laurentic*, a faster ship than the S.S. *Montrose*, intending to beat the *Montrose* to Canada. The *Montrose* seemed to have slowed a bit on its passage—under captain's orders of course. The *Laurentic*, which could make 16 knots, passed the *Montrose* in the Saint Lawrence Seaway while Inspector Dew was on deck; he knew then that he would soon have his man. Crippen had no idea that he was about to be captured. However, the press would be on hand to record the capture of the first murder suspect caught by way of the "Marconigram" on board ship. The truth of the matter was that even if Inspector Dew had not personally arrived in time to put the cuffs on Crippen, the fugitive was known to be on board and certainly would not have been allowed by local authorities to escape. It did, however, make some most interesting stories for the public to read in their morning papers.

Early on the morning of July 31, Inspector Dew, with Sergeant Mitchell in tow, boarded the S.S. *Montrose* from a pilot boat soon after the ship entered Canadian waters. Dew was taking no chance that the couple could escape. Along with the Scotland Yard men came a Canadian inspector because they were now in Canadian territory and they would need the inspector to effect an arrest in Canada. The group went first to the captain's cabin where "Mr. Robinson and son" were being held. Dew soon introduced himself in a manner of British understatement, which marked this senior detective. "Good morning, Dr. Crippen. I am Chief Inspector Dew of Scotland Yard. I believe you know me." The surprised and unsteady Dr. Crippen could only say, "Good morning, Mr. Dew." Dew continued, "I am arresting you for the murder and mutilation of your wife Cora Crippen in London on or about February 2 last." The chase was over and the legend began.

From Dew's 1938 memoirs we read:

> I had landed on July 29 by the liner *Laurentic*, arriving two days before the *Montrose*, which was already well out in the Atlantic when we first suspected

that Crippen was aboard, but which was a much slower vessel than the mail steamer *Laurentic*. Old Crippen took it quite well. He always was a bit of a philosopher, though he could not have helped being astounded to see me on board the boat. He was quite a likeable chap in his way. Much of my time in Canada was spent evading reporters and cameramen, who knew all about my arrival in spite of our efforts to keep it secret, and who frequently became personal when I did not give them a statement. As it happened, Crippen and his companion, Miss Ethel Le Neve, showed no desire to postpone our departure and waived their extradition rights, which enabled us to make the return journey after being only three weeks in Canada.

The doctor and Miss Le Neve were returned under police escort to London aboard the S.S. *Megantic* to face separate trials at the Old Bailey, Central Court. Edwardian England soon took excited note of the sensational crime and the 3,000-mile chase by Scotland Yard to get their man. Needless to say, the newspapers of the day did a brisk business.

Justice and Beyond?

Once again Richard Muir came to the bar for the prosecution. Muir went about building the case meticulously, taking the time to track down the source of the piece of pajama fabric, checking nearly every fabric merchant and clothing dealer in London. When he finally located the shop where it had been purchased, he learned that the shopkeeper actually remembered selling the pajamas to Mrs. Crippen! For their part, Dr. Pepper and Dr. Bernard Spilsbury invited the jurors to come to a bench they had set up in the court for a microscopic view of the abdominal scar he had located on the remains as well as a close look at some pubic hair which matched the known color of Mrs. Crippen's hair. It was for the prosecution *the* evidence that the corpse was the remains of Cora Crippen. For his work on this and other criminal cases Spilsbury would be long remembered as "the greatest medical detective of the century." His work certainly brought to the court a new confidence that medical science could indeed be viewed as positive evidence of criminal activity. The pathologist's close work with the police would also lead to the development of "murder bags," which are now used by detectives worldwide to secure evidence gathered from crime scenes.

On October 23, 1910, Crippen's five-day trial ended with his conviction and a sentence of death. Four days later Ethel's trial ended with an acquittal and she would walk free, never to see Doctor Crippen again.

On November 28, 1910, Dr. Peter Hawley Harvey Crippen was given a drop of six feet at Pentonville Prison by executioner John Ellis, which snapped his neck cleanly. His last request was that he be buried with a photograph of the very lovely Miss Le Neve.

In 1938, Inspector Dew would gain fame as the author of a book on the well-known case, entitled *I Caught Crippen*. In Walter Dew, Scotland Yard had its first "media star." As for Miss Le Neve, she soon faded from the spotlight, no doubt happy to be out of the minds of the press and public. She will, however, always find a place among the records held in the Black Museum along with her friend the doctor. There is of course at least one mystery still attached to this case. Scotland Yard detectives were never able to locate the head of Mrs. Crippen. How he disposed of this piece of his wife the good doctor took to the grave along with his photo of the lovely Miss Ethel Clara Le Neve.

Postscript to Pathology

For Dr. Spilsbury, the work he did on the Crippen case was to propel him in the public's mind as *the* man who could be counted on to use science in tracking down and helping convict criminals. As far as the Crippen matter is concerned, however, modern medical opinion on his ability to positively identify the victim in that famous case is questioned. Nevertheless, his fame continued as he worked on such well-known cases as the Brides in the Bath Murders, the Blazing Car Murder and the Brighton Trunk Murders. Sadly, following the deaths of two of his three sons, Spilsbury, then in failing health, committed suicide by gas in December of 1947 at University College, London.

A Final Postscript?

In recent years grave doubts about the identification of the remains in the Crippen cellar have caused a re-examination of this famous case. The results were remarkable. The remains were discovered to have been that of a male in his twenties! The scar on the skin was found to be a fold in the damaged skin. As for the cloth "found in the grave" by Inspector Dew, we are left with the understanding that if it was Mrs. Crippen's then how did it find its way into another man's grave?

As for what really happened to Cora—we may never know. The odds are that the quiet Mr. Crippen did indeed murder his wife, but it seems that what he did not do was bury her in the cellar!

Mr. and Mrs. Seddon and the Death of Miss Barrow (1911)

"What a terrible charge—willful murder! It is the first of our family that has ever been charged with such a crime!"

Miss Eliza Barrow (1862–1911) was a 49-year-old spinster who had moved into the upper floor rooms of Mr. and Mrs. Seddon's home in Crouch Hill in July 1910. She had been living with her relatives, the Vonderashes, but an argument over money—hers—forced her to decide that it was best for her that she moved away from these people who would be later portrayed as "hanging around her money like so many vultures." When she moved into her rooms she brought with her Ernie and Hilda Grant, who had been orphaned some years earlier upon the death of their mother. She was indeed a generous person but not one to be taken advantage of.

All seemed to go along quite normally until political events caused Miss Barrow to become concerned that her rather substantial funds would be insufficient in the years to come to allow her to live the easy life to which she had become accustomed. She had decided that a part-time job would not fill the void that she felt could arise, and at any rate working for the rest of her life was not appealing. Prime Minister Lloyd George was reportedly looking for ways to improve the cash flow into the British government. Miss Barrow feared that single people such as herself, who were completely dependent on the income derived from their investments, could be taxed so severely that she would not be able to make ends meet. She needed to find a way out of a potential problem.

Miss Barrow naturally spoke to her landlord, Frederick Seddon, who had some experience in matters of money. Seddon worked over the years as an insurance agent and in fact Miss Barrow was impressed that he was now a senior insurance agent. He offered to make a few calculations for her which could help her with a continued income. He never did any calculations, though, as he simply informed the gullible Miss Barrow that if she handed *all* of her capital over to him he could ensure that an annuity could be developed which would allow her to live in his home rent-free. In fact, he stated that she could live rent-free for the rest of her life. This seemed the solution that Miss Barrow had been looking for, so without checking further, she signed over to Mr. Seddon around £3,000 worth of "India stock" as well as the title for two homes she owned in Camden. There did not seem to be any plan for her to rent out her homes for some additional income. It would seem that Mr. Seddon was very good at convincing people of his sincerity. She thought she was now set for life, a life which Mr. and Mrs. Seddon would ensure was a short one.

The summer of 1911 saw an epidemic of gastro-enteritis spreading across England. This would prove a very good cover, at least for a while, for the opportunistic removal of Miss Barrow and her funds. Frederick Seddon made sure that Miss Barrow received her first annuity payment right on time. It was, of course, simply money taken from her own, a small amount of which he turned into a check. It would be her last "annuity payment." Mr. Seddon saw no reason to waste too much money on his tenant/victim. Miss Barrow was soon very ill with "gastro-enteritis" which involved several days of diarrhea and vomiting before she died. Mrs. Seddon would do her best to "care" for Miss Barrow during her "illness." Seeing another opportunity for some fast cash, Mr. Seddon gave Miss Barrow a pauper's funeral and pocketed a small commission from the undertaker. This would prove to be an error in the plan, as fast money was

Frederick Seddon was accused of killing his lodger, Miss Eliza Barrow, in order to steal her considerable fortune. He was hanged in 1911 for the crime.

foremost on his mind rather than a well-planned disposal of a body which was filled with critical evidence.

With Miss Barrow out of the way, at least for the moment, it was time to remove the burden of young Ernie and Hilda Grant. However, before any real moves could be made, the greedy and carefully watching relatives of Miss Barrow would need to be dealt with. They had learned of Eliza Barrow's death through published reports, and her cousins, the Vonderashes, wanted to know why they had not been informed of the death. Most important for them was the question of all of that investment capital which they wanted to get their hands on as soon as possible.

When confronted by the cousins, Mr. Seddon claimed that he had indeed written them. He further told the Vonderashes that Miss Barrow had died a pauper and had left them nothing. Naturally, having been aware of their cousin's wealth, the Vonderashes were not about to take Seddon's word for anything. They were soon off to the police, demanding an investigation. It did not take long for the authorities to see the possibilities of foul play and Miss Barrow was exhumed from her freshly dug grave for a medical examination. By 1911 medical and forensic science had moved forward enough to show quite conclusively that Miss Barrow had not died from gastro-enteritis. It was clear that she had been poisoned with arsenic! And there were very few suspects to investigate in this closely held case. Mr. Seddon, had he not been greedy for the undertaker's small commission, would probably have been in the clear if the body had been cremated.

An Arrest for Murder

The headlines read, "North London Landlords Are Accused of Poisoning Tenant." When Frederick Seddon was arrested in the Barrow matter he was quoted as saying to the officers, "What a terrible charge—willful murder! It is the first of our family that has ever been charged with such a crime." As it turned out he would not be the last. The police were soon following a trail of money, which included the cashing of £5 notes, which had been traced to Eliza Barrow's cashbox. Mrs. Margaret Seddon had been cashing them in, endorsing them with a false name and false address. She soon found herself under arrest when she could not supply the police with an adequate reason why she was cashing in someone else's £5 notes. Adding to the arrests the police soon had the Seddons' daughter in custody, as the police had discovered that she had purchased a group of flypapers from the local chemist. The flypapers Maggie Seddon had purchased were loaded with arsenic. The entire household was now in custody and the police court would soon conclude that there was enough evidence for a trial.

The Trial

The trial at the Old Bailey was prosecuted by Attorney-General Sir Rufus Isaacs with what was reported by the London dailies to be with "icy fervour." He was not a man to take a murder case lightly—he always went in for the kill! When it came to Mrs. Seddon she would say very little in her defense. She offered no defense or explanation whatsoever for passing the £5 notes, nor could she explain why she felt that she had to falsify the name and address of a dead woman. It would be clear by the end of the trial however that the jury actually felt sorry for Margaret Seddon, believing that she had been completely dominated by her husband. It would also go well for Maggie Seddon, as her arrest and presence at trial had not been on any firm ground. No connection to any murder plot could be proved in her case as she may very well simply have been directed by her father to purchase the flypaper. Frederick Seddon would be an entirely different matter. He had directed the fraud on Miss Barrow and was clearly the leader in how she had been dealt with.

Frederick Seddon was by nature a very calculating and cool individual. He was not one to warm to a jury or for that matter anyone else as he sat in the witness box. Even though he answered each question without hesitation Attorney-General Isaacs had no problem impressing the jury how cold he was as he detailed his answers. What came out in the court and reported in the newspapers was the feeling that both the victim, Miss Barrows, and her suspected killer, Mr. Seddon, were "both money-grabbing misers" who attempted to one up each other. There seemed to be little regard for the victim as far as her funds were concerned. A "mire woman" with that much money of her own and not being with a man was simply not proper! These opinions of money-grabbing courtside were soon displaced by the feelings of young Ernie Grant who stated that he and his little sister had been treated quite well both by Miss Barrow and then by the Seddons. These words by the orphaned Ernie contrasted with the feelings of the court and were further enhanced by Ernie's comments that the only time he felt mistreated was by Miss Barrow's cousins, the Vonderashes, whom he said only hung around Miss Barrow like a bunch of vultures circling for the money.

When the jury returned from their deliberations, Maggie Seddon was free and when Mrs. Seddon was acquitted Mr. Seddon leaned over to say, "You're well out of this." After his wife was acquitted Frederick was declared guilty, which did not seem to greatly disturb him. He did not seem to be surprised at the results and took it in stride, which continued to impress the reporters that he was indeed a cool customer. When asked if he had anything to say he gave a short speech covering a small financial point he wanted to make clear to the court which had not been part of the testimony. If anything he wanted the financial testimony to be complete as well as accurate. After this financial detail was cleared up in his mind Seddon, standing before the judge, made a Masonic sign which was clearly understood by the judge, Justice Bucknill, himself a Mason. This hand sign stopped the judge in his tracks and for a moment or two he did not seem to know what to do. When he recovered he told Seddon with a less than firm voice, "Our brotherhood does not encourage crime. On the contrary it condemns it. I pray you again to make your peace with the Great Architect of the Universe." He then sentenced fellow Mason Frederick Seddon to hang by the neck until he was dead. The papers would take note that a Mason had sent another Mason to the gallows.

The End Game

The newspapers were never satisfied with the verdict of murder in this case or that the Seddons had anything to do with it at all. Much of the dissatisfaction came from the testimony of Professor Willcox who came forward during the brief trial to discuss the new chemical process used to detect arsenic in Miss Barrow's body. Even the smallest error in the testing process could give a false reading reported as "a quite disproportionate difference to the final calculation." In other words, it was no more than a calculated guess and not clear proof of arsenic poisoning at any level. The papers would also bring up Mr. Seddon's "lower middle class vulgarity," which was used to show some kind of inbred guilt by the "smooth barristers" he was confronted with on the bench. Nevertheless, despite the many doubts, Frederick Seddon did indeed hang for the arsenic murder of Miss Eliza Barrow. And in the course of time the cousins Vonderashes did indeed inherit the remaining funds. Justice, one may argue, was not necessarily served in the death of Miss Barrow as the case finally came to a close.

George Joseph Smith and the Brides in the Bath Murders (1915)

"I am in terror!"

George Joseph Smith (1872–1915), alias Henry Williams, Oliver George Love, Charles Oliver James, and John Lloyd, was a womanizer and serial killer; one of many to call England home. His method of murder, however, would prove to be unique in the annals of British crime and one which would be labeled by the press as "The Brides in the Bath Murders." Unique or not, it would prove to be a method of murder which could not stand up under the heavy watch of a jury of 12, but not until three would die in one of his baths.

Smith was born on January 11, 1872, in the scenic town of Bethnal Green, England. He would marry his first wife, Caroline Beatrice Thornhill, in 1898. In 1908, quite forgetting to divorce Caroline, he married Edith Peglar using the alias Oliver George Love. In 1910 he married for a third time to Bessie Mundy using the alias of Henry Williams. Once again he failed to go through a divorce, but it must be said, considering his future activities, both Thornhill and Peglar could count themselves among the lucky ones. They were still alive, at least for the time being. From this point on in his much-married career Smith would correct that error as he then focused on the funds he could acquire from suddenly dead wives. Now he needed to find a good victim and he looked to the past to advance his future.

172   Section III: The 20th Century—A New Era for Murder

George Joseph Smith married five times and drowned three of those wives in the bathtub. Here he is shown with third wife, Bessie Mundy, murdered in 1912.

Bessie Mundy

Bessie Mundy had become Mrs. Bessie Williams in 1910, but it did not take long for Smith (Williams) to part with her. He had bigamously married the spinster when he found that she had some £2,500 of an inheritance available, but to Smith's horror he found that only £138 would go to him in the event of an accident. Not interested in such a small amount for all the work he would need to do, he simply deserted her with alacrity. However, in 1912 Smith returned and the still lonely Bessie took him in. After the reunion it did not take long for Smith to convince Bessie to change her will in his favor. In turn, Smith changed his will to favor his wife, which he knew she would never execute.

Five days later, on July 13, 1912, Mrs. Bessie Williams was found dead in the bath at their home at 80 High Street in Herne Bay. A coroner's inquest was held due to the strange and singular nature of the death and of course the new husband was closely examined. The primary evidence during the inquest would come from Dr. Frank French, who testified that it was his belief that the woman had had an epileptic fit while in the bath, allowing the body to slip under the water. His belief ran to "asphyxia brought about by drowning." When asked if the body had shown any signs of struggle or attack Dr. French would see none. It was a clean kill!

The final question the doctor was asked was what was his opinion on whether or not the death had been caused by anything other than a simple drowning. His reply was, "I have no reason to suspect any other cause than drowning." With that, the jury rendered a verdict of "Death by misadventure." Smith could now collect £2,579, 13 shillings and 7 pence.

Alice Burnham

Having gone through a good deal of the money he had acquired from Bessie, it was time for confidence trickster and by then, murderer, Smith to find a new victim. He soon found Alice Burnham of Aston Clinton. She married Smith late in 1913 despite the fact that Alice's father could clearly see grave things in his prospective son-in-law's manners.

During his daughter's engagement he described Smith as having "a very evil appearance" and he was not shy in reporting his feelings to Alice. Nevertheless, a marriage did occur and there was nothing he could do about it.

On the evening of December 12, 1913, Mr. and Mrs. Smith were staying at an apartment owned by Mr. and Mrs. Crossley. That night Alice went up for a bath and never came down. At the coroner's inquest held on December 13, Joseph Crossley would state that when Alice was found in the bath her head was "at the foot of the bath." This evidence would prove to be important at a later trial, but for this inquest the verdict would be "accidentally drowned through heart failure when in the bath."

It was time for the widower to collect another £500 for the loss of his second "wife"! Alice's father Charles knew that foul play had taken his daughter, but he had no real evidence to present to the police. Justice would have to wait.

Margaret Lofty

December 18, 1914, found Margaret Lloyd and her husband "John Lloyd" visiting her solicitor that cool afternoon. It was time for the newly minted Mrs. Lloyd, formerly Margaret Elizabeth Lofty, to change her will to include new life insurance in favor of her new husband. George Joseph Smith, alias John Lloyd, had found his latest victim and he was planning to cash in as soon as possible. That evening husband John informed the owner of the home he lived in with his new wife that he was going out to a local shop to purchase some tomatoes for his wife's dinner. They would be consumed after his wife had taken her bath. What he did not tell the unsuspecting landlord was that his wife was already upstairs in the bath dead!

Upon his return to the house, which he made certain was seen by the landlord, he called to his new bride to inform her that he had returned from the store to the boarding house at 14 Bismarck Road, Highgate, London. Smith then made his casual way to the bathroom where he "found" his wife's body. The "distraught" husband was soon running down the stairs with grave news.

On January 1, 1915, a coroner's inquest was held, with an unsurprising verdict of "accidental death" being recorded—case closed. Needing to end the situation with speed, Smith directed the funeral director Herbert Francis Beckett to move things along: "I don't want any walking. Get it over as quick as you can." The hearse had just drawn up when he spoke to Mr. Beckett. After the short funeral Smith would state, "Thank goodness, that's all over." Unfortunately for Smith that was not quite the end of the story as he placed a claim for the £700 life insurance on his new, now very dead, third wife. It seems that this serial killer for profit was moving just a bit too fast and people were beginning to pay attention.

A Closer Look

Matters were now moving away from Smith's deadly control. Charles Burnham, the father of Alice Burnham, was in the habit of reading the newspapers. When he read about the untimely death of Margaret Lofty (Mrs. John Lloyd) he became very interested in the details. The fact that this woman and his daughter's death by drowning in a bathtub were so similar caused him to bring these facts to the attention of the local police. At the same time Mr. Joseph Crossley, who had been the landlord of the property where Alice and her "husband" had lived when she died, noted the same similar events. On January 3, 1915, Crossley sent a letter to Scotland Yard expressing his concerns. He enclosed a newspaper clipping reporting details of Margaret Lloyd's death and noted the similarity to the reported facts in Alice Smith's death. The Yard took due notice and began to look at the particulars.

Detective Inspector Arthur Neil was assigned to the case. It would not take long for Scotland Yard detectives to establish that at the very least Smith was a bigamist, swindler, petty thief and very possibly a serial killer of lonely women. On February 1, 1915, Detective Inspector Neil walked up to Smith as he crossed Uxbridge Road in London. He informed his prey that he was being taken into custody for what amounted to a charge of bigamy—"false entry made in a marriage register." Smith would stand before the Bow Street Police Court on February 8. The court remanded him until February 15, which allowed the police to do a much deeper investigation of his other possible crimes.

The Final Days

On March 23, after several more remands, Smith was charged with the murders of Bessie Mundy, Alice Burnham and Margaret Elizabeth Lofty. It would be up to Dr. Bernard Spilsbury, the government's pathologist, to prove that it would be virtually impossible for anyone to accidentally drown in any of the baths that had been used by the victims in this case. From *Cops, Crooks, and Criminologists* we read:

> Spilsbury was the predominant authority in British forensics, a junior honorary pathologist to the Home Office, and the "murder man" on whom one called when probing a hard-to-prove poisoning death or other crime with few workable clues. In the "Brides in the Bath" case of 1915, he demonstrated how George Joseph Smith had overpowered a succession of girlfriends while they were bathing; Spilsbury's exhibition proved more than amply realistic when his courtroom model, a St. Mary's nurse, nearly drowned.

He would forcefully argue that these were murders for monetary gain and not accidents. His testimony was so clear and without fault which was exactly what the prosecution had needed. Needless to say, Smith was found guilty of murder and quickly sentenced to death.

Upon the conviction, Charles Matthews, director of Public Prosecutions, wrote a letter to the commissioner of the Metropolitan Police on July 1, 1915. His subject was Detective Inspector Arthur Neil.

> I feel I ought not to allow any interval of time to pass without expressing the acknowledgment which in my opinion, the administration of justice under Divisional Detective Inspector Neil, and to the officers who served under him, for their untiring, able, zealous, and intelligent efforts, which played so conspicuous a part in securing the conviction which was this day obtained of the above named malefactor.

Sir Charles Matthews had good reason to respect the efforts and professionalism of Inspector Neil. He had seen Neil's work in many other cases. Neil would eventually become one of Scotland Yard's top men.

On August 13, 1915, Chief Executioner John Ellis took the final measure of George Joseph Smith, dropping him the required amount on the gallows at Maidstone Prison. As he was led up the 13 steps Smith was heard to say, "I am in terror!" He was visibly shaking as he moved to the gallows. It was said by those close by to have been a good snap. Any struggle would be a short one. The black flag soon flew over Maidstone Prison to a cheer from those who had waited outside for news of the execution.

The Murder of Police Constable George William Gutteridge (1927)

"...who met his death in the performance of his duty..."

Police Constable George William Gutteridge (1891-1927) was on patrol duty during the evening and early morning of September 27, 1927, when he spotted a car coming along the road in Essex near Howe Green. Later investigations would show that Gutteridge probably thought that the vehicle was being driven by a local doctor named Edward Lovell. He flagged the car down, possibly noting that there were strangers driving the vehicle which had by then pulled to the side of the road. With pencil and pad in hand the officer approached the car. Evidence would show that before he could conduct any type of interview, two shots rang out, striking him in the face. He did not even have time to take out his flashlight. The cop killers then sped off down the darkened road. But not before pumping two more bullets into the officer's body.

Gutteridge was born in Downham Market, Norfork. He would join the Essex County Constabulary in April 1910 as constable #489. After only a month's training, not unusual at the time, he was posted to the Southend. As more and more men were needed to wage World War I, Gutteridge answered a new call to duty for king and country. He resigned from the police force in April 1918 as the war raged in France to join the British Army. He served for 10 months in a machine gun corps.

Finishing his military service, he rejoined the Constabulary on February 23, 1919. He served in the "Grays" upon his return, later transferring to Epping Division in March 1922. His posted station at Stapleford Abbotts included beats at Kelvedon, Lambourne End, Stanford Rivers and Stapleford. When he went on his final patrol, he lived at 2 Townsley Cottages, Stapleford Abbotts, with his wife, the former Rose Annette Emmerline, and their two children, Muriel and Alfred.

On September 26, 1927, Constable Gutteridge knew that it was going to be a long shift on patrol duty. He came home at 6 p.m., having finished his first patrols. After spending a few hours at home for some dinner and rest he returned to his patrol at 11 p.m. to later meet Police Constable Sydney Taylor who was posted to Lambourne End Station. At 3 a.m. the two men came together at the pre-planned location at Howe Green on B175 Romford off Chipping Ongar Road. The men exchanged information about the early morning events before parting for a well-earned rest at home. It was 3:05 a.m. as Gutteridge began his one-mile walk back to his home. His work was done but he was still an officer and one last job was on. It was the last time he was seen alive—except by the two men who murdered him as he walked along the dark and lonely road. No one would report hearing any gun shots that night.

The Discovery of a Body

Six a.m. on September 27 found postman William Alec Ward dropping off some mail at the Stapleford Abbotts Post Office. His early morning task completed, he continued driving on Ongar Road, across the familiar Pinchback Bridge in the direction of Stapleford Tawney. Before coming to Howe Green as he rounded the bend in the road he saw something he had not seen before along the grassy side of the road bank. Coming closer in the light of an early morning he realized that he was looking at the body of a man. The body appeared to be in an unnatural semi-sitting position facing the road with the legs pointed out. Coming closer, he was shocked to discover that he knew the man, Constable Gutteridge, and he had clearly been brutally murdered.

George William Gutteridge was a police constable in 1927 when he was shot and killed by William Kennedy and Frederick Browne in a stolen car (Essex Police Archive).

Mr. Ward quickly made his way to nearby Rose Cottage in Howe Green and summoned help at Alfred Perrit's home. From there Ward drove to Stapleford Tawney Post Office to the nearest telephone and made a call to the Romford Police Station. It is not clear what a bus driver named Mr. Warren did to notify the authorities because neither he nor the officer he summoned were called to testify at the trial, but we do know that he came across the body about the same time as Mr. Ward.

The first officer to make his way to the murder scene was Police Constable Albert Blockson. His first job was to secure the area to make certain that no critical evidence would be lost. He did not need to check on Constable Gutteridge as he was clearly beyond any mortal help. At 7:45 a.m. Detective Inspector John Crockford arrived to begin the official investigation. He was the first to closely look at exactly what had killed his fellow officer. From the Essex Police website we learn:

> The inspector examined George Gutteridge's body and noted that on the left side of the face just in front of the ear there were two holes which appeared consistent with the entry of two large bullets. On the right side of the neck he found two exit wounds. In addition, each eye had been shot away by two further bullets. George Gutteridge lay grasping a pencil stub while nearby his notebook lay in the road. His truncheon was still in the pocket where it was usually kept, as was his torch.

An Extensive Manhunt

A massive manhunt was soon underway and it was very quickly connected to the theft from Billericay of Dr. Edward Lovell's Morris Cowley car. The doctor had reported his stolen car and it soon became a focus of the search. Police reports were flashed nationwide to all stations to be on the lookout for registration number TW6120—the murder car. Within hours Scotland Yard detectives were called in, headed up by the very experienced Chief Inspector James Berrett.

Searching the area, investigators dug two .45 bullets out of the road that had passed through P.C. Gutteridge's body. At the later post-mortem surgeons recovered two more bullets. At about the same time the vehicle was discovered in Stockwell, London, where it had been abandoned. It would prove to be a storehouse of evidence linking the vehicle and eventually the killers to the murder. It was clear that there was a good amount of blood on the running board of the vehicle, suggesting that the constable had been right up against the vehicle when he was murdered. Certainly the evidence showed that he had no warning and no time to react. A close search also revealed an empty cartridge case on the floor of the vehicle. It was marked during its manufacture with RVIV. The clues and thus critical leads were starting to come together.

It was to be a long and detailed search and one of the toughest for the Yard. The area of search would eventually cover the entire country as well as require several investigations overseas. Nevertheless, by January 1928 the authorities had evidence that Frederick Guy Browne had been involved in the murder. Browne, a well-known criminal from London, had a somewhat shady garage business in Clapham and he was also known to be in the car theft business. Police set up a watch on his regular places of business and when Browne returned to his garage in Clapham he was taken into custody without incident. It would not be so easy to take the second suspect into custody. With Browne in custody, the authorities had developed information that an associate of Browne's, one William Henry Kennedy, was possibly involved in the murder.

A fast investigation showed that Kennedy was not at any of his usual haunts so it became a simple waiting game. He had fled London and traveled to Liverpool where he was also known for his criminal activities. Liverpool Police, in coordination with Scotland Yard, kept a close watch on several addresses known to be familiar to Kennedy. Liverpool Police Sergeant Mattinson spotted his man and attempted to take Kennedy into custody. Trapped, Kennedy pulled out a revolver and pushed the loaded weapon into Mattinson's side and pulled the trigger. The sergeant clearly heard the click as the hammer on the weapon dropped, but the gun did not fire. The bullet had jammed in the barrel, saving the life of the veteran officer. Kennedy was now in custody and would face a charge of at least attempted murder of a police officer. Conviction on that charge alone could have landed him in prison for the rest of his life. The ballistics, however, would up the charge to murder in the Gutteridge matter.

On to the Ballistics

Robert Churchill was a noted gunsmith and Scotland Yard's expert on ballistics when he was given the cartridge case and bullets which had caused the death of Police Constable Gutteridge. He would be Scotland Yard's top man on ballistics for many years. He soon discovered that although the cartridge was in good shape the bullets had been severely deformed in use. Nevertheless, Churchill was able to identify sufficient characteristics on the rifling to establish under microscopic examination that the bullets had been fired from a Webley revolver.

Several weapons had been discovered in Browne's business and other related areas, all loaded, including a Webley revolver. Using his laboratory microscope Churchill was able to compare a test cartridge to the one found in the stolen vehicle. This examination would prove conclusively that the weapon found in Browne's possession had fired the shots which had killed Constable Gutteridge.

End Game

From the first time he was arrested in connection to the murder of P.C. Gutteridge to the very end, Frederick Browne would deny any involvement in the murder. William Kennedy, upon first interrogation by Inspector Berrett, admitted to being at the murder scene and in fact would later admit his part in the murder. But he would point to Browne as the trigger man. Browne's defense would be that he had obtained the weapon from Kennedy, but only after the murder and did not know that it had been used to murder the officer. The confusing and contradictory statements could very well have caused the jury to dismiss the charge against at least one of the suspects. The prosecution, however, wanted both men to hang for the murder.

At the Central Criminal Court, London, Mr. Justice Avery presided over the case, which naturally focused on the ballistic evidence tying the murder to the two suspects. The prosecution brought forward some 40 witnesses, who described the events from before the murder all the way to the final post-mortem examination. Four ballistics experts, including Churchill, were called to give detailed information on how the bullets and cartridge were matched to the murder weapon and then to these suspects. Using enlarged photographs Churchill's testimony was devastating to the defense. It would not take long for the jury to convict both men and the death sentence was soon heard in the Central Court.

Both men were hanged on May 31, 1928. William Kennedy took his death drop at Wandsworth Prison by the fine work of Robert Wilson while Robert Baxter took the measure of Frederick Browne. Browne would go to the gallows still demanding his innocence, but Kennedy was not about to take his neck out of the noose. Only later would researchers looking into this case come to the conclusion that Browne may very well have been telling the truth and that Kennedy could very well have been alone when he murdered Police Constable Gutteridge. They hanged Browne, a career criminal, but not necessarily a cop killer.

Nevertheless, there are no memorials to Kennedy or Browne as both have by this time surely rotted into the ground of the prisons which still hold whatever remains of their bodies. That is not so for Police Constable George William Gutteridge. There are two small but sincere memorials to the officer. At Warley Cemetery there is a very well kept grave complete with ornate standing cross and memorial plaque. It reads:

> In proud memory of George
> William Gutteridge, Police
> Constable, Essex
> Constabulary, who met his
> Death in the performance of
> His duty on September 27th 1927.

Representing the police during the gravestone's unveiling was Essex Chief Constable, Captain A.J. Unett. The bullets which killed the officer are now held by the Essex Police Museum and as would be expected, other artifacts from this case may be found in the Black Museum.

The second memorial to the slain officer was placed close to where Gutteridge was murdered on Ongar Road, a section of which was renamed Gutteridge Lane. It was yet another reminder of his good works for the community and nation. The area he was killed in now lies between the Rabbits and Royal Oak public houses. It is said that the officer would have been pleased, having been known to take a draft or two at his local pub. The modest memorial is kept up with an annual check and clean-up by members of the Memorial Trustees to ensure that Constable Gutteridge will never be forgotten. And for the record the Essex officer was officially known as Police Constable 218, George William Gutteridge, serial number 2664.

Cecil Louis England (Toni Mancini) and the Brighton Trunk Murders (1934)

"Internal examination of the torso had not revealed the cause of death..."

Brighton, England, is a popular tourist town on the beautiful British seacoast. It is as popular today as it was in 1934. Nice breezes, good food and a seaside atmosphere all come together for a pleasant experience, even during the rains, for all who visit as well as those who call Brighton home. In 1934, however, this seaside town became the focus of intense police and press interest as two bodies in trunks were found in Brighton-by-the-Beach. The press would soon begin referring to Brighton as "The Queen of Slaughtering Places," much to the alarm of the town fathers. Tourism was not going to be helped along by such newspaper reports, or for that matter a couple of murders.

On June 17, 1934, William Joseph Vinnicombe, a cloakroom attendant working at the Southern Railway office at the Brighton Railway Station, discovered the first of the two unsolved murders when he noticed an unpleasant odor coming from an unclaimed plywood trunk held in the station storage area. He suspected that a crime might have occurred and as such called the Railway Police, who sent Detective Bishop to investigate. Bishop opened the trunk and discovered the dismembered torso of a woman. News of the discovery was flashed to Scotland Yard and Chief Inspector Robert Donaldson was soon on his way to Brighton. Other stations were notified to be on the lookout for trunks which had been abandoned recently. On June 18, a second trunk was discovered at Kings Cross Station. It contained two legs which would eventually be matched to the dismembered torso found the day before at Brighton. The arms and head were never found. The press would name the victim "The Girl with the Pretty Feet" or "Pretty Feet Girl." The body was not identified.

A post-mortem was conducted by Sir Bernard Spilsbury who was able to positively show that all of the remains belonged to a single victim. He stated that the remains were of a woman around 25 years of age. He also discovered that she had been pregnant at the time of her death. He would report to the coroner's inquest his findings.

> Internal examination of the torso had not revealed the cause of death [which was never discovered]; the legs and feet found at King's Cross belonged to the torso; the victim had been well nourished; she had been not younger than twenty-one and not older than twenty-eight, had stood about five feet two inches, and had weighed roughly eight and a half stones; she was pregnant at the time of death.

Naturally, Scotland Yard detectives began looking at the possibility that they had discovered the fruits of an abortion, which, having failed, caused the death of the woman. Doctors would be the first to be suspected. The seasoned Chief Inspector Donaldson soon had a suspect in mind, but it would be a very dangerous road politically because his suspect had well-known political connections reaching high into British society, including prominent politicians and royals! The suspect was the well-known and very well-connected Dr. Edward Massiah of Hove. Donaldson, well versed in the methods required at the time when powerful people are involved, would need to step lightly, so before he confronted Dr. Massiah he posted a watch on the man most covertly. His efforts at stealth would come to nothing when an inspector from Hove, who had been added to the investigation for some local coverage, decided to confront Dr. Massiah with all of the facts then known. The Hove inspector felt that when confronted, Dr. Massiah would "come quietly." Rather than coming along, the doctor wrote out a list of names of possible suspects on a piece of paper and handed it to the officer. The case was now blown wide open and people were going to be ducking for cover.

Donaldson did not learn of this encounter until he was confronted by an officer more senior in rank than himself. Donaldson was told in no uncertain terms to back off. Massiah's powerful friends in government had been informed and there was undoubtedly fear that if Dr. Massiah went down on a brutal murder charge he could very well take down powerful members of British society. Equal rights under the law were nowhere to be seen in England at the time. This was power politics. At all costs Dr. Massiah was not to be put into a position where he could talk. Donaldson was forced to drop his investigation. Nevertheless, that was not the last Dr. Massiah was heard from. He moved to London where in time a woman he was performing an abortion on died. He was not prosecuted for that death either, even though it was clearly a crime. (Abortion was against the law at the time.) He was still being protected by his powerful friends.

By 1952 Massiah had retired and moved to Port of Spain, Trinidad, and one would think, away from the prying eyes of Chief Inspector Donaldson.

Violette Kaye

One of the more interesting aspects of this case relates to the fact that there were two trunk murders in this time period. Almost certainly the two were completely unrelated. And even though the first victim was never identified the second certainly was. Her name was Violette Kaye and she was a well-known prostitute who worked the streets of Brighton as well as the dance halls as an exotic dancer to supply herself with drink and drugs. At the time of her death at age 42 Kaye, who also used the names Watts and Saunders, was living with a petty criminal named Cecil Louis England who at the time was using several aliases, including Toni Mancini, Jack Noytre, Tony England and just for good measure, Hyman Gold. When not involved in some petty crime, England worked many low-paying jobs, including waiting tables and as a bouncer at a club. For the most part, however, it was Violette who paid the bills, usually on her back.

The relationship between Kaye and England was not an easy one. It was in fact later reported to have been quite "tempestuous." The problems held by both parties came to a head at the Skylark Café which fronted the coast of Brighton. Kaye had come to the café on May 10, 1934, where England was working as a waiter, and drunkenly accused England of being overly friendly with one Elizabeth Attrell. Attrell was a good-looking teenage waitress and definitely a step up from Kaye in every respect. It was the last anyone ever saw of Violette Kaye—save her killer.

Before long, friends who had known both questioned England as to what had become of Kaye. England responded that she had gone to Paris and indeed Violette's sister had received a telegram stating that she had moved to France where she had taken on a new job. In the meantime, England was busy disposing of Kaye's clothing and other personal belongings, many of which were given to his new lady, young

Elizabeth Attrell. He also changed his lodgings, moving to a dismal flat near Brighton train station at 52 Kemp Street.

Kaye's absence was also noted by the local police, who were familiar with Kaye's work on the street, but only after a press reporter took note of her absence. When she did not return to "her usual patch" they naturally picked up England for a bit of conversation. The interview went nowhere and at the time the police did not even have any real evidence that a crime had been committed. What they did not look into was a newly acquired trunk which England had purchased, and which held the remains of Violette Kaye, whose real name was Violet Saunders. Not knowing what to do with the trunk he simply placed it at the foot of his bed and covered it with a cloth. He now had a new "coffee table" despite the fact that liquids soon begun to leak out of it.

Even though the police had nothing to go on, England decided that they were looking far too closely at him for England to remain comfortable. This was not to mention the fact that the body in the trunk was starting to smell. With these facts in mind the nervous petty criminal-turned-murderer panicked and ran. While he was gone the local authorities conducted a house-to-house search in the ongoing effort to find clues in the first trunk murder, which they were still attempting to solve despite the fact that Dr. Massiah was still a very good prime suspect. In fact he was truly the only real suspect. Because England had lodgings near the railroad station where the first remains had been found the authorities naturally searched his residence. They were soon opening the large trunk at 52 Kemp Street and accidentally discovered a second body. It can be argued, perhaps, that had England not run, his room might not have been searched. Luck, it would seem, was not on his side—yet!

The new body found its way to the table of pathologist Spilsbury who conducted the post-mortem. He was able to show that the victim had died by blunt force trauma to the head. The hunt was soon on to find alias "Toni Mancini," the petty criminal who had chosen an Italian alias because he thought it made him sound like a tough guy. It did not take long for Scotland Yard detectives to track him down and he was soon arrested hiding in South East London. He had been spotted on July 17 by two police constables from R Division (Greenwich) on Eltham Road, Lee. The charge would be murder and he knew full-well that his neck would be on the line. Once again Inspector Donaldson was assigned to the case as it was felt at the time that the two murders were somehow related.

The Trial

The five-day trial was held in December 1934 at Lewes Assizes and England was quite skillfully defended by Mr. William Norman Birkett (1883–1962). Birkett would become 1st Baron Birkett, Privy Council, in 1947 and later served as an alternate judge for the British during the famous Nuremberg War Crimes Trials conducted after World War II. For this trial the prosecution had assembled a tough team to conduct this well publicized case, led by J.C. Cassells and Quintin Hogg (1907–2001). Hogg would later become a prominent Conservative politician and eventually became Baron Hailsham. During World War II he served as captain in North Africa as a platoon commander in a rifle brigade. A wound to his knee and his age at the time caused him to be removed from front-line service. By the end of the war he would leave army service as a major.

The case seemed to be relatively straightforward, focusing on the victim's head injury, the handwritten form used to send the sister the telegram from Paris which matched England's handwriting and the fact that England had boasted days after the murder of giving (the missus) Kaye "the biggest hiding of her life." Doris Saville also stepped forward to testify that England had told her to supply a false alibi for the time period the victim was thought to have been killed. Saville decided that giving false witness would decidedly not be in her best interest, as she could easily have been sent to prison as an accessory after the fact in a murder.

The defense would focus on Kaye's rather unflattering background as a prostitute and exotic dancer (stripper), claiming for the jury that any of her numerous clients could have killed her. It would not have been an uncommon end for a prostitute. Birkett was also able to highlight the fact that morphine had been found in the victim's blood, throwing some doubt on exactly how she met her end. Finally, the defense was able to prove that the bloody items of clothing which had been presented in court by the prosecution had in fact been purchased *after* Kaye had been murdered! They could not have been part of this murder case, a fact which had escaped the eyes of the prosecutors.

England's story, although not complete by any means, did throw some confusion into the mix. The petty criminal stated that he had simply come home to the flat he shared with the victim in Park Crescent to find Kaye's body on the floor—she was dead. Knowing that the police would suspect him because of his lengthy criminal record he decided to hide the body rather than report what he had found to the police. To this tall tale, defense council added that Kaye could easily have fallen down the stairs having taken too much morphine. It was not an unlikely story by any means and the jury would have a tough time sorting out fact from fiction. All the defense would need was reasonable doubt and there was plenty of that to go around.

For two and a half hours the jury of twelve reviewed the case before returning a verdict of not guilty. The verdict seemed to surprise just about everyone in court, including the judge and England. England was so shocked that he thought he had heard the reading of the verdict incorrectly. He stared at his attorney and said, "Not Guilty, Mr. Birkett? Not Guilty, Mr. Birkett?"

A Final Word on Murder

With this verdict, the Brighton Trunk Murders would officially stay open and unsolved—or at least one of the murders would. In 1976 an aging and very ill Cecil England gave an interview to a London Sunday newspaper. During that interview he freely confessed to murdering Violette Kaye 32 years earlier and still expressed his surprise that he had actually gotten away with murder. England told the reporter from *News of the World* that during a violent verbal confrontation with Kaye she had picked up a hammer England had been using to break up large pieces of coal for the fire. She had threatened him with it. With difficulty he had gotten hold of the hammer and taken it from her. When the luckless Kaye demanded that he return the hammer he threw it at her, hitting her on the left temple. That was the blow which had killed Kaye instantly, confirming the doctor's report during the inquest. In fact, it had not been a planned murder but manslaughter at best.

It would not be possible to try the case again. England had missed his date with the hangman. A few days later England died of age-related problems. The second trunk murderer, however, never came forward, but it is still suspected of being the case of a botched abortion by the very well-connected Dr. Edward Massiah, who also seems to have gotten away with at least one and perhaps many more murders. He could very well have been a serial killer, protected by powerful men and women in government. Which murders could he have been responsible for would only be speculation.

Gordon Frederick Cummins, the Blackout Ripper (1942)

"...a savage sexual maniac."

The London blackout during the early days of World War II brought a whole new set of criminal problems to the people and to the government in Great Britain. As they attempted to lower the visibility of their homes and businesses against vicious German bombers, they created a shadowy environment that eased the efforts of the criminal element, an element that was by no means slowing their efforts during the war. It was an environment of fear and darkness tailormade for a serial killer. It was in fact a golden opportunity for death along the blacked-out cobblestone streets of London. A serial killer had stepped upon the dark stage of World War II and he had his targets well in sight.

London's many wartime streetwalkers were forced to adapt to the new darkness in unique ways. Along Piccadilly and Haymarket streets, the prostitutes began to illuminate their feet with flashlights shaded from above. It soon became the norm for these good-time girls to ply their trade with such devices.

Gordon Frederick Cummins (1917–1942) was a 25-year-old pilot trainee (#525987), training to fly the venerable Spitfire fighter and working at the time as an aircraftsman in the Royal Air Force (RAF). School records show that he was a poor student, lazy, and his work record was less than satisfactory; he was cited as an "irresponsible worker." In 1935 he enlisted in the Royal Air Force as a flight rigger, which he seems to have done well at.

Cummins, at age 19, had been married in 1936 to a young lady who worked as a secretary to a theatre producer. He was, however, not happy with his lot and began to present himself as a well-heeled man of noble birth with a good deal of income. He would pass himself off as the "Honourable Gordon Cummins," claiming to be the illegitimate son of a member of the aristocracy, whom he managed never to name. He presented himself to those in the clubs and local pubs as being well educated, which did not endear him to his fellow airmen who knew better. They began to refer to him as "The Duke" or "The Count" and laughed behind his back.

His fantasy life did not pass at his Royal Air Force unit, but he could pull it off for a while on the dark streets of London supported by the money he stole from his female victims. He would soon graduate to serial murder during a brutal six-day murder spree which dramatically captured the attention of all London despite the war which raged all around them. The press soon dubbed this new dark menace "The Blackout Ripper" because he chose his victims in the darkness, and the way he killed them invoked memories of a serial killer some 54 years earlier—Jack the Ripper. His crimes were also called the London Blitz Murders.

Margaret Evelyn Hamilton

Cummins's first known murder victim was not a professional prostitute, though she may have been adding to her meager income during those most difficult times. Margaret Evelyn Hamilton was a 40-year-old pharmacist with a good reputation. On the night of Sunday, February 9, 1942, she was attacked by an unknown assailant in Montague Square (Place) in Marylebone, London. She was strangled with her own scarf and her body was left to be discovered in the air raid shelter. There were no marks of mutilation on her body nor were there any signs of a sexual assault. That part of his work would come later. It was later discovered that the primary reason for this attack was the money the killer hoped to find in her handbag, which was missing. The killer had earned £80 for his trouble.

Evelyn Oatley

The next day, as deadly German bombers rained their terror onto the population of London, the naked body of 35-year-old Evelyn Oatley, also known as Nita Ward, was found in her flat on Wardour Street in Soho. Oatley had been married to a poultry farmer but decided that she preferred the excitement of London to the life of a dutiful wife on a farm during a war. Coming to London, she took a job dancing topless at the Windmill Club. After work she would walk the dark streets of London picking up men and bringing them back to her Wardour Street apartment. Her final pickup would be the Blackout Ripper! Now Cummins had all the time he needed to do his work and with such time the mutilations began.

After Cummins strangled Oatley with a silk stocking he cut her throat to make certain that the job had been done. At that point he began to attack and mutilate her body with, of all things, a can opener. He also used a razor blade and a short knife. The mutilations were mostly directed to suggest a sexual need on the part of her killer, which told the police something about the killer. The fingerprints found on the can opener revealed the fact that the killer was left-handed. The fingerprints at the time could not be matched to a known suspect because the crimes were being committed by someone who did not have a criminal record on file at Scotland Yard. What they did know was that it was probable this new threat would kill again, but the authorities had no idea how fast the murders would come. At the time Scotland Yard detectives did not connect the two murders because of the differing circumstances and suspected motives of each murder.

Margaret Florence Lowe

Before the war, Margaret Florence (Pearl) Lowe, alias Peggy Campbell, was a boardinghouse keeper in the South End of London. On Tuesday, February 11, she could be found walking the darkened streets of London near her Gosfield Street, Marylebone, apartment. The 43-year-old full-time prostitute met Cummins on the street and invited him up to her flat. It would not be long before her well-heeled customer took hold of her and strangled her with one of her silk stockings. This trademark was still around her neck when she was found. After she was dead Cummins attacked her naked body with a variety of "tools" he found around the flat. The many brutal injuries committed were later reported by pathologist Sir Bernard Spilsbury as being "quite dreadful," committed by "a savage sexual maniac." Cummins had used a candlestick, a straight razor and a kitchen knife, slashing as he went. As before, he had all the time he needed to do whatever he wanted. There were still no clues which would lead Scotland Yard detectives to the killer. The press was beginning to wonder if this killer would be able to evade police capture. Detective Cherrill would write that the "vicious mutilations which had been wreaked upon the dead woman, ... were even more shocking than those inflicted upon Evelyn Oatley."

Doris Jouannet

Doris Jouannet was the wife of the manager of a hotel located in Sloane Square, London. However, the pair had a two-room ground floor flat they shared away from the hotel, which afforded Doris the opportunity to bring men home at times when her husband stayed overnight at the hotel. On Wednesday, February 12, 32-year-old Doris, better known as Doris Robinson when she was looking for men in the West End of London, was carousing around her familiar dark haunts in Leicester Square when she ran into a good-looking young chap in an airman's uniform. He seemed to be well-off and quite taken with Doris. It was not long before the pair was back at her ground floor apartment in Sussex Gardens, Paddington. Shortly thereafter Doris was dead, strangled with her scarf and stripped naked. The mutilations then conducted on her body by Cummins would make their way to the press who after this murder began to describe the sadistic killer as "the Blackout Ripper." The Yard would need a break in the case and as far as this series was concerned that meant a new victim.

Writing in his autobiographical work in 1954, *Cherrill of the Yard*, Scotland Yard detective Fred Cherrill would remember how this case terrorized a section of London.

> In the pitch-like darkness of London in 1942 terror stalked the blitz-shattered streets. It was not just the terror from the sky, as Hitler's Luftwaffe flew overhead. It was the terror created by a ghoulish slayer. Not since those panic-

ridden days of 1888, when Jack the Ripper was abroad, had London known such a reign of terror when death—[fearful], revolting, and gruesome—came to four unsuspecting women in the heart of the metropolis.

Greta Hayward

The German air raids continued and so did the blackout. Friday, February 14, found Mrs. Greta Hayward having a drink at the Captain's Cabin near Piccadilly Circus in London when she was approached by a man wearing an RAF uniform who offered to buy her a drink. The offer of a drink and his sexual advances were both rejected by the married woman. The young man left and was soon forgotten by Mrs. Hayward. The good-looking man, however, had not forgotten Mrs. Hayward. When she left the pub and entered the darkness near Piccadilly Circus she was attacked by the same man who had approached her at the Captain's Cabin. Her attacker punched her in the face and began to strangle her. She was soon unconscious, but luck was on her side. Fortunately for Mrs. Hayward a delivery boy on his rounds passed by, which forced her attacker to beat a fast escape into the darkened streets. He would escape, but he left behind a vital clue. In his haste he had dropped his gas mask, leaving it behind at the scene of the attack. He had signed his own death warrant! Before the service number on the mask could be traced, though, the killer had one last murder to commit.

Katherine Mulcahy

The attack on Mrs. Hayward had not been successful and by this time the serial killer needed to kill. His bloodlust was up and he soon located Mrs. Katherine Mulcahy, alias Kathleen King, a full-time prostitute. Cummins found her near her apartment just around the corner from Paddington Railway Station. She brought him back to her apartment and before long she was undressed but her client had a "strange look come over his face" and he soon began his attack. This time, however, he would fail to kill, as Katherine, fighting for her life, kicked him in the shins. It was too much for Cummins who ran off before anyone could come to the aid of his latest victim. In his haste to escape he left his belt behind and strangely gave Katherine an extra £5 for her trouble!

It did not take long for the London authorities to find the name of the man whose service number was found on the gas mask. On February 16, 1942, Airman Gordon Frederick Cummins was arrested on murder charges and brought to Bow Street Police Station for a chat with police. He denied any knowledge of the attacks and interestingly enough he was able to demonstrate that during the Journnet, Lowe and Oatley murders records would show he was signed in at the base. It did not take long for detectives to establish that it was common enough at St. John's Wood Base to sign each other in, so the alibi soon evaporated. A search of his quarters on the base located several items he had collected from his victims and his fingerprints were matched to those on the can opener and other items he had used on Evelyn Oatley. Because this was the most damaging evidence against Cummins the Yard called in Detective Chief Superintendent Frederick Cherrill. Cherrill was the leading expert on fingerprints at the Yard which was critical to proving the case against Cummins.

The Old Bailey

Trial was held at the Old Bailey on April 27, 1942. Cummins was charged with two attempted murders and four counts of murder to which he pled not guilty. However, the trial was halted when the prosecution brought forward erroneous evidence. The trial was restarted on April 28 and lasted for a single day. Cummins was defended by Mr. J. Flowers with the prosecution case presented by Mr. G.B. McClure, before judge Mr. Justice Asquith. Needless to say, the prosecutor's case was well-grounded and easily conclusive as the defense could not escape the testimony of eyewitnesses nor the evidence of Cummins's fingerprints on a bloody murder weapon. This time, however, the charge would be a single count of murdering Evelyn Oatley. The jury took only 35 minutes to bring a verdict of guilty in the death of Evelyn Oatley.

An Air Raid and an Execution

Sentenced to death by Justice Asquith, his appeal was rejected on June 9. Cummins was executed on the gallows at Wandsworth Prison on June 25, 1942, by Albert Pierrepoint with an able assist by Harry Kirk, during one of the frequent air raids. Scotland Yard detectives would later report that Cummins could very well have been the killer of two other women who had been murdered during air raids on London conducted in October of 1941. Investigations showed that he was certainly available at the time. It was later noted that neither executioner during the hanging seemed to be bothered the least by the air raid, both calmly going about their official duties to a fine drop. No reason to allow war to interfere with the progress of justice.

Neville George Clevely Heath, the Gentleman Vampire of Bournemouth (1946)

"It has fetishistic and compulsive components."

Clinical vampirism (Renfield Syndrome) is a set of behaviors known to psychiatrists, involving the delusion that the individual is indeed a vampire with a critical need to feast on the blood of others. This set of behaviors relate to an erotic attraction to blood and the idea that to feast on blood transfers certain powers from the victim to the individual involved with the feeding. This fantasy of power over others through the blood is reportedly enhanced by film and books, which can move the individual from personal fantasy through sexual excitement and on the ultimate act of taking a life and ingesting the victim's blood. There is however, limited data on people suffering the delusion. Psychologist and author Richard Noll has studied clinical vampirism and has given a broad description of the mental affliction.

> The first stage is some event that happens before puberty where the child is excited in a sexual way by some event that involves blood injury or the ingestion of blood. At puberty it becomes fused with sexual fantasies, and the typical person with Renfield Syndrome (named after a character from *Dracula* named Renfield) begins with autovampirism. That is, they begin to drink their own blood and then move on to other living creatures. That's what we know from the few cases we have on record. It has fetishistic and compulsive components.

196   Section III: The 20th Century—A New Era for Murder

One such possible rare case came to the attention of the people of post-war London in the guise of Neville George Clevely Heath (1917–1946), known as "the Gentleman Vampire of Bournemouth." Heath, born in Essex, England, was a petty criminal with a long record of housebreaking and jewelry theft (he served a six-month sentence at Borstal for forgery and housebreaking), but there is no record of his committing violent crimes before he began his work as a serial killer. That is to say that there are no known murders which can be confidently placed into his murder column. He was, to be sure, quite charming and handsome at 29 years of age and would prove to be a most suitable escort for the ladies—until he killed them! He also used false identities and passed a series of bad checks. He spent more than he could earn to impress the ladies.

His story for the ladies was that he had been a well-decorated group captain in the Royal Air Force, Lord Dudley, or perhaps an Army lieutenant colonel, depending on his mood or whom he was trying to impress. World War II had just ended, and reminders of its terror were still very much evident in the cities of Great Britain and in the minds of those who lived through its horrors. Heath actually had been in the Royal Air Force in 1937, but he had been dismissed "for cause" having gone AWOL. Nevertheless, he certainly could talk the talk. And for a while he did actually serve as a flying instructor for the South African Air Force as one Lt. Col. Armstrong. It has been reported that he was such a good instructor that he was kept on for a while even after his false identity was discovered. He was, however, eventually released from service and he returned to London to

Neville George Clevely Heath was 29 years old when he was hanged in 1946 for the brutal and sadistic murders of two women.

continue his rakish activities. He was soon married with a new son, but as the war had come to an end he deserted his wife who took advantage of his desertion to divorce him. She was able to walk away.

Margery Gardner

June 16, 1946, found Heath taking a room at the Pembridge Court Hotel in Notting Hill Gate. Not hiding from anyone at the time, he registered under his real name but added Lieutenant-Colonel just for the effect. With him was a woman named Yvonne Symonds whom he had just met. They registered as man and wife which was just fine for Symonds as her new friend had promised to marry her. She would spend only one night with Heath and returned home the next day very much alive.

On June 20, 1946, it was at the well-known Panama Club in Knights-bridge that the "Group Captain" or "Lt. Col." would meet a part-time actress who went by the name "Ocelot Margie." A cab driver would recall that the man he identified later in a lineup had picked up 32-year-old Margery Gardner that evening.

The pair had met before, in May. It was a perfect match of killer to victim. Gardner was a self-styled masochist who had separated from her husband and daughter and Heath was a sadist looking for a "subject to work with." After their arrival at the hotel, binding and beating soon followed and is thought to have been enjoyed by both partners—at least for this first sadistic sexual encounter. Something seems to have gone wrong, however, at least from Gardner's point of view, at perhaps their second encounter that night. This time, however, hotel staff seem to have interrupted events, which probably saved Gardner's life—at least for now. Years later attorney J.D. Caswell would write of this part of the case stating, "It is almost certain that a month before her death she had been with Heath in another hotel room, and had only been saved by a hotel detective." Her luck would not hold.

Taking a great risk but needing to be brutalized by her escort, Gardner agreed to meet Heath again. She knew what he was capable of, but went anyway to the same hotel they had visited in May. There was no night porter at the hotel, but Heath was able to use his own key to room number four. Once again masochist and sadist were together and before long events turned deadly.

On June 20 Gardner had not been so lucky. The next day Margery Gardner's body was discovered by the chambermaid. She had been gagged with a scarf, suffocated, stripped naked and tied up. Her ankles and wrists had been tightly bound with a large handkerchief and there were signs that she struggled greatly in an attempt to escape her bonds. Later medical examination revealed the tremendous whipping she had suffered with a metal-tipped whip thought at the time by police to be most likely a riding crop, which left unique diamond-patterned marks over her body. Professor Keith Simpson told the investigating officers, "Find that whip and you've found your man." Her nipples had both been bitten off and there were deep bite marks on her breasts. It was also found that her vagina had been torn and mutilated by some type of blunt instrument which had been forcefully inserted and subsequently rotated with great force. The police examiner, Home Office pathologist Professor Simpson, felt that it was possibly a poker which had been found in the fireplace. Clearly, not all of these wounds were inflicted after she had died. There were a total of 17 slash marks on the body. Despite the damage done to the body the most puzzling aspect of the brutal murder for investigators was the fact that her face had been either licked or washed clean of the blood. This was proven by the congealed blood still clogging her nostrils, indicating that a good deal of blood had been present before the cleaning. The actual cause of death, thought to have occurred sometime between midnight and 1:30 a.m., was suffocation.

A quick check of the hotel's registry showed the room had been taken by "Lt. Col. and Mrs. Heath." However, the colonel was long gone. Nevertheless, he did write to authorities claiming that he had nothing to do with the murder and that he had discovered the body upon returning to his room after Margery had slept with a friend. The police would never discover any evidence that sexual intercourse had occurred that night and did not believe the note, but they did feel that it had come from her probable killer. The hunt was on.

From the hotel Heath made his way to Worthing to visit his declared fiancée Miss Yvonne Symonds. Yvonne's parents were very impressed with the "lieutenant-colonel." He did not stay long, perhaps knowing that the authorities were closing in. His name had appeared in the newspapers as a possible suspect in the murder of Margery Gardner. As Heath was moving to another hotel at the seaside resort town of Bournemouth, Scotland Yard detectives were expanding the hunt for a depraved and bloodthirsty killer. Heath checked into the Tollard Royal Hotel on Sunday, June 23, as Group Captain Rupert Brooke and relaxed near the beach. He soon found his last victim.

Doreen Marshall

Twenty-one-year-old Doreen Marshall was checked into the nearby Norfolk Hotel and was recovering from influenza when she came into contact with Heath. It was felt that the sea air and rest would take care of her brief illness. She was soon having tea and dinner at the West Cliff hotel in Bournemouth with Group Captain Rupert Brooke and on the evening of July 3rd she simply disappeared. She had last been seen around 11:30 p.m. being escorted out of the hotel lobby by the group captain as he walked her to her room. Naturally, the group captain was concerned about Miss Marshall, so he went off to the local Bournemouth police station to file a report and offer any help he could in the matter. The meeting did not go well for Heath as he was immediately recognized as Neville Heath, a man wanted in connection with the murder of Margery Gardner. Detective Constable Souter stated, "Isn't your name Heath?" Naturally, Heath denied it and asked that he be allowed to return to his hotel room to retrieve his coat. That ploy did not work as Heath was held while the police searched his room. During the search they found a cloakroom ticket from a local railway station. There they recovered an attaché case which held the riding whip with the unusual diamond weave pattern. It would not take long for Professor Simpson working for the police to match that pattern to the wounds found on the body of Margery Gardner. The police had their man. He was immediately taken into custody and charged with murder.

Five days later, a swarm of flies alerted authorities to the shallow grave which had been dug near a clump of rhododendron bushes. The body, near the path of the hotel, had been stripped naked except for a yellow shoe still held by her left foot. The rest of her clothes had been dumped on top of the body and her empty handbag was found nearby. The medical examiner was able to discover a wide variety of wounds on the body. They were a near match to the first victim. As before, this last victim's nipples had been almost bitten off along with other bite marks on the breasts. Her throat had been cut in two places, which had caused severe hemorrhaging, later determined to be the probable cause of death. There were also several defensive wounds on her hands as she attempted to fight off her attacker. Clearly she had not submitted to the needs of her attacker as the first victim had. As before, the victim's hands and ankles had been tightly bound. The examination also found a series of deep slashes said to be jagged all the way from her breasts to her vagina along with several deep stab wounds. Her vagina and anus had also been violated by a jagged weapon thought by authorities to have been a branch taken from a nearby tree. It had certainly been a brutal inhuman attack. For many involved with this case it would be the most brutal attack they would ever encounter. They had captured a true serial killer who clearly would kill again given the opportunity.

As authorities were questioning Heath, officers went over his room with great care, locating a gold mine of evidence. Handkerchiefs and scarves belonging to both women were found, apparently trophies of the kills, as were tickets and several bloodstained weapons which would later be shown to match the blood type of both victims as well as the wounds.

The Trial

It would not be a long trial in which Heath pled not guilty due to insanity. It began on September 24, 1946. Heath was defended by J.D. Casswell KC, who early on decided not to call Heath to the stand. To push his defense strategy forward, Casswell called Dr. W.H. de Bargue Hubert to the stand. Hubert, billed as a well-known and respected criminal psychiatrist, testified that Heath knew what he was doing to the victim on a simple level but that he was unable to understand that what he was doing was wrong, or, for that matter, criminal.

The prosecution attacked this defense with the testimony of two prison doctors who had interviewed Heath to the effect that he was indeed a psychopath and a brutal sexual pervert—however, he was decidedly not insane as he knew right from wrong even though he had done nothing to cover up the first murder. After debating the issue for an hour, the jury of 12 returned their verdict of guilty for Heath in the murder of Margery Gardner which had been the only case heard. The second murder case would be held in the unlikely event that the jury voted not guilty in the first matter.

The End of Days

On October 26, 1946, Neville George Clevely Heath was hanged by Albert Pierrepoint at Pentonville Prison after the prisoner requested a double shot of whiskey. Reports would make note that he made his way to the gallows in a jaunty manner and with a spring to his step. Did this showcase his insanity or an act to the very end? Whether he suffered with Renfield's Syndrome or not is still an issue of some debate. The fact that he was properly hanged for a brutal and sadistic murder is not. The Gentleman Vampire of Bournemouth would never again be on the hunt for blood victims along the vacation shoreline of southern England. Residents of Bournemouth could soon forget that at one time they had hosted a bloodthirsty killer.

John George Haigh and the Acid Bath Murders (1949)

"If I told you the truth, you would not believe me."

Serial killer John George Haigh (1909–1949) is known to have murdered at least six people, but he would claim nine as his full count. It is difficult to know for sure, as he dissolved all of their bodies in a bath of sulfuric acid. Haigh is an uncommon serial killer in that he did not murder for any personal pleasure, a cause known to be the case in many serial murders. Haigh murdered simply for the money he would gain as each victim fell prey to his drum of acid. And his gains were substantial as he then forged papers which allowed him to sell his victims' possessions.

Haigh was born in Wakefield, Yorkshire, England. The family soon moved to the nearby village of Outwood where he would spend part of his childhood. It is to his parents, John and Emily Haigh, that we may look to perhaps find some of the reasons why this child would grow up to become a serial killer. Haigh's parents were members of the nonconformist Plymouth Brethren, a Christian cult with strict religious rules that served to oppress all who became members. The "church" preached that any form of amusement was a sin. Haigh himself would be confined for years in the small garden surrounded by a 10-foot high fence erected by his father "to lock out the outside world." Haigh would later claim that during his childhood the repression caused him to have recurring religious nightmares, at times quite violent ones. Visions of blood spouting trees in a bloody forest were common. These could be early signs of hematomania, a psychological obsession with blood. He would never escape this obsession.

Despite the torment at home Haigh was able to win a scholarship to Queen Elizabeth Grammar School in Wakefield. It is reported that one may still find a small desk in the school where he carved his name. Continuing his early education, he earned a second scholarship. His parents had by then changed their religious ideology to Anglican, attending the High Church of Wakefield Cathedral. Young John would become a choirboy at the cathedral. It was not enough to keep Haigh on the straight and narrow and in fact the intense religious confinement was thought to have pushed him towards less socially acceptable behavior. The change from his earlier religious indoctrination to this new and open one seems to have completely confused the young man.

As a young man Haigh developed a passion for cars and tried to learn as much as he could about them. After school he apprenticed himself to a small company involved with the repair of car engines. Haigh soon found that despite his passion for cars, he did not enjoy the grease, oil and general grime one finds in repair garages and so he sought out cleaner work. Within a year of his work starting at the garage he was hard at it in the insurance and advertising game. After stealing from the petty cash box the 21-year-old was fired.

By 1934 he had had enough of church, which he had still been attending with his parents. He quit the church and never looked back. In that same year, on July 6, Haigh married 21-year-old Betty Hammer. His new wife was generally known as a "good-time girl," which caused the marriage to end quickly. He deserted her. Within months (in November) Haigh was jailed for fraud, ending up in prison for the first time. His roving wife Betty gave birth while he was in prison, giving up the child for adoption. It is debatable as to whether or not Haigh was the father.

After his release from prison Haigh once again turned to petty crime which landed him back in prison for his second term, lasting some 15 months. His fraud scheme to purchase cars had fallen through with great speed. After he was released Haigh actually did try to go straight, putting together a legitimate dry cleaning business with a partner, but fate soon stepped in. His business partner was killed in a motorcycle accident, leaving Haigh unable to continue in the business. It was on to London for more mundane work.

After moving to London Haigh worked as a chauffeur for a wealthy amusement park owner, William McSwann. Despite becoming good friends, Haigh was not satisfied, wanting to own his own business. Working for others was simply not his style, but neither was honesty. He soon found himself in prison for the third time, having been convicted of fraud in a scheme featuring himself as a bogus solicitor. The start of World War II would see his release and new conviction for theft, which as one would expect landed this career petty criminal back in prison for the fourth time. Haigh, it would seem, was doing life in prison on the installment plan! And plan he did.

He spent his time in prison attempting to create a plan for committing the perfect murder, having made a step up (or down depending on one's point of view) from petty criminal to serial killer, even though at the time he had yet to murder anyone, at least as far as the record can indicate. His plan focused on the

Serial killer John George Haigh has six confirmed victims, but the count could be as high as nine. Misunderstanding laws regarding murder, he dissolved his victims' bodies in acid, believing that if no body could be found, he could not be charged with murder. This mistake cost him his life in 1949.

disposal of the body once the deed had been done. The best method seemed to be a bath of acid which Haigh found could completely dissolve the body of a mouse in around 30 minutes. Mice of course are quite small when compared to your average human body, but a larger acid bath would seem to do quite nicely.

The Acid Work Begins

He was out of prison at the end of 1943 as the war continued. The year 1944 found Haigh working in an engineering firm as an accountant. It could be assumed that with manpower shortages due to the all-out war effort that his "resume" was not looked at with any great zeal.

By chance, as Haigh was having a draft at the local pub, the Goat, he ran into his old boss, 21-year-old William McSwann. McSwann was out with his aged parents, Donald and Amy McSwann. During the conversation the elder McSwanns mentioned that they had invested in some local Kensington property. Haigh saw his chance to use his rented basement to his advantage.

On September 6, 1944, Haigh lured William McSwann to 79 Gloucester Road, London. Once he was in the basement, not unlike endless horror movies, Haigh hit him over the head with a hammer. It is not known if the blow killed McSwann because no one would be able to examine the body. McSwann, dead or alive, was dragged to the sidewall, dismembered and the parts placed into a 40-gallon drum and then covered with a bath of sulfuric acid. Haigh allowed the acid to do its work and upon returning two days later found that the body was now fully dissolved into a sludge. William McSwann was then disposed of by being poured down a manhole and into the sewer! Only later would Haigh state that after McSwann had been hit on the head his throat was slashed and his blood was drained for Haigh to drink. Haigh was then able to take over a pinball arcade which had been owned by McSwann.

Naturally, William's sudden disappearance caused his parents to question where he could have gone. The police were not called in, rather, Haigh visited them to tell them that their son had been called up for military service, a very real possibly at the time, but that he had declined the government's generous offer, deciding instead to flee to Scotland. Keeping up the fraud, Haigh made many trips to Scotland where he forged letters in William's hand to his parents. The story began to fall apart when William failed to contact his parents and subsequently failed to return to England as the war was coming to an end. Something would need to be done, so on July 2, 1945, Haigh was able to lure Mr. and Mrs. McSwann to the basement at 79 Gloucester Road where he murdered both of them with the hammer. As he had done before, both followed their son, disappearing for good down the storm drain.

With the McSwanns gone, Haigh was able to steal Mr. McSwann's pension checks as well as sell their estate, which included five homes and some securities. He had forged a power of attorney to effect the deeds. His efforts rewarded him with around £8,000, a considerable sum at the time. He was now able to move into the Onslow Court Hotel in South Kensington. However, his newfound wealth did not last as his gambling habit had taken a toll on his funds. Poor investments and a lavish lifestyle were also taking their toll. Running low on funds he began to search for more likely victims, which appeared before him in the guise of Dr. Archibald Henderson and his wife Rosalie.

The Hendersons were looking for a buyer for their home and Haigh was quick to show interest in the property. Keeping in touch with his new friends, Haigh rented a small workshop on Leopold Road in Crawley, West Sussex, south of London. He would move his now well-used drums and acid to the new workshop. On February 12, 1948, Haigh had convinced Mr. Henderson that he had invented something in the workshop and asked him to look at it. As he arrived at the shop Haigh immediately shot him in the head with the doctor's own revolver. Haigh had earlier taken it from the Hendersons' home. Returning to the Henderson home he convinced Mrs. Henderson to go with him to the workshop in Crawley with the story that her husband had taken ill and needed her. Upon her arrival he immediately shot her in the head. Once again he would report that he would sample blood from both of his latest victims before disposing of their remains.

Both of the Hendersons were soon cut into smaller pieces and placed in drums which were then filled with sulfuric acid. It did not take long for the acid to do its work. After the job was done Haigh went about the work of forging a letter from the Hendersons showing that he was now the owner of their property. Before long he had rid himself of their possessions which included their house and car. With that he increased his income by another £8,000.

The Hendersons' funds kept Haigh in comfort until the beginning of 1949. He was still gambling at the dog track and would need a new infusion of cash before his funds once again ran out. This latest chance came in the form of Mrs. Olivia Durand-Deacon. Olivia was a 69-year-old widow who was living out her life at the Onslow Court Hotel. She had been known to Haigh for a time. He had presented himself as being an engineer and an inventor. With this in mind Mrs. Durand-Deacon mentioned that she had an idea for artificial fingernails. Haigh immediately spotted his opportunity. He invited his neighbor to visit his Crawley workshop to possibly work out some manufacturing and marketing details in the event that he could help bring the new invention to market.

On February 18, 1849, the pair drove down to the workshop and as soon as she was inside and the door was closed Haigh shot her in the back of the head. Again the knife came out, slitting her throat and a quaff of blood was consumed. The widow was stripped and dumped in one of his handy drums. The acid bath followed, doing its usual good job, but this time the disposal took a full week to finish. Perhaps the mix was getting a bit weak for the work expected. Haigh of course kept her valuables, including a singular Persian lamb coat she had worn to the shop. It was a poor job all around as this murder earned Haigh around £150 for the jewelry he sold which had belonged to the victim.

Haigh had made three grave errors. First, he had murdered a woman who not only lived very near his rooms at the hotel, but he had murdered someone who would be missed. Second, he had left a good deal of evidence at his workshop which would prove a gold mine to detectives. Last, he had not completely removed all evidence of human remains in his well-worn drums.

Two days after the widow seemed to simply vanish, her close friend Miss Constance Lane reported to local authorities that her friend was missing. It did not take long for local detectives to uncover Haigh's long criminal record during a routine check of all residents in the hotel. A search of his room and later workshop revealed an attaché case. In the case were records which referred to the McSwanns, the Hendersons and a very new dry cleaner's receipt for Mrs. Durand-Deacon's Persian lamb coat which had been stained with blood. However, it would be the close examination of the foul-smelling drums which would prove critical.

Pathologist Keith Simpson had been called into the case and his examination of the sludge, much of which had been dumped on nearby waste land, revealed three very human gallstones, as well as a set of false teeth.

Needless, to say, the sewer would have been a better place to pour away the remains. In all, some 28 pounds of human fat was skimmed off the top of the acid drum. Small bone fragments were also found which had yet to be completely consumed by the acid.

Under questioning, Haigh asked Detective Inspector Albert Webb about his chances of somehow working his way out of his situation. "Tell me frankly, what are the chances of anybody being released from Broadmoor?" To which the good detective reported that he would not be able to make any comments involving those possibilities. Haigh, seeing that he really did not have many options replied, "Well, if I told you the truth, you would not believe me. It sounds too fantastic to believe."

He began to tell the story of his nightmares, which were filled with blood, crucifixes and the overpowering thirst to drink human blood. He stated that he had killed so that he could open each of his victim's jugular vein and fill a cup of blood that he would then consume. He would then dissolve the bodies in one of his acid baths. Pressed for more details on Mrs. Durand-Deacon, Haigh blurted out, "Mrs. Durand-Deacon no longer exists. I've destroyed her with acid. You can't prove murder without a body." He then continued his rant by confessing to murdering the Hendersons and McSwanns, as well as three other victims. Two of these other murders were named as simply Mary and Max, said by Haigh to have been killed simply to drink their blood. The police were never able to prove that any of these other murders actually occurred.

The Trial and a Body of Evidence

Haigh had been in error when he thought murder couldn't be proved without a body. To convict for murder, one does not need a body, one only needs a body of evidence. The legal term *corpus delicti* refers to "body of the crime." The overall weight of the evidence, which could very well be completely circumstantial, demonstrates that a crime took place and then focuses on the most likely suspect, in this case John George Haigh, petty criminal turned serial killer. The fact that Haigh had admitted that he had "destroyed her with acid" was enough to show that he had purportedly prevented a burial and had thus concealed evidence of a murder. It would prove to be a fatal error!

Held in cell number 2 at Horsham Police Station, Haigh was charged with capital murder at the Old Town Hall courthouse near the jail on Barttelot Road. Haigh's trial began on July 18, 1949. At the Lewes Assizes, Attorney-General Sir Hartley Shawcross, later Lord Shawcross, led the prosecution team. For the defense, Sir David Maxwell Fyfe would stand for Haigh, hoping to get his client off by reason of diminished capacity.

Fyfe put up a determined defense, calling many witnesses who were able to testify as to the mental state of the accused. This group included the well-known psychiatrist Dr. Henry Yellowless who presented the idea that Haigh was more than a bit paranoid and that this paranoia overrode clear thought. He testified that Haigh's vampire like activity was "pretty certain" and that he was clearly insane. "The absolute callous, cheerful, bland and almost friendly indifference of the accused to the crimes which he freely admits having committed is unique in my experience."

Despite the flood of testimony which alleged Haigh's incapability to fully understand his crimes, Shawcross brought forth evidence of malice aforethought which showed that though the act of murder may have been spontaneous, the fact that Haigh had planned ahead of time for the disposal of the bodies proved that he was able to think clearly and was therefore not insane.

It would take the jury only a few minutes to agree with the prosecution that Haigh was sane when he killed and was therefore guilty of capital murder. Thanking the jury, Mr. Justice Humphries then donned the black cap and sentenced the prisoner to death by hanging.

He would spend the last few days of his life in the condemned cell at Wandsworth Prison. On August 6, 1949, Haigh walked the final steps of his long criminal life to the gallows at Wandsworth guided by London's chief executioner, Albert Pierrepoint. It was a clean drop and a fast kill for one of the most prolific executioners in British legal history. Students of crime on both sides of the issue may now seek out this case well-stored within the quiet walls of the Black Museum.

John Thomas Straffen, British Serial Child Killer (1951–1952)

"What would you do if I killed you? I have done it before!"

There can be no doubt that John Thomas Straffen (1930–2007) was an insane serial killer of innocent children. It is also quite clear that if he had ever been released upon the British people he would seek out a victim at the earliest possible time and murder again. What is less clear, albeit only based upon law and not upon physical realities, is whether or not this disturbed killer with an I.Q. of 58 could be fully responsible for his brutal actions. The British legal system would decide that he was not, before deciding at a later trial that he was, but it would cost the life of another innocent child before that would occur. No matter how one views Straffen, in the end he would live the rest of his life as the longest serving prisoner held by the British legal system.

Born on February 27, 1930, Straffen was the third child of John Thomas Straffen, Sr., at the base hospital at Borden Camp, Hampshire, England. Two years later his father was posted to India where the family would spend the next six years. In March of 1938 John Sr. was discharged from the army and the family moved to Bath in Somerset, England.

The Early Signs

By October of 1938 Straffen's stealing, truancy, and other petty crimes had become so bad that he was referred to a child guidance clinic. They could do nothing that would stop the eight-year-old's delinquent behavior. June of 1939 found him standing before a juvenile court accused of stealing a young girl's purse. The court sentenced him to two years of juvenile probation. It soon became apparent to the probation officer that Straffen did not understand what probation meant nor what the difference was between right and wrong. Based on his interviews the probation officer took the nine-year-old to a psychiatrist, who after the examination certified Straffen as a "mental defective." A report issued in 1940 would give his I.Q. as no better than 58.

In June of 1940 he was sent by the local authorities to a residential school. The school, St. Joseph's School in Sambourne, was designed to hold and instruct mentally ill children. Straffen fit right in for the two years that he was there.

Straffen's next move at the age of 12 was to Besford Court, a senior school for mentally ill teens. At this new school he was noted for being a depressed loner who would act up when corrected or disciplined. He would strike back when he could. In 1944, at the age of 14, he was suspected of manually strangling two geese owned by one of the school's officials. By 1946 Straffen was thought to be ready for the outside world and would be discharged, despite the fact that after years of training his new testing had shown him to have no better than an I.Q. of 64, reported as equal to a mental age of 9 years and 6 months. So it was in March 1946 he returned to his home in Bath. Examined by the local medical officer of health, he was certified once again as being mentally deficient.

Even with his limited mental abilities he needed to work and, after working a series of short-term jobs, he found a job as a machinist in a factory that produced clothing. He did the work well enough, but it would not be long before he began to steal things. He targeted unoccupied homes in the area and began to steal small items. He never kept anything; he simply hid the things he was stealing.

An Arrest and Commitment

July 27, 1947, could have ended very badly for a 13-year-old girl who met up with John Straffen. On that date she ran into a local police station to report that a boy had come up behind her and put his hand over her mouth. He had told her, "What would you do if I killed you? I have done it before!" The police were unable to locate "John" and only later were they able to link Straffen to this attack. This was only one of several attacks and other incidents that Straffen had recently been involved in. Six weeks after the incident with the 13-year-old, Straffen strangled five chickens that had belonged to a man whose daughter had quarreled with Straffen. When Straffen was arrested for suspicion of a number of burglaries, officers found that he was happy to confess to a series of incidents which had yet to be connected to any one suspect.

He was held in jail until the medical officer at Horfield Prison was able to examine him. The doctor was able to certify that he was severely mentally retarded.

On October 10, 1947, 17-year-old John Thomas Straffen was committed under the Mental Deficiency Act to Hortham Colony in Bristol. Hortham Colony was called an "open" colony which did not house violent offenders and specialized in the eventual resettlement of their "guests" back into the community. Unfortunately, Straffen had been suspected only of burglary and as such his report would state that he was "not of violent or dangerous propensities."

In July 1949 he was transferred to a very low security hostel in Winchester that specialized in agricultural studies. He had not been a problem at Hortham so the officials felt it was safe to transfer him. For a while he seemed to do well, keeping mostly to himself, but before long he began to steal. When he stole a bag of walnuts in February 1950 he was sent back to Hortham. In August 1950 Straffen escaped from Hortham, which was not difficult to do, and had to be recaptured by the police.

A Reassessment of the Mind of a Killer

Before the age of six Straffen suffered an attack of encephalitis while his military family lived in India. In 1951 doctors at a Bristol hospital examined him to reassess his mental state. The electroencephalograph examination showed that he had "wide and severe damage to the cerebral cortex, probably from an attack of encephalitis in India before the age of six." This was confirmation of major brain damage which could never be repaired. Nevertheless, Straffen was judged to be "sufficiently rehabilitated" so the doctors allowed him to visit his family at their home for short periods of time. Using his newfound freedom, he found a job at a local market garden using the skills he learned at the school in Winchester. Hortham officials were so impressed that Straffen was allowed to keep his job and authorities subsequently gave his mother permission to keep him at home (known as a home license). Once he celebrated his 21st birthday, the law required that he be reassessed by Hortham doctors, who decided to continue his certificate of mental deficiency for the next five years. This did not fit well with his family and they appealed the decision. This appeal led to a re-examination on July 10, 1951, and a finding that he now had a mental age of ten. The final decision was to keep the certificate for only six months with an expected discharge from the government's care at the end of that period. Straffen was almost a fully free man.

The Murders

Some have speculated that the reason Straffen targeted children went beyond the fact that mentally he was a child, albeit a rather demented one. Speculation focuses on Straffen's supposed "smoldering hatred and intense resentment" he felt for the police and the feeling that the murder of a child would be the most difficult for them to solve. Whatever the true reasons for his killings one fact is clear. The first murder attributed to Straffen occurred on the very same morning of his mental assessment. His target was a young girl named Christine Butcher, who was found strangled. The 21-year-old serial killer had begun his murders, which would end with three dead children in a little less than four weeks.

Now allowed to move around town unescorted, Straffen walked towards the movie house on July 15, 1951. As he walked along he saw five-year-old Brenda Goddard picking flowers outside of her home at 1 Camden Crescent in Bath. He walked up to her and, seeing what she was doing, offered to show her a better place to find flowers. Straffen took hold of her and lifted her over a fence, preventing her from being seen

John Thomas Straffen, whose I.Q. was measured at a mere 64, was a serial killer of children. He committed the murders in the space of just a few weeks when he was 21 (U.K. *Daily Mail*).

from the road. After he climbed over the fence he strangled the child. In a later statement to police Straffen would speak of his frustration at the child not attempting to scream. Enraged, he took her head and bashed it on a stone. After the murder there was no attempt to cover up the crime. Straffen simply climbed back over the fence and continued on his way to watch a movie—reportedly *Shockproof*. After the movie he went home, passing by the yard which still held little Brenda Goddard's body.

It did not take long for the local police to suspect John Straffen of murdering the child. The Bath police force would at the time report that Straffen was not considered violent, but his mental record would show otherwise.

On August 3, Straffen was interviewed by the Bath police. They had earlier investigated his work record with his employer to check on his location at the time of the murder. It was easily shown that he was available to do the killing. On July 31 Straffen was dismissed from his job because his employer wanted nothing to do with anyone who was a possible child killer. The police had no evidence to charge him with any crime so he had to be released. What the police did not do was place an around-the-clock surveillance on Straffen, which allowed him to commit the last murder in this series.

August 8 found Straffen once again attending a movie in town. He was not hiding from anyone. At the movie theater he found nine-year-old Cicely Batstone. Straffen was able to convince Cicely to go with him to another theater to watch a different movie. After the movie he took Cicely on a bus ride to a locally known meadow called "Trumps," which lies on the outskirts of Bath. He had taken no precautions to cover up the fact that he was with little Cicely. He would strangle her in the field and simply walk away and go home. It would not take a great deal of detective work to solve this case. There were numerous witnesses at the theater that had seen Cicely with Straffen. The bus driver had been a former workmate of Straffen's so he was easily able to identify him as being with the little girl. He was even seen in and around the meadow by a young couple and the wife of a policeman. The next morning as the alert was sent out about the missing child, the policeman's wife told her husband of what she had seen. She would be the one who would direct the authorities to the area she had seen the little girl with the young man. Cicely Batstone's body was soon discovered. The killer's description clearly matched John Straffen who had earlier been questioned.

The Arrest and Trial of a Serial Child Killer

On August 9 Straffen was finally arrested for murder. Straffen made a statement to the police that he had indeed murdered the Batstone girl. He also confessed to Brenda Goddard's murder. "The other girl, I did her the same." He did not confess to murdering Christine Butcher, but the circumstances of her death were very similar so there is very little doubt that Butcher was also on his list of victims.

After a two-day hearing, which ended on August 31, the Bath Magistrates Court ruled that Straffen was to be held for trial in the murder of Brenda Goddard. On October 17, 1951, Straffen would stand in the docket before Mr. Justice Oliver at Taunton Assize Court. There would be only one witness called before the court. Dr. Peter Parkes, medical officer from Horfield Prison, was called to detail Straffen's mental history. His testimony would be that in his opinion Straffen was "unfit to plead," as he did not know right from wrong nor did he understand what this trial was all about. And yet, if Straffen did not truly know right from wrong the question must be asked: Why was he released from custody even though he was suspected of violent behavior? The doctor would state, "In this country we do not try people who are insane. You might as well try a baby in arms. If a man cannot understand what is going on, he cannot be tried." The jury agreed with the doctor and a verdict of "unfit to plead" due to insanity was entered into the record.

Broadmoor and a Final Escape

Long ago Broadmoor was referred to as a "criminal lunatic asylum." However, in 1948 the British Parliament passed the Criminal Justice Act. Within that act was the responsibility for Broadmoor, which was then by law transferred to the Ministry of Health. The criminally insane murderers held within the walls of Broadmoor, including child killer John Thomas Straffen, became "patients." Newly minted patient/child murderer Straffen was assigned a job as a cleaner. On April 29, 1952,

Straffen along with another patient were sent to some outbuildings with a single attendant to do some cleaning. Under his work clothes Straffen was wearing regular street clothes. This fact alone proves that he was able to pre-plan with a good deal of detail an effective escape and was well aware of his criminal activities. Clearly this serial killer was "fit to plead!"

The buildings to be cleaned were near the external ten-foot-tall wall which enclosed Broadmoor. Over that wall was the freedom Straffen was aiming for. In the small yard which faced the wall was a small low-roofed shed whose roof sloped down. It was only eight-and-a-half feet high at the top of the roof. Large empty disinfectant cans were already in place in the yard which could easily be used to access the low roof. Straffen requested that he be allowed to go into the yard to clean off his dust broom. Permission granted, Straffen simply went into the small yard, climbed up the empty cans to the roof and easily hopped over the wall. Serial killer Straffen was once again able to prey on little children. His well-thought-out escape plan had worked!

The Last Murder

Mrs. Doris Spencer was working in her garden when Straffen came up her private driveway in Crowthorne. Meeting Mrs. Spencer only twenty minutes after escaping from Broadmoor, he asked for a glass of water. While Straffen drank his water, he discussed the fact that Broadmoor was very nearby and wondered how easy it would be to escape. He stayed for only ten minutes before taking his leave and moving along down the road. Mrs. Spencer was too old and too big to kill. He was able to walk to Farley Hill, arriving around five in the afternoon. It had been a little more than two hours since his well-planned escape from Broadmoor. It was at this point that Straffen came upon five-year-old Linda Bowyer. The little girl was spending the day riding around the village on her new bicycle. Within the hour she would be dead by the hands of John Straffen. Her murder would cause the British legal system to take another hard look at this serial killer.

After murdering the little girl Straffen quite calmly walked up to the home of Mrs. Kenyon to ask for a cup of tea. It was at this point that he asked to be driven to the bus stop on the edge of town. Arriving at the bus stop Straffen spotted several men in uniform. He asked Mrs. Kenyon if they were police officers. Her reply, that they were, sent Straffen out of the car and on the run. As it turned out the men were actually staff members of Broadmoor who were on the lookout for the escaped patient. Mrs. Kenyon pulled them aside to inform them about her suspicious passenger and before long Straffen was in custody being driven back to Broadmoor. In the car he told his captives, "I have finished with crime." Clearly, he knew what crime was and that he was fully involved. Linda Bowyer's body was found around sunrise the next day.

Investigation and Trial

It did not take long for the police to drive over to Broadmoor to interview Straffen. They arrived at 8 a.m.—critically, before any information of the murdered child had reached the institution. The police woke up the serial killer, who was sleeping comfortably in his private room. He was asked if he had been involved in any "mischief" while he was away from Broadmoor. His reply ended any speculation that he was possibly not the right suspect: "I did not kill her!" The Scotland Yard inspector informed Straffen that there had been no suggestion of anyone being killed and they were merely seeking to understand his whereabouts during his time away from Broadmoor. Straffen replied, "I know what you policemen are. I know I killed two little children, but I did not kill the little girl."

Stunned, the inspector confirmed that there had been a murder and that the victim had been killed near where Straffen had been taken back into custody. "I did not kill the little girl on the bicycle." That was all the officers needed. Straffen then made a long confession once it was explained that only the killer could have known about "the little girl on the bicycle." After checking his confession for accuracy, on May 1 he was charged with the murder of Linda Bowyer.

On May 2, 1952, Straffen stood before the Reading County magistrates. Even though he was still committed to Broadmoor and technically the responsibility of the Ministry of Health, the magistrates decided that they could not take any more chances with this serial killer. Broadmoor had failed to hold him, but Brixton Prison would not have that problem.

Straffen's trial began on July 21 with a plea of not guilty. His defense team decided to leave the question of whether or not he was insane to a jury. This trial and conviction was considered to be so important that the prosecution was led by Solicitor-General Sir Reginald Manningham-Buller. Once the facts of the death of the little girl had been established, the prosecution moved to bring forward evidence of two other murders Straffen had committed in Bath. Naturally, the defense team felt this new evidence would prejudice their case, but the evidence was ruled admissible. The jury would be allowed to learn about this killer's brutal past.

At this point a rather singular event occurred. William Gladwin, one of the jurors, had taken his leave that evening, popped off to a local club in Southsea and told all who were in earshot that he was on the Straffen case as a member of the jury and that Straffen was not guilty. Further, he claimed that the little girl had been murdered by one of the prosecution witnesses! Needless to say, the court had to fix this problem. The next day the judge, who had come into court late, explained to the remaining members of the jury that "owing to the alleged conduct of one of your members" he was required to dismiss all of them and call forward a new jury. He then ordered ex-juror William Gladwin to remain in attendance for the entire trial at which point he was required to apologize for his "wicked discharge of your duties as a citizen." It would take the new jury less than an hour to return a verdict of guilty. The death sentence was soon passed by Mr. Justice Cassels.

Fifty-Five Years in Prison

John Straffen was scheduled to be executed on September 4, 1952. He would, however, miss his date with the hangman. On August 29 the British government announced that David Maxwell Fyfe, the British Home Secretary, had recommended that Straffen be reprieved.

After being reprieved he was removed from the death cell and taken in chains to Wandsworth Prison. In 1956 Straffen was transferred to Horfield Prison in Bristol after prison officials at Wandsworth uncovered a plot by a group of prisoners to use Straffen as a diversion, taking him with them while they effected an escape. Needless to say, the residents in Bristol were not pleased to have a child killer in their neck of the woods. Within weeks local residents, numbering some 12,000 people, had signed a petition demanding his removal and relocation away from their town and their children. In August 1958 Straffen was transferred to Cardiff Prison.

In early 1966 a new 28-cell high security wing was completed at Parkhurst Prison on the Isle of Wight, just off the south coast of England. Straffen was transferred there on January 31, 1966, without warning or any public announcement. When his rumored transfer found its way to the British press, the Home Office would not deny the rumor. Straffen was the first to be housed at the new facility. Seemingly to keep him on the move, Straffen left the Parkhurst facility in May of 1968 to be housed at Durham Prison where he found a bed in the top security section known as the "E wing."

The Final Page

Straffen was held as a life prisoner and could not be released unless the British Home Secretary agreed to his release. To say the least, no Home Secretary would allow that to happen. With that in mind in 1994 then British Home Secretary Michael Howard decided to dispense with the yearly reviews of life prisoners and set up a list of twenty prisoners sentenced to life who must never be released under any circumstances. At the time the list was a government secret. Only by rumor were the British public informed that Straffen was on that much-too-short list. By December of 1997 the secret was out when the entire list was published by *News of the World*. John Thomas Straffen was indeed on that list. He was slated to die an old man in prison for his three confirmed brutal murders.

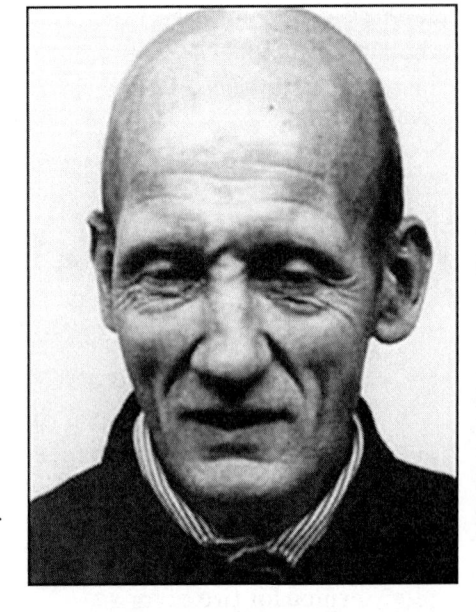

When John Thomas Straffen died in prison at 77 years of age in 2007, he was the longest-serving prisoner in Britain, having served 55 years.

In May of 2002 the European Court of Human Rights attempted to interfere with British justice, stating that they did not approve of the British holding a British serial killer of British children for life if he was being kept there under orders by a human being called a Home Secretary instead of being held there by a European Court of Human Rights. The British would ignore the ruling and the serial killer of children would remain in prison. Needless to say, none of the nations represented by the court were willing to allow Straffen free movement in their own countries!

In March 2006 *The Sun* published a story about Straffen and what prison life was like for this serial child killer. They quoted an unnamed fellow inmate who reportedly saw Straffen on a daily basis: "He's still lively. He works as a cleaner in the craft shop and makes tea for the officers. They treat him well, call him by his first name and often take time to chat with him."

On November 19, 2007, John Thomas Straffen died while in custody at Frankland Prison in County Durham. He was 77 years old and had spent 55 years in prison, which is a record as the longest-serving prisoner in British history. How many children are alive today due to the fact that he was never released is a matter of conjecture. However, one fact is clear. Since he was never released his record of kills during those 55 years he spent behind prison bars was zero!

John Reginald Halliday Christie and His Special Gas (1953)

"John Waddington of 35 Westbourne Grove."

That John Reginald Halliday Christie (1898–1953) was a serial killer there is no doubt. His conviction was solid and his confession was detailed and accurate. What makes Christie's crimes unique is the method he used, the disposal and use of the bodies and the man who was executed for two of his suspected murders. The story of the abused Christie begins in West Riding, Yorkshire, in 1898.

Records would show that he was completely dominated by his mother and sisters and was abused by his father and grandfather, abuse which is strongly suggested to have been of a sexual nature. Beatings at home were a frequent occurrence. Unhappy and shy throughout his childhood, he was later able to state that there was indeed one happy childhood memory that he could go back to and remember fondly. At the age of eight his grandfather died, and as young John stood staring at the corpse laid out in the coffin at the family home, he stated that he felt a new feeling of power. The dead man could no longer cause any fear or pain to John, which he had done for all the years of John's still young life. Now John had the power, at least while he viewed the body. He would never forget the feeling of power in that moment and it is perhaps at that time he became for all intents and purposes a killer.

As a young man Christie began to associate death and violent aggression with sex. From this point on he had to be in complete control or he was for the most part impotent. Investigators would uncover tales of his adolescence where his fellows would taunt him with names such as "Can't-do-it-Christie" and "Reggie-no-Dick." It did not take long for his first failed attempts at sexual encounters to get around. He would blame his un-conquested female acquaintances for his not-so-charming nicknames. Despite the fact, or perhaps because of it, that he had an I.Q. of 128 and skills at detail work, he made few friends. He was also a hypochondriac, tending towards hysteria.

Along with millions of others, World War I found Christie in uniform and in service to the king in the muddy trenches of France. Reports relate that after a mustard gas attack Private Christie was temporarily blinded and ended up in a military hospital. This, however, may have only been a ploy, as author Ludovic Kennedy writes that there is "no record of his supposed blindness." Christie may have also exaggerated a mute condition which was said to have been ongoing for three years. True or not, there was one very good reason why Christie may have faked these injuries—they kept him out of the front lines and very much alive. Christie's military service was over, and it was back to the safety of England.

On May 10, 1920, Christie married Ethel Simpson, a 22-year-old from Sheffield. It was not a good match. For four years Ethel hung on to a very dysfunctional married life. It seems that Christie was not able to perform his husbandly duties and was impotent with his wife. He was only able to function with the prostitutes he frequented. It did not take long for those who knew the couple to whisper that the only reason Ethel stayed with her husband was out of an unspoken yet overwhelming fear of what he was capable of. When Christie moved to London in 1924 Ethel took the opportunity to escape her fears and moved in with her relatives. She was safe, at least for a while.

For the next decade Christie engaged in a series of petty crimes, many of which would end with periods in custody. April 1921 found Christie working as a postman, but the temptation to steal postal money orders became too much and he ended up receiving a three-month jail sentence. Beginning in September 1924 he would spend nine months in the Uxbridge Jail, again for theft. In May of 1929 Christie was living with a prostitute and his violent nature came to the forefront. He was convicted of assaulting her and received a sentence of six months' hard labor for his trouble. The year 1933 was no better for Christie, as he stole a car from a priest who had become friendly with him. He would spend a few months locked up in jail before becoming free once again late in 1933. It was at this point that John Christie decided to look up his wife who for some reason decided to give her strange marriage a second chance. It would be a fatal error!

In 1934 Christie was hit by a car and suffered a very serious head injury and nearly died. His other wounds healed but there is some doubt about that head injury. Is that what pushed him over the edge to serial murder?

John and Ethel Christie were married in 1920, had separated by 1924, but reunited in 1933. They remained together until John murdered her in 1952. He had killed others previously but another man had hanged for two of his murders in the late 1940s.

After the couple reunited, they moved around London, but by 1938 they settled on a ground floor flat at 10 Rillington Place, Ladbroke Grove, Notting Hill. Christie's "work" at this London flat would in time turn this address into an infamous location, so much so that the street was renamed a short time before the entire street was demolished for a long overdue redevelopment. Christie, it seems, was not good for business.

World War II brought new opportunities to Christie, but not in a manner which may have been expected based upon his recent history. Christie seems to have ended his career as a petty criminal, at least for the time being, and applied for a job as a police officer! In the early critical period of the war when manpower was at a premium he was accepted and assigned as a war reserve police constable posted to the Harrow Road police station. Records show that Christie seems to have done a very good job, as he was noted for his hard work and efficiency. This, however, did not seem to be enough for Christie even though he genuinely enjoyed the newfound respect his work as a police officer gave him. He soon took advantage of his situation and the on-going war, beginning a relationship with a woman who worked at the police station. Her husband was in the British army fighting the Germans in France.

The Christie Methodology

Christie began his work as a serial killer even as he continued his work as a police constable. The first to fall was Austrian immigrant Ruth Fuerst, reportedly his mistress. He was still married to and living with his wife Ethel, but prostitutes were his mainstay as far as sexual contacts were concerned. Ruth was murdered, apparently on impulse, while having sex with Christie. Christie was unable to ejaculate until he strangled her to death and only then could the necrophiliac continue on her corpse until he was satisfied. It was August 1943 and Christie had completed his first known sexual murder, however, considering how old he was at the time—45—and considering how violent he was towards women in general, it is entirely possible that he had been getting away with murder for years without ever being suspected.

Muriel Eddy had bronchitis. She also worked with John Christie. When Muriel complained about her bronchitis to her work colleague, he was more than happy to take advantage of the situation. He offered to cure her bronchitis with a gas he called a "special mixture." Muriel was soon on the table at Christie's home as he administered a mixture of regular gas used in cooking, which had an amount of carbon monoxide in the mix. Muriel was soon rendered unconscious as Christie removed both his and her clothing. Now prepared for "work" he slowly strangled her to death but not during sex. He would only have sex with her after she was dead. The Christie method of murder by gas and manual strangulation, then rape of the corpse, was now fully established. It would remain his methodology for the rest of his murderous career. He would add one other habit to his method—he collected the pubic hairs of his victims in an old tobacco tin.

The end of December 1943 was not a good time for Christie. While Christie and the wife of a soldier were having sex, her husband, coming home quite unexpectedly, walked in. Christie got the beating of his life. It would not be long before Police Constable John Christie resigned his position as an officer for another line of work.

The Graveyard in the Garden

The ill-kept building, badly needing repair, that Christie and his wife lived in had a communal garden in the small back yard. The garden was in good repair and Christie kept the area neat and proper for all to see. Although it was a communal area it was Christie who did most of the work and all of the digging. The garden did seem to be one of the better features of the building. It was to all appearances a very proper British garden.

It was also a small graveyard which held the rotting corpses of Ruth Fuerst and Muriel Eddy! A later photograph of serial killer Christie would show him standing against the vine-covered wall on the same piece of ground which held their remains. In that photo Christie appears to be somewhat pleased with himself and his little garden. For a few years there do not seem to be any new murders by Christie who seems to have been able to satisfy himself with the knowledge that his conquests were close by even though they were underground. He could always enjoy the local prostitutes. Relations with his dutiful wife, it would seem, were still out of the question—for the moment.

224 Section III: The 20th Century—A New Era for Murder

The back garden at 10 Rillington Place, where sexual serial killer John Christie disposed of some of his victims (U.K. *Daily Mail*).

The Evans Case

In April 1948 Timothy John Evans and Beryl Evans moved into the top-floor flat of 10 Rillington Place. They had been recently married and were delighted to find a kindly older couple living in the same building on the ground floor. They also liked the fact that there was a very nice garden in the back of the building. Six months after moving into their new flat Beryl gave birth to a daughter who was named Geraldine. It was a happy time for the Evans family, but things would soon turn dark. Beryl became pregnant a second time in November of 1949. Timothy, who was illiterate and reportedly had an I.Q. of only 70, was known to be quite gullible and did not feel he could earn enough money to care for a second child. After he relayed his fears to his older neighbor, Christie came up with a solution, and another opportunity for himself. For months Christie had been trying to figure out how he could use Beryl for his needs. Christie told Evans that he could abort the baby as he had a "medical background," which he did not have, and a special gas, which of course he did have. As Evans went to work on the morning of November 8 he left his pregnant wife in the hands of Christie, who had set up his equipment in his flat.

It did not take long for Christie to begin his work. Mrs. Evans was soon incapacitated by his special gas mixture. When she was unconscious Christie removed her clothes, strangled her and proceeded to rape her corpse. When the slow-witted husband returned from his job as a van driver he was informed that his wife had suddenly died due to the failure of the procedure. It was not very difficult for Christie to convince Evans that both of them could go to prison for the death even though Evans had not been involved. Evans was instructed to run and hide which he did, going to Wales to live with his relatives. Christie let him know that he would be happy to take care of little Geraldine.

Evans would return and several times he attempted to see his daughter, but Christie kept putting him off, telling him that it was too early to see her and that he needed to stay away from London a bit longer. Nevertheless, Evans finally went to the police on November 30 in Merthyr Tydfil. At the station he made a full statement confessing to accidentally killing his young wife by giving her abortion pills. "I would like to give myself up. I have disposed of the body of my wife." He also stated that he had disposed of the body by pushing it into the sewer drain by the apartment, but the police found no evidence of a body.

A new series of questions was then put to Evans as he changed his story. Part of his confession this time was true. Evans reported that his neighbor Mr. Christie had offered to perform an abortion on his wife and that when he came home from work he found his wife dead. Continuing his second confession he stated that it was Christie who had disposed of the body. He also stated that he had made arrangements to have his daughter Geraldine looked after while he hid out in Wales. When Christie was confronted, he of course reported that he had nothing to do with any murders. Nevertheless, police inspectors began a search of the flats and the backyard. They were literally standing on the graves of Christie's first two victims when they discovered the bodies of Beryl Evans and her daughter in the back garden wash house. It would later be learned that while Christie stood by talking to the detectives a dog had dug up a shallow buried skull. As the conversation continued with the unsuspecting officer Christie shooed the animal away from his find and stood on top of the skull, pushing it back into his little garden. Clearly both victims had been strangled to death. When the victims had been strangled to death was a question for the coroner. When the victims' clothes were shown to Evans he was asked if he was responsible for their deaths. The slow-witted Evans, now confronted with the death of his little girl for the first time, said that he was responsible. He confessed to strangling both.

Before his trial, which began on January 11, 1950, Evans recanted his confession, but it would remain as strong evidence against him as it seemed to match what was known of the case. One of the key witnesses for the prosecutors was John Christie, who did everything he could to place the noose around the head of Evans. Christie would be referred to by the prosecution as "this perfectly innocent man." It would take two days for the trial and only 40 minutes for the jury to bring in a verdict of guilty. Within minutes the death penalty was declared, and Evans was led away. All of his appeals were denied and Timothy Evans was hanged by Albert Pierrepoint on March 9, 1950.

The Sexual Serial Killer Continues

Evans's trial had led to his execution, but it also led to Christie losing his job. He was at the time working at the Post Office Savings Bank. He had held the job for four years and by all accounts had done good work. However, when his criminal past, including theft of postal money orders, was exposed during the trial his present employers fired him. He fell into a deep depression and was unemployed for the next six months. In September of 1950 he finally found work with the British Road Transport Service. He would hold this job until December 5, 1952, when he resigned, telling his employer that he had located a new job in Sheffield. He also informed his former employer that he would be moving to Sheffield with his wife the following January. In fact, he was moving nowhere, and his wife would soon be dead!

On the morning of December 14, 1952, John Christie murdered his long-suffering wife Ethel, strangling her with a stocking. True to form, he had sex with her corpse. To keep up appearances he wrote letters to Ethel's sister who lived in Sheffield, at one point changing the date of a letter Ethel had written from December 10 to December 15. He would later claim that Ethel's arthritis prevented her from writing herself, but her dutiful husband was more than happy to fill in for her. And fill in he did as he prepared to "plant" his wife, but he decided to put her in a special place separate from "his other women." He placed his wife with some difficulty under the floorboards of the sitting room.

On January 6, 1953, Christie began to clean house. He needed the money, as he was not working. Most of the furniture was sold to a local dealer, including his bed, but he did keep the mattress. He also began to empty out his wife's bank account, forging her signature, and of course there were a few pounds to be made selling his wife's wedding ring and old watch. When he finished he had a few chairs, his old kitchen table and the mattress he had saved to sleep on. Adding to his slim cash flow he put in for unemployment benefits even though he had quit his job.

Christie was now ready to begin a new series of murders which would all include necrophilia. From January 19 through March 6, 1953, Christie brought at least three prostitutes to his flat and incapacitated them with his special gas followed by manual strangulation. He was now a true serial killer! First was Kathleen Maloney, who had come to London from the southern English port city of Southampton. Next was Rita Nelson from Belfast, Ireland. Finally, Christie invited Hectorina MacLennan from Scotland. Christie had been lucky with the first two prostitutes as no one had seen him with them. That was not the case with MacLennan. He had been seen with her by her boyfriend, Alex Baker, and Baker knew who Christie was. When Baker asked Christie if he had seen MacLennan Christie simply reported that she had "wandered off," which Baker assumed meant that she had gone back to Scotland. The flat at 10 Rillington Place was starting to become crowded.

On March 20, 1953, Christie moved out of his old flat, but not before he defrauded a couple out of three months' rent. The money never made it to the actual landlord so they would need to move out the next day. Within the week the flat was properly rented to a new couple, Mr. and Mrs. Beresford Brown from Jamaica who, while moving in, discovered that they were sharing the flat with three corpses! Mr. Brown had decided that he needed to install some brackets on the wall to hold his new radio set. When he went about the wall tapping for the studs he located the hidden cupboard. "There's a woman's body inside." Christie had placed Maloney, Nelson and MacLennan in an old coal cellar attached to the kitchen and had covered the opening with thin wallpaper.

The End of Days

Scotland Yard detectives were soon doing a detailed search of the flat and the grounds at 10 Rillington Place. The police would find the remains of Ruth Fuerst and Muriel Eddy as well as the now moldy remains of his long-suffering wife Ethel. One of the corpses was seated in a chair. The second was simply propped up against a wall and covered with a blanket. Standing in the corner was the final corpse wrapped in another blanket. The medical examiner would later conclude that Christie had had sex with each of the corpses. It would not take long for the press to begin front-page coverage of Christie and his "Cupboard Crimes." They were also on the hunt for 55-year-old John Christie who was clearly the only suspect. Christie must have known that it was only a matter of time before he was captured. Nevertheless, he rented a room at King's Cross Rowton Houses using his real name and address. He had intended to stay for a week but left after four days when he heard news reports that the police had begun a nationwide manhunt for him.

On March 28 Christie made a call to a reporter from the *News of the World*. He arranged a meeting in the middle of the night for an exclusive interview with only one stipulation. He wanted a meal of two fried eggs, baked beans, a gammon rasher and chips. The reporter quickly agreed to the terms and waited for Christie. However, when Christie arrived at the arranged meeting he spotted two local constables on regular patrol and decided that he could not afford to wait for the reporter. He was now on the run believing that he had been set up and he was very close to being out of money.

The end came on the morning of March 31 at Putney Bridge when he was challenged by a constable on regular beat duty. The officer asked him for his name and address and Christie said "John Weddington, 35 Westbourne Grove." Not believing the story, the constable asked him to remove his hat and told him, "You are Christie, aren't you?" The game was up and Christie told the constable who he really was. When he was searched the officer found his identity card as well as his old ambulance badge, a union card and a ration book. They also found a newspaper clipping about the arrest of Timothy Evans which included details of the murders he would eventually hang for. Christie would be charged with murdering his wife as well as Kathleen Maloney, Rita Nelson and Hectorina MacLennan. Before he came to trial Christie would confess to all of these murders as well as the murder of Beryl Evans. However, he never admitted to killing the child.

His trial began on June 22, 1953, for the murder of his wife. If unsuccessful, the government still had three more chances to convict him. It was the same court which had convicted Evans of murdering his wife and child. Christie pled insanity with the further excuse that he did not recall the murders. The fact that he was clearly a sexual pervert would also become part of the trial, however, the prosecution argued that despite the fact that he was a necrophiliac he was not insane. He knew very well what he was doing and the fact that he tried to hide the bodies showed that he knew it was a criminal offense. It would take the jury 22 minutes to agree with the prosecution and find Christie guilty of murdering his wife. He was soon sentenced to death.

On July 15, 1953, Albert Pierrepoint took the measure of John Reginald Halliday Christie and hanged him on the same gallows he had earlier used on Timothy Evans. It would not be long before the flat Christie had used for his series of murders was demolished to make way for redevelopment. In 1966, as a postscript to these events, Evans was cleared for the murder of his wife and child, posthumously of course! Artifacts and papers related to Christie are now securely held by the Scotland Yard's Black Museum.

Ruth Neilson Ellis and the Public House Murder (1955)

"It is quite clear to me that I was not the person who shot him."

Ruth Neilson Ellis (1926–1955) was born in the northern seaside town of Rhyl in Wales. While at Rhyl her father made a living playing the cello on the Atlantic cruise line run to the United States and Canada. Her mother, Bertha, was a refugee from Belgium after the First World War and was of Jewish decent. After the birth of Ruth's older sister, Muriel, her father changed his surname to Neilson. Ruth, who left school at fourteen to work as a waitress, was one of five children in the family. In 1941, as German bombs rained down on London in the early stages of World War II, Mr. Neilson moved the family to the British capital.

In 1944 18-year-old Ruth gave birth to a son named Clare Andrea. The boy was fathered by a Canadian soldier who was already married. His visits and monetary support would last only as long as he remained on duty in England. That support ended when he returned to his wife and family in Canada. She had heard the last of him. After this period she supported herself and her son via factory and clerical jobs. Later she did some low-paying, part-time modeling work as well as working as a nightclub hostess. Prostitution may have also been part of the mix just to make ends meet.

In 1950 she met 41-year-old George Ellis while she worked at the Court Club on Duke Street, London. Ellis was a divorced alcoholic dentist with two sons when they married later that year. The marriage did not last, due to Ruth's possessive jealousy. She believed that he was having an affair, which added to George's drunk violence with her. In 1951 when Ruth gave birth to her daughter Georgina her husband would not admit paternity. Separating, she moved in with her parents and back to the clubs as a hostess. She was once again part of London's nightlife.

Working her way up, she became the manager of a nightclub in 1953. It would be at the Little Club nightclub where she would meet 24-year-old David Blakely. Blakely was an amateur racecar driver with expensive tastes in all things, including women (and as it turned out men). He was also a hard drinker, which seems to have been an attraction to Ruth. It seemed that alcoholic men were her weakness. It did not take him long to move into the flat above the club with Ruth. He was at the time engaged to another woman who was soon cast aside. Moving on to Ruth, he proposed a marriage of sorts, and although she was still married to George Ellis, she accepted the offer.

From the beginning there was jealousy on both sides of the equation as Blakely, who had another woman on the side that he was "maintaining," began to spend a good deal of time keeping an eye on Ruth in the club as she attended to her male customers. Taking care of the customers was a large part of the job but that did not make much of an impression on Blakely—he saw it differently. Her income did not take long to decline due to Blakely's interference. As for Blakely, he had gone through most of his inheritance. Both were now in need of money. Violence from both, enhanced by alcohol, became frequent as money became an even worse problem. At the same time Ruth was also "reacquainting herself" with a former boyfriend, Desmond Cussen. Blakely was aware of the "arrangement" and was extremely jealous.

Six Shots!

Blakely was doing his best to dump Ruth, as he had become tired of the "older woman." Keeping up with his work on his new racing car, he was spending the weekend with engineer Anthony Findlater. Findlater, who worked on designing new racing cars, was working out some details with Blakely. Findlater's wife was also with the two men and she took a call from Ruth, who was looking for Blakely. She would not put Blakely on the phone which caused Ruth to believe that the Findlaters were conspiring with Blakely and the Findlaters' babysitter for a sexual weekend. For two days Ruth's frustration grew until she finally decided to borrow a gun and go hunting for Blakely. She would wait for him at his favorite pub.

On the evening of Easter Sunday, April 10, 1955, Ruth confronted Blakely at 9:20 p.m. outside of the Magdala Tavern in Hampstead. Blakely had driven out to the pub for beer and cigarettes. Taking a .38 caliber revolver from her purse, and in front of several witnesses, she began firing at Blakely. He saw her coming and he also saw the gun as she chased him around his car. Just before her execution Ruth would admit that not only had the gun been supplied by Desmond Cussen, but he had actually driven her to the pub that night so that she could "confront" Blakely. It would not be established, however, whether or not he knew a murder was about to be committed. The first shot missed Blakely and wounded Gladys Kensington, who was simply passing by. The shot had ricocheted off of the pavement and hit Gladys in the hand. The second shot hit Blakely and he went down to the pavement. Calmly walking over to Blakely as he lay wounded on the street, Ruth pumped four more bullets into Blakely's body, emptying the revolver. He would be pronounced dead on arrival at the hospital. Ruth made no effort to escape and even asked a witness to call the police. She had remained calm throughout the entire assassination.

At her trial when she was asked by the prosecutor, Christmas Humphreys, what she had intended to do that evening, Ruth calmly replied, "It is obvious that when I shot him I intended to kill him." It would take the jury just 14 minutes to convict her of murder. She of course received the mandatory sentence of death by hanging from Judge Sir Cecil Havers.

The Last Execution

The last woman hanged in England, at least for the present time, was Ruth Ellis, who went to the gallows in the hanging shed at Holloway Prison on July 13, 1955. The gallows, it was reported, had to be erected especially for her as Holloway had no execution shed at the time she was scheduled to be put to death.

Visiting Ruth in her death cell came the Bishop of Stepney, Joost de Blank, seeking, it seemed, a bit of fame for himself rather than offering comfort for the condemned. He would later report that when he visited her he "was horrified and aghast beyond words." It seems that the Bishop discovered upon his visit "that prisoners could hear the hammering as the scaffold was being erected." His words of concern for violent killers did make the evening papers as reported in *The Star*. He was therefore able to get the publicity that he had wanted.

The day of Ruth Ellis's execution saw the *Daily Mirror* also muse liberal about the loss of a brutal killer, probably because she was a beautiful woman. "The one thing that brings stature and dignity to mankind and raises us above the beasts will have been denied her—pity and the hope of ultimate redemption." Interesting to note, there were no words of "hope of ultimate redemption" for the family of David Blakely or for Blakely himself, who had been pumped full of bullet holes on a quiet London street.

On the evening before Ellis was executed, Home Secretary Major Gwilym Lloyd George rejected a petition for clemency, which had been signed by 50,000 people. This final rejection by the Home Secretary allowed Chief Executioner Albert Pierrepoint and his assistant Royston Rickard to continue their preparations. On July 13 they earned their fee and disposed of murderer Ruth Ellis with a fast drop and a final snap. A French reporter made his opinion known on the Ruth Ellis matter as well as his general contempt for all things British in a Paris newspaper. He would report, "Passion in England, except for cricket and betting, is always regarded as a shameful disease." He made no comment on the "shameful disease" of colonial murder, nor were there any words for the parents and friends of David Blakely.

After the work was completed on Ellis her corpse was allowed to cool for the prescribed period of time before being cut down for burial in a prepared unmarked grave within the walls of Holloway Prison. However, that was not to be the last resting place of the last woman executed in England. During the early 1970s the prison underwent extensive renovation. At the time all of the women who had been executed at Holloway were exhumed. All of them were reburied in Brookwood Cemetery in London except Ruth Ellis. In 1971 Ellis would make her final escape to Saint Mary Churchyard in Amersham, Buckinghamshire. Her headstone would read, "Ruth Hornby 1926–1955." In 1982 her son Andrea destroyed the headstone a short time before he committed suicide at the age of 38. It is said that there is now no trace of the grave of this killer, now reportedly overgrown with yew trees.

A Controversy—of Sorts!

The Ruth Ellis case was soon being used as a weapon to help end the death penalty in Great Britain. Grasping at any straw, those who would attack the death penalty could soon be heard to declare that the diminutive Ruth Ellis at five feet two inches and weighing 105 pounds could not possibly have fired six shots from such a large "manly" weapon. The British public was expected to ignore the powder burns on her hand, the wounded innocent woman, the death penalty David Blakely received from Ellis and the witnesses who saw her pump five bullets into his body. They also seemed to have conveniently forgotten her statement in court—"I intended to kill him!" Disregarding the easy to understand and witnessed facts, her supporters would still focus on medical myths that she could not have squeezed the trigger.

On May 27, 1955, in a report prepared for Mr. Bickford, Ellis's solicitor, the medical register at St. Giles Hospital in London, W. Mackenzine, would write of a bout of rheumatic fever Ellis had contracted as a teenager. He wrote that the fever had destroyed "the bones in her left ring finger" which had been "destroyed by septic arthritis." He further wrote, "I should be interested to know, from a medical point of view, the present state of her joints."

Earlier, the prison medical officer at Holloway would note on April 11, 1955, that she had "contracted rheumatic fever, which was followed with arthritis in the fingers of the left hand and of the ankles." This medical report was to be used as an excuse for murder by her defense team. It would of course fail.

In 1955 the director of the Metropolitan Police Laboratory, Lewis Charles Nickolls, would report on the weapon proven to have been used in Blakely's murder.

> On receipt the Smith & Wesson revolver was in working order, and during the course of firing in the Laboratory, the cylinder catch broke as the result of a long standing crack in the shank…. The trigger pull is 9.5 to 10 lbs uncocked…. These are normal figures for this type of weapon…. In order to fire these six cartridges, it is necessary to cock the trigger six times, as in the case of a revolver pulling the trigger only fires one shot. To pull a trigger of 10 lbs requires a definite and deliberate muscular effort.

This report would later be pointed to as evidence that little Ruth could not have fired the shots. However, the operative section of the report would be ignored by those who are *still trying to reprieve* convicted and executed murderer Ruth Ellis. "On receipt the … revolver was in working order, and during the course of firing in the Laboratory, the cylinder catch broke…." Ellis, painful hand and fingers or not, proved that she could fire the weapon. The evidence being the corpse of David Blakely and the witnesses to the cold-blooded murder on a London street. Try as they might, her supporters are simply not able to remove the murder weapon from the hand of Ruth Ellis. That would not stop their efforts over the next 50 years.

On May 21, 2005, *The Mirror* would report on the latest effort. "Fifty years on, government turns down reprieve for hanged Ruth Ellis.—Hanged killer Ruth Ellis has been secretly denied a pardon by the government, documents reveal. The decision has been kept under wraps for fear of unleashing protests which could embarrass ministers."

Final Words?

Only a few weeks after Ruth Ellis's execution, her 18-year-old sister suddenly died. In 1958, three years after his wife's execution, widower George Ellis hanged himself, having turned into a hopeless alcoholic. As stated above, in 1982 her son Andrea committed suicide reportedly in "a squalid bed sit." The newspapers were quick to report that his mother's execution for murder had caused him to suffer "irreparable psychological damage." The prosecutor at Ruth's trial, Christmas Humphreys, paid for his funeral. In the end the six shots fired by Ruth Ellis killed more than just David Blakely. How long efforts to reprieve Ellis will continue is unknown. What is known is that murderer Ruth Ellis will have no more opportunities to kill again.

Peter Thomas Anthony Manuel, Scottish Serial Killer (1956–1958)

"I'm standing on her now."

Psychopath Peter Thomas Anthony Manuel (1927–1958) was a brutal serial killer who was born in the United States to Scottish parents. In 1932 at the tender age of five he moved with his parents from New York to Coventry, England. From the very beginning Manuel was trouble; a reported juvenile delinquent as far back as records can show. At the age of 12 he was involved in a burglary which caused him to be convicted of the crime; he spent the next three years in reformatory institutes. He became a full-fledged criminal by age 16 when he was finally jailed for more than just a few days on a conviction of sexual assault. Upon his release he continued his criminal activities, serving several more sentences for rape. While he was in prison on a rape conviction his family moved to Glasgow, Scotland. He would join his family in Glasgow when he was released in 1953.

In 1955 Manuel was charged with assaulting another woman. At the time his attorney advised him to plead guilty, but Manuel would have none of it. It turned out to be a lucky call as a majority of the jury voted to acquit the rapist. During his post-trial medical/psychological interview with Dr. Angus MacNiven, Dr. Anderson, Dr. Inch and Dr. Boyd, Manuel would relate that this acquittal had brought the wrath of the police on him. "His acquittal, he says, rankled with the Inspector of Police who was involved in the investigation of this particular crime and this man determined to be revenged upon him, the accused, and this man involved other police officers in the conspiracy against him." In that same report the doctors would write an account given to them by Manuel's sister Teresa. At the time she was a certified mental health nurse undergoing training as a general nurse practitioner. "[Teresa Manuel] said that she had always thought that the accused was a psychopath." "She told me that three years ago when the accused was detained on a criminal charge in Barlinnie Prison she went to the Procurator Fiscal in Hamilton and suggested that he should be certified insane." He now began his known killing spree which would be random and conducted for the thrill of the hunt, even though none of his victims were armed. Along with being a psychopathic killer, he was also a coward.

Anne Knielands

Anne Knielands was a 17-year-old schoolgirl in 1956. She would meet her death in northwest Lanarkshire, Scotland. At the hands of Peter Manuel she was brutally beaten with an iron pipe after being assaulted. Her body was found on an East Kilbride golf course. Although

Manuel, a known sexual criminal, was picked up for questioning soon after the murder there was no evidence to connect him to the crime so he was released without being charged. He was not yet ready to brag about any murders. Two years later he would confess to this rape and murder. The murder of Anne Knielands is officially considered his first murder; however, considering his advanced age of 29 at the time the crime was committed and his continuous criminal background, including a series of sexual assaults, it is unlikely that this 1956 murder was Manuel's first. True serial killers rarely begin their murders so late in life, but there is no real way of knowing.

Three at a Time

The bodies of 45-year-old Marion Watt, her sister 41-year-old Margaret and Marion's 16-year-old daughter Vivienne were found in Marion Watt's home in Burnside, Glasgow, on September 17, 1956. They would be discovered by the mailman on his route. All three had been shot in the head at close range by a single killer. The evidence was very slim and could not be traced to any one suspect. Manuel had broken into master baker Mr. Watt's home while he was on a fishing trip and it is possible that he did not know anyone was home at the time he planned the break-in.

Even with thin evidence, the inspector in charge of this case suspected that the killer was Peter Manuel. Checking his suspect he found that Manuel had recently been arrested on a burglary charge at a local colliery and the motive for these murders did seem to be a botched burglary. When the three murders were being committed he was on bail awaiting

Between 1956 and 1958, Peter Thomas Anthony Manuel killed at least eight people, but perhaps many more.

trial. Once again Manuel was picked up for questioning, but there was no solid evidence. Manuel denied being anywhere near the home. The police, with nothing to connect him to the murders, had no choice but to release him.

For a time the police suspected that Mr. Watt, Marion's husband, was the killer. He was on a fishing trip but the authorities believed that he would have just been able to drive home, murder his family, and make it back to his fishing spot. He would be remanded in Barlinnie for questioning, but would never face trial. There was simply no case to be made against the grieving Mr. Watt who had lost his family at the hands of a serial killer.

Manuel would not be free for long, as two weeks later he was found guilty of the colliery burglary and sentenced to 18 months in prison. However, he would only serve 13 months before being released to once again prey upon the people of Scotland. He would soon take advantage of his freedom to add to his bloody body count. At least five more people would die during the five months that Manuel should have still been in prison.

Sydney Dunn

During the early part of December 1957 the newly released Peter Manuel decided to visit Newcastle Upon Tyne. It would be in Newcastle Upon Tyne that he would casually murder cab driver Sydney Dunn. Dunn was shot in the back of the head at close range for no reason whatsoever. He was now definitely killing randomly and the murders had just begun. No one seemed to be safe from this serial killer and the police had no real list of suspects. At the time no one connected Manuel to Dunn's murder because it did not seem to match the MO of the man they were looking for. Police would later be able to confirm that Manuel had indeed been in Newcastle at the time Mr. Dunn met his death.

Isabelle Cooke

As Manuel returned to Lanarkshire the newspapers were reporting on the brutal unsolved murders and asking if this was the work of one killer. Fear of random murder was beginning to come to the area of eastern Glasgow as more and more officers were assigned to the case.

On December 27, 1957, 17-year-old Isabelle Cooke set out from her home in Mount Vernon, intent on going to a dance at the local grammar school in Uddington. She was assaulted and murdered on her way home. Police would find her body only after Manuel pointed out where he had buried her in a nearby field in Burntbroom, near the school. That would come later; for the present all the authorities had was a missing person's case and no body. They could not be certain that she was part of the murder spree. At the time she had simply disappeared.

Three More—The Smart Family

On January 1, 1958, 45-year-old Peter Smart, his wife Doris and their 10-year-old son Michael were shot to death by Manuel in their home in Uddington. It would be a week before they were missed and the police entered the "death house" in Uddington. Once again evidence at the scene of the crime would show that a murder had been committed in connection to a home burglary. With three new murders matching aspects of earlier attacks, the public outcry was intense as the police went after any clue they could find to help track down this brutal serial killer. As it turned out, Manuel would be trapped by a banknote he had stolen from the Smart home.

It was a lucky break in a case that had very few clues to follow, and it turned out to be just the one needed to trap a serial killer. Manuel decided to spend some of his murder money at a local pub. When the bartender saw the notes he became suspicious of Manuel. Taking no chances, he called the police. It was January 13, 1958, and Peter Thomas Anthony Manuel was arrested, banknotes in hand. The police were able to trace the new banknotes to Peter Smart who had recently withdrawn them from his bank. That and other evidence, including his background and general movements, were sufficient enough to arrest Manuel for eight murders.

End Game

"The accused denies that he has ever suffered from any gross form of mental illness. At the present time he states that he is feeling well and he is not aware of any mental disturbance in himself."—Medical report by Dr. Angus MacNiven, March 28, 1958

The police would need a good deal more than a banknote and circumstantial evidence to bring this case to a jury and they believed the killer would have to be the one to supply the evidence. Manuel was informed that the police had arrested his father for possible involvement in the Smart murders. Police had taken him into custody after finding property from some of Manuel's victims in his father's home. Manuel decided it was time to confess. During questioning he would admit to eight murders and agreed to take police to the place where he had buried Isabelle Cooke. While they were standing in the field one of the officers asked him to point out the exact spot where he had buried her. He replied, "I'm standing on her now!" The brutal killer was very proud of his work and was extremely arrogant about it. The officer took little time to pull the killer off the shallow grave he was standing on.

The trial was held at Glasgow High Court. The prosecution had a very easy task of proving that Manuel had been the killer of at least seven of the victims he was charged with. The defense was handled by Manuel himself after dismissing his counsel Harold Leslie, attempting to prove that he was innocent due to insanity. It was not an easy thing to do when one is defending one's self. The court was not impressed with his less than able defense even though some news reports published his skills as "remarkably skillful and with aplomb." Nevertheless, he was found guilty of seven murders in May of 1958. He was acquitted of the murder of Ann Kneilands only because the prosecution had no other evidence of his guilt besides his confession, which Manuel had withdrawn before the trial began. The state would have to settle for seven convictions, which would do nicely for justice to be served. Needless to say, he was soon sentenced to death by judge Lord Cameron. There was to be no reprieve for the Scottish serial killer. In his report on the trial Judge Cameron wrote, "I saw no sign indicative to a layman of any illness or abnormality beyond callousness, selfishness and treachery in high degree, but I did inform the impression that he was even then laying the foundation of a suggestion that he might in the end of the day be presented not as a criminal, but as one in need of medical care."

On Friday, July 11, 1958, 31-year-old serial killer Peter Manuel was hanged in Barlinnie Prison, Glasgow, Scotland. It was 8 a.m. and the hangman did a fine job. Before he took his drop Manuel asked the hanging party to "turn up the radio, and I'll go quietly." Manuel would become the third to the last to be hanged in Scotland and the second to the last to be put down on the gallows at Barlinnie Prison. To this date investigators still believe that he was involved in at least 15 murders, but evidence in those other cases was found to be too weak to prove in a court of law. If he had been convicted of all 15 murders his total body count would be more than the infamous Yorkshire Ripper. As for this killer, despite interrogation efforts, he would be satisfied to keep his known murder count at eight, leaving the other killings in the unsolved column.

Edwin Bush and the Antique Shop Murder (1961)

"Speaking personally, the world is better off without me."

Edwin Bush (1940–1961), coming from an Indian background, was raised in a troubled home. Records show that in 1953 the British National Society for Prevention of Cruelty to Children had looked into his troubled family. Investigating the general living conditions, the organization discovered six children and two adults living in a tiny three-room flat. Due to the overcrowded conditions, 12-year-old Edwin was taken from his home and sent to a government home. In 1955 he was relocated to a training farm near Uckfield in Sussex County. His training did not take, as he was soon involved in several cases of breaking and entering. These as well as other stealing cases landed him in Borstal detention center on several occasions.

March 2, 1961, found Edwin Bush at an antique shop located at 23 Cecil Court, looking to all the world a regular shopper examining the wares. Cecil Court was little more than an alley off Charing Cross Road, London. Entering the business, Bush met antique dealer Louis Meier. When Mr. Meier inquired what Bush may be looking for he told the shop owner that he was interested in purchasing a present for his girlfriend. Mr. Meier would later recall, "He told me his father was an Indian and that it was a common thing to carry a dagger in India." With this in mind Meier showed the young man a large curved dress sword Bush had shown an interest in for the low cost of £15. He also laid out several other daggers for his customer's selection. Bush would leave the shop without making a purchase, promising that he would return in the near future.

Having made his criminal plans, Bush soon returned but Louis Meier had left for the day. Elisa May Batten, who worked for Mr. Meier, was on duty at the time and was happy to help the customer make a selection. It would be a fatal error. Bush would leave with the sword, and Elisa Batten would soon be dead.

The next day a 15-year-old apprentice sign writer named Peter Albert King left his workplace for lunch, intending to use his free time to do a bit of shopping. He had also planned on stopping in at a firm in St. Martin's Lane to inquire about some signs they wanted painted. At around 11:30 a.m. Peter looked into Louis Meier's Antique Shop. He had wanted to purchase a billiard cue and found the shop open. When he found no one in the front after he called out, he took a look in the back. He found a partly opened curtain which covered the back rooms and spotted what he thought might have been a store front dummy lying on the floor. He also thought that it might have been a woman who had fainted. Leaving the shop, King was disturbed by what he had seen and reported it to several people, but no one did anything until after the body had been discovered by Mr. Meier. Meier seems to have found the body of his employee only a short time after Peter King had beat a hasty retreat. It was a bloody scene and clearly Mrs. Batten had been long dead. He immediately called the police.

Home Office Pathologist Dr. Keith Simpson was called to the scene. He soon discovered that the victim had been stabbed to death. Three deep stab wounds had been inflicted on Mrs. Batten by an antique dagger that had been for sale in the shop. There was one wound in the back which was very deep, a second stab in her neck had buried the dagger around nine inches deep, and a third stab wound of around eight inches to the chest, the blade was buried completely up to the ivory handle which remained in the victim. Certainly there had been a brutal and cowardly murder. There would not be much to go on as there had been no weapon taken into the shop and no one had seen the killer enter or leave.

Identikit

Despite the many problems presented by this case the first real lead would come quickly. Detective Sergeant Raymond Frederick Dagg from

Bow Street Station was assigned to interview Mr. Meier on March 4. Mr. Meier was able to relate the story of the young Indian man who had shown a good deal of interest in the daggers earlier in the week on March 2. His recollection of the man's appearance was so detailed that Detective Sergeant Dagg was able to put together a facial composite of the possible murder suspect using a new "identikit." The identikit was not a true portrait or police sketch; the method was more of a complicated jigsaw puzzle. Witnesses pick out the closest nose, eyes, ears, lips, and other features from several choices of these features and the best are combined to build up a "right look" of the suspect.

Continuing his investigation as he canvassed the local area he located Mr. Paul Roberts, the son of a gun dealer who worked in his father's shop in St. Martin's Lane. Roberts related to the officer that a young Indian man had come into his father's business attempting to sell the sword which was suspected of coming from Mr. Meier's Antique Shop. The sword would later prove to have definitely come from Mr. Meier's shop and was thus a direct link to the killer of Mrs. Batten. With Roberts's description the officer was able to put together a second composite of the suspect. Upon Dagg's return to headquarters, Divisional Detective Superintendent Pollard saw the two composites and decided that they were so close to each other that they must be very close to the actual appearance of the killer they were looking for. Pollard ordered the composites to be photographed and published side-by-side internally to all police stations. These two composites were also released to the media in the hope that the public would be able to identify this "person of interest" as they had been asked to many times before, beginning with the 1881 Mapleton murder on the Brighton Train Line. Though what had developed was reported to not be up to press standards, it was published with notes that the suspect appeared to be an "awkward-looking and fiercely dark-haired young man." The identikit work was about to pay off much faster than anyone in the police force could have hoped for.

Capture

March 8, 1961, found Police Constable Arthur John Hilton Cole on patrol duty on Old Compton Street in the well-known fashionable Soho area of London. Cole was attached to the West End Central Police Station and had done his work studying the composite sketches and it was about to pay off. He spotted a young Indian man on Old Compton Street whom he thought was a dead ringer for the suspect being sought for the murder of Elsie Batten. The suspect was walking with his girlfriend, 17-year-old Janet Wheeler. Both would be held by P.C. Cole as he waited for backup. The man he held was 21-year-old Edwin Bush. It had taken less than four days from the issuance of the composite and the arrest of the suspect. The identikit had found its place in Scotland Yard.

At the police station Bush would relate to the officers that the composite sketches did indeed look somewhat like him. He had actually seen them in the newspapers, yet he continued to go about his business as if nothing was about. As he was being interviewed, other officers interviewed Janet Wheeler, who was soon found to have no knowledge of the murders. She was later released and one would think somewhat wiser for the experience. Bush's mother was also questioned. Police were able to discover from her that her son had left home on the morning of the murder, supposedly for work, at 7:30 a.m. She could not alibi her killer son. Only later would she learn that her interview had helped hang her murderous son.

On March 8 at 7:40 p.m. Bush was re-interviewed by Divisional Detective Superintendent Pollard along with Detective Inspector Howlett who had charge of the case. Naturally, Bush denied any knowledge of the murder and denied that he had been in the shop. He stated that he had been at home with his mother "at the reported time of the murder." He did not know that his mother's previous statement had already contradicted his claim. At 10:15 that evening Inspector John Child set up an identification parade at the Bow Street Police Station. With Edwin Bush in the line-up Louis Meier was unable to positively identify Bush as the Indian he had seen in his shop. This was a setback for the officers who had good reason to believe that they did indeed have the right man. It was left up to Paul Roberts who stepped into the darkened room, took one look at the assembled men on parade to immediately identify Bush as the man he had spoken to about the sword in his father's shop. No fewer than two other Cecil Shop owners were able to give positive identifications of the man with the sword.

With the positive identifications now in hand Pollard informed Bush that he was being charged with the murder of Mrs. Elsie Batten.

With that he left Bush with Detective Inspector Howlett who was soon taking down a full confession from Bush. He admitted the murder and stated that his girlfriend had nothing to do with it. In his statement he would report:

> I went back to the shop and started looking through the daggers, telling her that I might want to buy one, but I picked one up and hit her in the back. I then lost my nerve and picked up a stone vase and hit her with it. I grabbed a knife and hit her once in the stomach and once in the neck. I am sorry I done it. I don't know what came over me. Speaking personally, the world is better off without me.

The End of Days

On May 12, 1961, Edwin Bush stood before Judge Stevenson and was given a verdict of guilty for his brutal attack on the unarmed woman. During his trial he had attempted to play the race card by claiming that Mrs. Batten had said to him, "You niggers are all the same. You come in and never buy anything." Needless to say, this was no excuse for murder and Mrs. Batten was never heard to voice those types of words when she was alive. Clearly, the vicious killer had lied to save his cowardly neck. Stevenson soon sentenced Bush to death by hanging for the brutal murder. Justice would see to it that the world would soon be "better off" without Edwin Bush. On July 6, 1961, after the defense had failed in their attempts to remove Bush from the condemned cell and replace the death sentence with life in prison, Bush was executed at Pentonville Prison. It had been a little longer than four months from the murder to the execution of the killer. British justice indeed worked with great speed in the case of the Antique Shop Murder.

Peter William Sutcliffe, the Yorkshire Ripper (1975–1980)

"In this truck is a man whose latent genius, if unleashed, would rock the nation; whose dynamic energy would overpower those around him. Better let him sleep?"

246   Section III: The 20th Century—A New Era for Murder

During his five-year reign of terror the Yorkshire Ripper would murder 12 women and attempt to murder at least four others in Northern England as he waged war on prostitutes and innocents while working as a long-haul trucker, always armed with his deadly ball-peen hammer.

At an early age Peter William Sutcliffe was disturbingly interested in corpses. He was born on June 2, 1946, in Bingley, West Yorkshire, England. His father was a mill worker while his mother tended to the home. Never popular, he left school at the age of fifteen and began a series of low-paying jobs, which included a period as a gravedigger. He finally settled for a night shift job at Anderton International.

In 1966 he met Sonia Szurma who came to England from Czechoslovakia. On August 10, 1974, Peter and Sonia were married and things seemed to be going along reasonably well. However, shortly after the marriage he was laid off from his factory job. He had been employed long enough to receive a buy-out, which he used to train for an HGV license. Finishing his training in June of 1975, he would begin work as a truck driver on September 29. The Yorkshire Ripper now had a job which would allow him to move around a good deal, and he would use it to good advantage. However, before he hit the road there was work to be done somewhat locally.

Anna "Annie" Rogulskyj

Thirty-six-year-old waitress Anna Rogulskyj is thought to have been the first victim of the Yorkshire Ripper, but no one can be certain. On the evening of July 5, 1975, she was walking alone in Keighley when she was suddenly and brutally attacked from behind. An attacker came up on her and hit her on the head with a ball-peen hammer. Rendering her uncon-

The Yorkshire Ripper, Peter William Sutcliffe, murdered 12 women and attacked at least four others over five years (1975 to 1980), mostly using a ball-peen hammer, though he had other tools in his "murder kit" (U.K. *Daily Star*).

scious, he began slashing her stomach with his knife. He would have continued if not for the fact that a neighbor came by, requiring a hasty retreat. After an extended hospital stay and repeated surgeries Anna recovered from her attack, including the most severe of injuries to her head. Pointedly, she would later meet Sutcliffe's father and she encouraged him to feel the two remaining indents in the back of her head, which had been made by the ball-peen hammer.

Olive Smith

In August of 1975 office cleaner Olive Smith was attacked in Halifax by an unknown man with a ball-peen hammer. The attack on the 46-year-old matched the MO of the previous victim and the police were concerned that a mad attacker was starting to attack women in the general area. As before, the attacker was interrupted and he made off, leaving the woman badly injured but alive. She would eventually recover and as before, the attacker would escape—at least for the present. Unfortunately, these were only the start to a devastating and cowardly series of attacks on unarmed women in Northern England.

Tracy Browne

Later that August Sutcliffe came up behind 14-year-old Tracy Browne in Silsden. Tracy had been walking along a country lane when she was attacked by Sutcliffe, who proceeded to hit her on the head five times with his hammer. He would not be convicted of this attempted murder, but he would eventually confess to being the man who committed the brutal attack on the youngest victim in the series. This attack on a child would show that no woman was safe from this madman. The attack would also put aside any myth that the attacker targeted only prostitutes.

Wilma McCann

Twenty-eight-year-old Wilma McCann of Chapeltown Leeds was the fourth known victim of the Yorkshire Ripper and she became the first to die at his bloody hand. On October 29 or 30, 1975, the mother of four and part-time prostitute was attacked from behind with a ball-peen hammer. The slaughter of prostitutes had begun. It would take two blows to the head to bring her down before he stabbed her fifteen times. Her body was found on the Prince Phillip Playing Fields in Leeds. With her death came an extensive investigation which eventually numbered some 150 police officers headed up by Scotland Yard inspectors. Nevertheless, with more than 11,000 interviews conducted, the officers were unable to focus on a proper suspect. They would need more evidence to close in on the killer and the only way to acquire that would be to investigate the next crime!

Emily Jackson

The killer's next victim was 42-year-old housewife and prostitute Emily Jackson who was also from the Leeds area. After she had been ambushed, Sutcliffe proceeded to stab her to death. Fifty-one times he attacked with his knife in a bloody frenzy. It was January 20, 1976, and clearly the killer was increasing the ferocity of his attacks on his victims as they lay unconscious. There was also a sexual implication to these attacks which would not be released to the general public until 2003 when it would find its way into publication in a book on the murders. The sexual connection was verified when Sutcliffe was finally taken into custody much later and stripped by police officers. Along with his "attack kit" he was wearing a V-neck sweater beneath his trousers. The sweater arms had been pulled over his legs leaving his groin exposed through the V-neck opening. The elbows of the sweater also had padding on them to protect his knees so that when he knelt down over his victims he would not hurt his knees!

Marcella Claxton

> Any street-girls, models on the seamier side of Leeds, and the prostitutes who may know or suspect a client that may be this way inclined and violently opposed to their way of life, should come forward and see us.—Detective Chief Superintendent Denis Hoban

In March of 1976 Sutcliffe was fired from his job as a driver due to his absenteeism and would not find another position until October. In the meantime, he went back on the hunt for his next victim. He found her in the form of Marcella Claxton, a 20-year-old prostitute from Leeds. He would attack her in Roundhay Park in Leeds. As before, the attack began with Sutcliffe hitting Marcella on the head with his ever-ready hammer. It was May 9, 1976, and he had enough time in the darkness to continue the attack with 25 stab wounds. However, this victim did not die even though the knife wounds had been extensive. Certainly her attacker thought that he had finished her off. Because of the nature of the attack, however, Marcella never saw her attacker.

Irene Richardson

Irene Richardson was a 28-year-old prostitute from Chapeltown on February 5, 1977, when she was brutally attacked in Roundhay Park in Leeds. The attack began with a number of hammer blows to the head. This surprise attack was followed, as had become usual, by a number of stab wounds inflicted on the dead woman. This attack, however, left a clue which would lead to a great number of inquiries. Tire tracks were located near the body, but they turned out to be of a very common kind, resulting in a very long list of possible cars which could have been used by the killer. The evidence could not be used to trace any one person, but could be used to match a suspect's car once he had been captured.

Patricia "Tina" Atkinson

The next murder took a different turn as the victim was murdered in her own flat. Thirty-two-year-old prostitute Patricia Atkinson lived at Flat 3, 9 Oak Avenue, Bradford. On April 23, 1977, she had unknowingly taken the Yorkshire Ripper to her home and paid the ultimate price for the error. She would be the fourth woman murdered by this serial killer. Once again, the police gained a clue to the killer's identity. A boot print was found on the blood-soaked bedclothes, allowing detectives to learn the shoe size of the killer. It was, however, not crisp enough for them to be able to match it to a particular shoe. Luck was still on the side of the killer.

Jayne MacDonald

On June 26, 1977, 16-year-old shop assistant Jayne MacDonald had found her way to the Adventure Playground on Reginald Street in Leeds. She would find the Yorkshire Ripper waiting there in the darkness for a victim. Jayne MacDonald was *not* a prostitute, but would nevertheless become the youngest to die at the hands of this serial killer who seemed to always attack from behind. She was murdered almost close enough to home to see her house. Her death would once again refocus the British public's perception that only prostitutes were in mortal danger of becoming victims of this insane killer. The murder of an innocent changed all of that. No woman or young lady was safe from this madman in the northern counties of Scotland, and the press would make certain that their readers were reminded of that fact.

Maureen Long

Forty-two-year-old Maureen Long was a prostitute working in Bradford in July of 1977 when she was attacked by the ever-present hammer of the Yorkshire Ripper. She survived the attack on her skull only because her attacker was interrupted, and he had to flee before he could be identified. This attack would also leave the police with a false lead when a car, thought to have been driven by the killer, was misidentified. The result cost the efforts of more than 300 police officers and more than 12,500 witness statements before the error and thousands of checked cars proved that it was a false lead.

Jean Jordan

The next murder would bring the police and Peter Sutcliffe face-to-face. Jean Jordan was a 20-year-old prostitute from Manchester. She was murdered on October 1, but her body was not discovered for 10 days on an allotment next to the Southern Cemetery in Manchester.

Her skull had been crushed with 11 hammer blows, which had been followed by 24 stab wounds after she was already dead. Investigating the murder, detectives discovered that the body had been moved to that location several days after the murder. There was a very good reason for the move. Sutcliffe knew that he had made a grave error. He had given Jordan a £5 note, presumably to purchase sex. She had placed the note in her handbag which had been lost during the attack. A week after the murder Sutcliffe returned to the murder site to find the bag and retrieve the £5 note. Failing to locate the handbag or note, Sutcliffe moved the body and proceeded to work on removing the head with a hacksaw and a broken pane of glass. This late evening movement and attack on the body occurred after he had hosted a party for his family at his home.

This time the authorities got a break and located the handbag. The £5 note was a new one, easily traced to one of the Midland Bank branches in Shipley or Bingley. Further investigation over a three-week period developed a list of some 8,000 local employees, as the note had been used in a wage package. With this information in hand 5,000 men were soon interviewed by the police, including Peter Sutcliffe. There would be no follow-up interview with Sutcliffe in reference to the £5 note. The police were being overwhelmed by information. Later investigation would show that the Ripper Squad would eventually interview Sutcliffe at least nine times. He was disregarded as the Ripper each and every time. There were too many suspects and too little hard evidence to work with in order to point to a single killer. As with Jack the Ripper, it was starting to look like the only way the authorities were going to catch the Yorkshire Ripper would be if he was discovered leaning over a body! Or perhaps sitting next to a live one.

Of mildly historic interest comes the report that this victim was discovered by one Bruce Jones. Jones would later appear on the long-running British soap opera *Coronation Street* in the part of Les Battersby.

Marilyn Moore

Twenty-five-year-old Marilyn Moore was a working prostitute from Leeds when she was brutally attacked by the Yorkshire Ripper in December 1977. She would survive the attack and would be able to supply the police for the first time with a general description of her attacker. Further investigation proved that the tire prints found at the scene matched the tire prints at the murder site of Irene Richardson. There was no doubt that this attack was committed by the same serial killer. But scant clues were still costing lives.

Yvonne Pearson

In January 1978 Scotland Yard detectives attached to the Ripper Squad ended their inquiries into the £5 note and moved on to other areas of investigation. In that same month, prostitute Yvonne Pearson met her death at the well-practiced hands of the Yorkshire Ripper. There was no doubt that her killer used the same method. This time he would hide the body under an old sofa on a piece of waste ground just off Arthington Street in Bradford. It seemed that he was now hiding his victims in order to have time to get away.

Helen Rytka

Helen Rytka, 18 years old, was a prostitute working the darkened streets of Huddersfield when she met the Ripper on January 31, 1978. She was raped before she was murdered and mutilated. Her body would be discovered three days later in a timber yard on Great Northern Street. Her body would display all of the hallmarks of the Yorkshire Ripper. Once again a hammer had been used to take a life along with the ever-present chisel taken from the killer's murder kit.

Vera Millward

Vera Millward was found dead in the car park of the Manchester Royal Infirmary. The 40-year-old's death on May 16 would be the last one for 1978. After the murder of this prostitute the killer would not kill again for nearly a year. It was during this hiatus that Sutcliffe's mother died. She would die before her son was positively identified as the killer so she would never really know the truth. The question must however be asked: Due to his many police interviews during this ongoing series of crimes did she ever suspect that her son was responsible for any of these brutal murders and attacks? Did he tell her the truth?

Josephine Whitaker

Josephine Whitaker was a 19-year-old bank clerk from Halifax. She was *not* a prostitute. She was assaulted and murdered on April 4, 1979, as she walked home from her job on Savile Park moor in Halifax. This murder came at the same time a clue was sent to lead investigator Superintendent George Oldfield. The clue, however, turned out to be a hoax that sent the police on a months-long fruitless search for a suspect with a "Wearside accent." The hoax was in the form of a taped message taunting the police generally and Superintendent Oldfield by name. The same hoaxer had earlier sent two letters to the authorities the previous year, both signed "Jack the Ripper." He would soon be dubbed "Wearside Jack." It would not be until October 2005 that an unemployed alcoholic named John Humble would be arrested and charged with "attempting to pervert the course of justice." On March 21, 2006, Humble was sentenced to eight years in prison for sending the tape and letter. The police are as of this writing continuing their investigation into John Humble, trying to link him to the murder of 26-year-old Joan Harrison, who was murdered in November 1975 in Preston. "Wearside Jack" had boasted of her murder in one of the hoax letters. As far as the police can determine she was not one of the Ripper's victims.

Barbara Leach

Barbara Leach was also not a prostitute. Leach was a 20-year-old student at Bradford University. On September 4, 1979, she was attacked and murdered very near the university behind her lodgings at 13 Ashgrove, Bradford. Once again it appeared that the Yorkshire Ripper had attacked a random female victim who was, as the press would report, "totally innocent." This was the seventeenth attack attributed to this serial killer and the eleventh murder. The public alarm was intense which caused the police to produce a publicity campaign in order to enlist the public's help and perhaps calm concerns. The campaign proved to be fruitless as it focused on the Wearside connection. Nevertheless, Sutcliffe was picked up twice in 1979 and even though he was on the list of 300 men who had been connected to the £5 note there was no strong case that he was the killer—yet!

In April of 1980 Peter Sutcliffe was arrested for drunk driving. In his vehicle was his murder kit, but since he was arrested for drunk driving and not as a Ripper suspect, the kit was not discovered. A search of the vehicle was not required for the charge. Sutcliffe was soon out on bail.

Marguerite Walls

While Sutcliffe was out on bail and awaiting his trial on drunk driving he murdered 47-year-old Marguerite Walls at Pudsley on August 20, 1980. Walls was a civil servant and had never been a prostitute. For this murder the killer would try strangulation as his method of death before mutilating her body. Her death had most of the hallmarks of the Ripper. She would be found in the back garden of a home known as Claremont on New Street in Farsley.

Jacqueline Hill

Twenty-year-old Jacqueline Hill was a student at the University of Leeds when she meet Sutcliffe. On November 17, 1980, she was murdered by the Yorkshire Ripper, becoming the thirteenth to die at his hands and also the last. Her body would be found on a piece of waste ground just off Alma Road in Headingley, Leeds. Once again the killer had attacked a woman not involved in prostitution. In this case he also stabbed the victim in the eye. It would later be reported that he could not stand to see her "reproachful stare."

Theresa Sykes and Upadhya Bandara

During this general time period Sutcliffe also attacked 16-year-old Theresa Sykes in Huddersfield and 34-year-old Upadhya Bandara in

Leeds. Upadhya Bandara was an older student at the University of Leeds and in fact was a doctor. She would be strangled and beaten by the Ripper in Leeds in September but would survive the attack to continue her work in the medical field. Both of these women would survive their injuries. No one at the time could know that the rampage of the Yorkshire Ripper had ended.

Finally an Arrest

> "13 murders and eight other brutal attacks."

On November 25, 1980, a friend of Sutcliffe's named Trevor Birdsall made a report to the police to the effect that Peter Sutcliffe was the Yorkshire Ripper.

> I have good reason to [know] the man you are looking for in the Ripper case. This man [has] dealings with prostitutes and always had a thing about them.... His name and address is Peter Sutcliffe, 6 Garden Lane, Heaton, Bradford. [He works] for Charles Transport, Shipley.

This report became lost in the enormous amount of data held by the police in this case. Before he could be interviewed for the tenth time in response to this report, fate would place Sutcliffe finally into police hands for the last time.

Sutcliffe had placed false number plates on his car. This was the reason why he was pulled over by the police. It was January 2, 1981, as Sutcliffe pulled into the driveway of Light Trades House, Melbourne Avenue, Broomhill, Sheffield, South Yorkshire. With him in the car was 24-year-old prostitute Olive Reivers. Sutcliffe was arrested because of the false plates and transported to Dewsbury Police Station for processing. Before he was taken in, Sutcliffe used the pretext that he needed to urinate. For a short period of time he was out of sight of the arresting officer which allowed Sutcliffe to dispose of a rope, a hammer and a knife he had been carrying in anticipation of another murderous attack.

At Dewsbury station the fact that he matched many of the known characteristics of the Yorkshire Ripper and the fact that he was in the case file caused the police to begin questioning him about the murders. The next day the area of his arrest was closely searched and the police found his murder kit. The police felt that they had their man, but they needed more. They obtained a search warrant and began a detailed search of his home at 6 Garden Lane, Bradford. The police also brought in his wife for questioning, but she was never thought to be involved with any of these brutal attacks.

The police continued to question Sutcliffe for two days, bringing up a series of circumstantial clues as they tracked his movements and possible connection to this series of murders. On the afternoon of January 4, 1981, Peter Sutcliffe suddenly declared that he was indeed the man they were looking for—he was the Yorkshire Ripper. On January 6 he was charged with 13 murders and numerous assaults. He would go to trial in May claiming that he was only a "tool of God's will." That would be his stated defense.

The Trial

Sutcliffe's trial lasted two weeks. He pled not guilty to the 13 Ripper murders, but using a defense of diminished responsibility, he pled guilty to manslaughter on the deaths he had caused. He added a plea of guilty to seven counts of attempted murder. Four psychiatric reports were entered into the record, all showing a diagnosis of paranoid schizophrenia. After proposing to accept the plea, the prosecution was charged by Judge Mr. Justice Boreham to prove in detail how they had made their decision to accept this plea. This was most unusual and took the prosecution by surprise. Answering the judge's demands, Attorney-General Sir Michael Havers stood and delivered a detailed two-hour presentation to the court. Returning from an hour and half lunch, there began a 40-minute legal discussion of the matter. After this unusual session, Judge Boreham rejected the plea of diminished responsibility and informed the court that the matter would be decided by a British jury.

Guilty of manslaughter, no matter how many counts, would clearly allow Sutcliffe to be released upon the British public much more easily than if he had been convicted of murder. That problem was corrected when the jury returned with a verdict of guilty on 13 counts of murder. With the death penalty removed, for the moment, from the British legal system, Sutcliffe was sentenced to life imprisonment at "Her Majesty's pleasure." With the sentence, Judge Boreham declared that Sutcliffe was beyond redemption and that he should never be released from prison. He recommended a minimum sentence of at least 30 years before any type of parole could be discussed for this brutal convicted serial killer.

Aftermath

Her Majesty's Prison Parkhurst began playing host to Sutcliffe on May 22, 1981. He had been found sane at the time of the murders despite the diagnosis of schizophrenia. Even as he arrived, efforts were made to send him to a secure psychiatric unit. These efforts were blocked for a while but eventually efforts succeeded in upgrading Sutcliffe's residence. Their chance came after an attack was made on Sutcliffe by an inmate at the prison. It seemed that even brutal convicts at Parkhurst felt that the Yorkshire Ripper had not been properly dealt with by the British legal system.

On January 10, 1983, a 35-year-old career criminal named James Costello attacked Sutcliffe with a broken coffee jar. Costello, known for his violent attacks, stabbed Sutcliffe in the left side of his face, which caused four deep wounds needing 30 stitches to close.

Sutcliffe's protectors demanded that he be moved and in March of 1984, having spent less than three years in prison for his 13 brutal murders, Sutcliffe was sent to Broadmoor Hospital. It seemed to be a good move for the serial killer, who now had a nice room and a comfortable bed to sleep in, at least until 1996. On February 23 of that year Sutcliffe was relaxing in his private room

The death penalty being repealed at the time of his conviction, Peter William Sutcliffe, the Yorkshire Ripper, is serving a life sentence.

in the Henley Ward at Broadmoor when fellow resident Paul Wilson stepped in to borrow a videotape from Sutcliffe's private collection. Wilson then attempted to strangle Sutcliffe with the flex cord from a pair of Sutcliffe's stereo headphones. Sutcliffe's screams brought Jamie Devitt and Kenneth Erskine, both murderers, to the rescue.

March 10, 1997, brought a third attack on the Yorkshire Ripper when a fellow resident stabbed him with a pen. This attack would cause the serial killer to become blind in his left eye and severely damaged his right eye. He is still able to view his videos, however, with what remains of his right eye.

The Byford Report

In 1981 the Inspector of Constabulary, Sir Lawrence Byford, delivered a detailed investigation report into the Yorkshire Ripper murders and the problems that developed during the hunt for this serial killer. There was plenty of blame to go around, partly due to the realization that the authorities needed a better method to handle cases with a large amount of data. Eventually this realization would lead to a new computer system known as HOLMES (Home Office Large Major Enquiry System). By all accounts the system is very useful in the investigation of major crimes.

Byford's report, partly released to the British public on June 1, 2006, also related the fact that the police do not believe that all of Sutcliffe's crimes have seen the light of day.

> We feel it is highly improbable that the crimes in respect of which Sutcliffe has been charged and convicted are the only ones attributable to him. This feeling is reinforced by examining the details of a number of assaults on women since 1969 which, in some ways, clearly fall into the established pattern of Sutcliffe's overall modus-operandi. I hasten to add that I feel sure that the senior police officers in the areas concerned are also mindful of this possibility but, in order to ensure full account is taken of all the information available, I have arranged for an effective liaison to take place.

As of this writing Sutcliffe has yet to be charged with any more murderous attacks. If he is convicted of another murder there will be no doubt that he will die in custody. There are at least four unsolved murders and seven brutal assaults of women in Scotland which could one day be placed in the column marked the Yorkshire Ripper.

Bibliography

Books

Beal, Edward. *The Trial of Adelaide Bartlett for Murder, Held at the Central Criminal Court from Monday, April 12, to Saturday, April 17, 1886.* London: Stevens & Haynes, 1886.
Berry, James. *My Experiences as an Executioner.* London: Newton Abbot, 1972.
Burney, Ian. *Poison, Detection and Victorian Imagination.* Manchester: Manchester University Press, 2007.
Fido, Martin. *The Chronicle of Crime: The Infamous Villains of Modern History and Their Hideous Crimes.* London: Carlton Books, 2004.
Gribble, Leonard R. *Triumphs of Scotland Yard: A Century of Detection.* London: J. Long, 1955.
Hall, John Richard, ed. *Trial of Adelaide Bartlett.* Edinburgh and London: Wm. Hodge & Company, 1927.
Jones, Richard Glyn. *Unsolved Classic True Murder Cases.* New York: Peter Bedrick Books, 1987.
The National Archives of Scotland. Records relating to the trial and execution of Peter Thomas Anthony Manuel.
Newton, Michael. *The Encyclopedia of Serial Killers.* New York: Checkmark Books, 2000.
O'Donnell, Elliott, ed. *Trial of Kate Webster.* Edinburgh and London: Wm. Hodge & Company, 1925.
Parry, Leonard Arthur, ed. *Trial of Dr. Smethurst.* Edinburgh and London: Wm. Hodge & Company, 1931.
Phillips, Charles, and Alan Axelrod, with Kurt Kemper. *Cops, Crooks, and Criminologists: An International Biographical Dictionary of Law Enforcement.* New York: Checkmark Books, 2000.
Roughead, William, ed. *Trial of Dr. Pritchard.* Edinburgh and Glasgow: Wm. Hodge & Company, 1906.

Online Sources

Casebook: Jack the Ripper, www.casebook.org
Dr. Thomas Neill Cream (1850–1892)
Mary Eleanor Wheeler Pearcey
The Camden Town Murder
Broadmoor Asylum
Crime Library, www.crimelibrary.com
The Vampire Killers: Renfield's Syndrome
The Trial of the Century: The Madeleine Smith Story
en.citizendium.org, Frederick Porter Wensley
Geocities, www.geocities.com
John "Babbacombe" Lee—The Man They Could Not Hang
Mary Eleanor Wheeler (Pearcey)
History by the Yard, www.historybytheyard.co.uk
The Infamous Charlie Peace (1832–1879)
Jonathan Whicher and the Road Hill House Murder
Scotland Yard
Percy LeFroy Mapleton
Why is it called "Scotland Yard"?
hometown.aol.com, Baby Farmer's
London Metropolitan Police, www.police.uk/history

Bibliography

"The Notorious Case of Dr Crippen (1862–1910)"
"Neville Heath—A Dangerous Man for a Woman to Have Known"
"The Crime Museum"
Constance Kent and the Road Hill House Murder
The Brighton Trunk Murders 1934
The Metropolitan Police Service Historical Archives
PC Gutteridge murder—1927
The Antique Shop Murder
The "Brides in the Bath" Murders
Brief definition and history of policing
The Newgate Calendar, www.exclassics.com
James Greenacre
George Fursey
Mary Young, alias Jenny Diver
Serial killer true crime library, www.crimezzz.net
Amelia Elizabeth Dyer
Neville George Clevely Heath
Wikipedia, en.wikipedia.org
The Blackout Ripper
The Black Museum
Brighton trunk murders
Broadmoor Hospital
Norman Birkett, 1st Baron Birkett
Juana Bormann
Brighton trunk murders
Mary Ann Cotton
John Reginald Halliday Christie
Thomas Neill Cream
Amelia Dyer
Dartmoor (HM Prison)
Walter Dew
Ruth Ellis
Edgware
Execution Dock
Henry Fielding
Antonio Grajera
Irma Grese
Neville Heath
John George Haigh
Edmund Henderson
Josef Kramer
Bruce George Peter Lee
John "Babbacombe" Lee
Peter Manuel
Percy Lefroy Mapleton
Peninsular War
Mary Pearcey
Charles Peace
John Straffen
Peter Sutcliffe
Walter Sickert
Bernard Spisbury
Special Branch
Madeleine Smith
Scotland Yard
Sratton Brothers case
William Herbert Wallace
www.bbc.co.uk, John "Babbacombe" Lee
www.bmj.com, Adelaide Bartlett and the Pimlico Mystery
www.btp.police.uk, Murder on the Brighton Line
www.capitalpunishmentuk.org, Kate Webster—The "Barnes Mystery"
www.edp24.co.uk, Spooky Norfolk
www.electricscotland.com, Rev. Dr. Norman MacLeod's account of the execution of Dr. Pritchard
www.essex.police.uk, Essex Police Memorial Trust: George William Gutteridge
www.essex.police.uk, The Moat Farm Murder
www.everything2.com, The London Blitz Murders (idea)
www.fact.on.ca, Off with her head
www.fileysurgery.com, The Regrettable Dr. Edward William Pritchard
www.findagrave.com, Peter Thomas Anthony Manuel
www.fprints.nwlean.net, Michele Triplett's Fingerprint Terms
www.grangeassociation.org, Dr. Pritchard
www.historic-uk.com, Victorian Poisoners
www.ianwaugh.com, John "Babbacombe" Lee
www.ianwaugh.com, The Man They Could Not Hang
www.jewishvirtuallibrary.org, Elizabeth Volkenrath
www.johngrievecentre.co.uk, John Grieve Centre
www.murderuk.com, Murder in the UK, Mary-Ann Cotton
www.murderuk.com, Murders in the UK, Gordon Frederick Cummins

Bibliography

www.mustrad.org.uk, Constance Kent and the Road murder
www.norfolkcoast.co.uk, The Tabernacle Murder
www.old-time.com, The Black Museum
www.scrapbookpages.com, The Belsen Trial
www.sl.nsw.gov.au, Convict Life
www.staffspasttrack.org.uk, John Parsons Cook
www.stephen-stratford.co.uk, Edwin Bush
www.stephen-stratford.co.uk, Gordon Cummins
www.stephen-stratford.co.uk, Ruth Ellis
www.trutv.com, Charles Peace: King of the Cat Burglars
www.womenofbrighton.co.uk, Christiana Edmunds

Index

Abbot, Newton 102
Abbotskerswell 97, 99
Abley, Mr. 28
Acid Bath Murders 201–8
Adelaide, Frederick 105
Adolphus, Mr. 17
Adventure Playground 250
Alabama 112
America 134, 159, 161, 230
American Civil War 127
Anderson, Detective Constable 138
Anderson, Dr. 236
Andrea, Clare 230
Anscombe, Henry 91
Anstee, Edward 120
antimony 55
Antique Shop Murder 241–5
Armley Prison 88
Arrow, Chief Inspector Charles John 5
arsenic 37, 42, 112, 117, 118
Asquith, Justice 194
Athenaeum Club 57
Atkinson, Sergeant Albert 152
Atkinson, Patricia "Tina" 249–50
Atkinson, Under Sheriff T.D. 35
Attercliffe Railway Station 83
Attrell, Elizabeth 185
Australia 18, 44
Avery, Justice 181
Aylesbury 119

Babbicombe 98
Baby Farmer 136–43
Babylonians 4
Baker, Alex 227
Balcombe Tunnel 92
RMS *Ballic* 112
Bamford, Mr. 30, 32
Bandara, Upadhya 254–5
Banister, Detective Inspector 123
Banner Cross 82
Banner Cross Murders 79–88
Barker, Sidney Albert 61
Barlinnie Prison 236, 240, 241
Barnes Bridge 76

Barnes Mystery 76
Barnes Police Station 76
Barrow, Eliza 166–8, 169–70, 171
Bartlett, Adelaide Blanche 104–111; trial 109–11; *see also* Pimlico Mystery
Bartlett, Edwin 104, 105, 106, 107, 109
Barton, Dr. 137
Bart's Hospital 28
Batstone, Cicely 213, 214
Batten, Elisa May 244, 248
Battlecrease House 112
Battley's Sedative Solution 55
Baxter, Robert 182
Baxter, Coroner Wynne Edwin 93
Beard, Mrs. 58–9, 60, 61, 63
Beard, Dr. Thomas 58, 61
Beckett, Herbert Francis 174
Belgium 105, 230
Bennett, Curtis 155
Beplar Committee 155
Berkshire 138
Berrett, Chief Inspector James 179, 181
Berry, James 100–1, 125, 126
Bertillon, Alphonse 154
Besford Court 210
"Big Five" 5
Billington, James 127, 136, 142
Birdsall, Trevor 255
Birkett, William Norman 187
Birtistle, Mr. 17
Bishop, Detective 183
Black, David 61
Blackheath 85, 86
Blackout Ripper 189–95
Blakely, David 230–2, 233, 234, 235
Blandon, Mr. 30
Blank, Joost de 232
Blockson, Police Constable Albert 179
Bloody Sunday 9
Bly, Mr. 30
Bodkin, Mr. 17
Book of Scoundrels 79
Boreham, Judge 256
Borough Poisoner 124
Bournemouth 199, 201

263

264 Index

Bow Street Police Court 162, 175
Bow Street Police Station 194, 243, 244
Bowyer, Linda 215, 216
Boyd, Dr. 236
Bradford 252, 256
Bradford University 253
Bratten, Mrs. 245
Brides in the Bath Murders 171–6
Brierley, Alfred 114, 116, 118
Brighton 58, 61, 63, 90
Brighton Railway Station 183
Brighton Train Line 93, 96, 243
Brighton Trunk Murders 183–9
Brighton University 58
Brinnand, Detective Sergeant Matthew 6
Bristol 217
Bristol Times & Mirror 139
British and Prudential Insurance Company 65
British Medical Association 159
British National Society for Prevention of Cruelty to Children 241
British Road Transport Service 227
Brixton Prison 216
Broadbent, Dr. William 131
Broadmoor Asylum 62, 207, 214, 215, 216, 257
Brompton Barracks 96
Brooks, Anne 28–9
Brooks, Colonel 28
Brooks, Flora Elizabeth 128–9
Brookwood Cemetery 233
Brown, Mr. & Mrs. Beresford 228
Brown, Hannah 15, 16, 17
Browne, Frederick 178, 180, 181; execution 182
Browne, Tracy 247
Bryning, Police Superintendent Isaac 118
Buckinghamshire 119, 233
Bucknill, Justice 170
Bulled, Jessie Augusta 102
Burgess, Emma 145
Burham, Charles 175
Burke, William 70
Burney, Dr. Ian 65
Burnham, Alice 173, 175, 176
Bush, Edwin 241–5; execution 245; *see also* Antique Shop Murder
Butcher, Christine 212, 214
Butler, Inspector Thomas 3
Byford, Lawrence 258

Calcraft, Chief Executioner William 18, 24, 35, 56
California 161
Camden 167
Cameron, Lord 240
Canada 128, 129, 130, 131, 143, 162, 163, 164, 230
Cane, Chief Inspector Paul 5
Capstick, Detective Inspector John 6
Captain's Cabin 193
Cardiff Prison 218

Carter, Dr. William 117
Cassells, J.C. 187
Cassels, Justice 217
Caswell, J.D. 197, 200
Central Criminal Court 181
Chamber of Horrors 126
Chamberlain, Clara 104
Channel Islands 38
Chapham 180
Chapman, George 124
Charing Cross Hospital 109
Chatham 133
Chatham Dockyard 96
Chatham Prison 81
Chelmsfold, Essex 35
Chelmsford Prison 149
Cherrill, Detective Chief Superintendent Frederick 192, 194
Cherrill of the Yard 192
Chicago 129
Chidley, Head Turnkey Mr. 35
Child, Inspector John 244
Child Guidance Clinic 209
chlorodyne 108
chloroform 108, 109, 110, 129
Chocolate Cream Poisoner 57–63
Christie, Ethel Simpson 220–1, 227, 228
Christie, John Reginal Halliday 10, 219–29; execution 229; trial 229
chronic dyspepsia 115
The Chronicle of Crime 70
Church, John 75, 76, 77, 78
Churchhill, Robert 180, 181
Clark, Detective Inspector Nobby 6
Clarke, Edward 109
Clarkson, Mr. 17
Clavering 144
Claxton, Marcella 248–9
Cleveland, President Grover 119
Clover, Matilda 131, 134
Cock, Police Constable Nicholas 82
Cold Harbour Lane 15
Cold Meat Shed 79
Cole, Police Constable Arthur John Hilton 243–4
Coleridge, Lord Chief Justice 17, 94
Collins, Detective Inspector Charles Stockley 153, 156, 157
Comptroller-General of Convicts 8
Conan Doyle, Sir Arthur 9
Condy's Fluid 108
Conquest, Chief Inspector John 63
Cook, John Parsons 31–2, 33, 34
Cooke, Isabelle 238–9, 240
Coronation Street 251
corpus delicti 207
Costello, James 257
Cottingham 83
Cottman, Mr. Justice 17
Cotton, Charles 67, 68, 69
Cotton, Frederick 67

Index 265

Cotton, Frederick, Jr. 67, 68
Cotton, Margaret 67
Court Club 230
Court of Chancery 29
Cream, Dr. Thomas Neill 10, 127–36; execution 135–6; trial 134–6; see also Lambeth Poisoner
Creighton, Charles 121
Crime Museum 7
Criminal Investigation Department (CID) 89
Criminal Justice Act 214
Crippen, Cora (aka Kunigunda Mackamotzki) 157
Crippen, Peter Hawley Harvey 10, 157–66; execution 165; trial 164
Crockford, Detective Inspector John 179
Cromarty, Annie 154
Crossley, Joseph 174, 175
Cummins, Gordon Frederick 189–95; execution 194–5; trial 194; see also Blackout Ripper
Cussen, Desmond 231, 232
Cuthbert, Inspector 9
Czechoslovakia 246

Dagg, Detective Sergeant Raymond Frederick 242–3
Daily Mirror 232
Daily Star 246
The Daily Telegraph 89
Davidson, Thomas 128
Davis, Inspector James 22
Dawson, Mr. 29
Deepdene Lane 21
Denman, Justice 77, 124
Devon 142
Dew, Chief Inspector Walter 5, 161–2, 163, 165
Dewsbury Police Station 255
Dismemberment Killer of Edgware Road 13–19
Doggett, Frederick 106
Donaldson, Chief Inspector Robert 183, 184, 185, 186
Doncaster Sessions 80
Donworth, Ellen "Nellie" 130
Dougal, Samuel Herbert 143–49; execution 148–9; trial 148; see also Moat Farm Murder
Dracula 195
Dressmaking Serial Killer of Durham 63–71
Dugay-Trouin 97
Dunn, Sydney 238
Durand-Deacon, Olivia 206, 207
Durden, Mary 78
Durham County Jail 70
Durham Prison 218
Dyer, Amelia Elizabeth 136–43; execution 141–2; trial 141; see also Baby Farmer
Dyer, Polly 139–40
Dyott, High Sheriff Lt. Col. 35
Dyson, Arthur 82, 83, 86, 87, 88
Dyson, George 106, 107, 108, 109, 111
Dyson, Mrs. 82, 83, 87

East Dulwich 105
Eddy, Muriel 222–3, 228
Edgeware Road Tragedy 14
Edmunds, Christiana 57–63; trial 61–2; see also The Chocolate Cream Poisoner
Ellis, Andrea 233, 235
Ellis, George 230, 235
Ellis, Georgina 230, 231
Ellis, Chief Executioner John 165, 176
Ellis, Ruth Neilson 10, 230–5; execution 233; trial 232; see also Public House Murder
Emmerline, Rose Annette 177
England, Cecil Louis 183–9; trial 187–8; see also Brighton Trunk Murders; Mancini, Toni
English Channel 97
English cholers 31
Epping Division 177
Essex County Chronicle 147
Essex County Constabulary 177
Essex Police 179
Essex Police Museum 182
European Court of Human Rights 219
Evans, Beryl 225, 226, 229
Evans, Geraldine 225, 226
Evans, Timothy John 225, 226, 229
The Examiner 43
executions (hangings): Browne, Frederick, by Robert Baxter 182; Bush, Edwin, by Henry Bernard Allen 245; Christie, John Reginald Halliday, by Albert Pierrepoint 229; Cream, Thomas Neill, by James Billington 135–6; Crippen, Peter Hawley Harvey, by John Ellis 165; Cummins, Gordon Frederick, by Albert Pierrepoint 194–5; Dougal, Samuel Herbert, by William Billington 148–9; Dyer, Amelia Elizabeth, by James Billington 141–2; Ellis, Ruth Neilson, by Albert Pierrepoint 233; Greenacre, James, by William Calcraft 18; Haigh, John George, by Albert Pierrepoint 208; Heath, Neville George Clevey, by Albert Pierrepoint 201; Kennedy, William Henry, by Robert Wilson 182; Manuel, Peter Thomas Anthony, by Henry Bernard Allen 240–1; Mapleton, Percy LeFroy, by William Marwood 96; Palmer, William, by George Smith 36; Peace, Charles Frederick, by William Marwood 88; Pearcey, Mary Wheeler, by James Berry 125–6; Pritchard, Williams, by William Calcraft 56–7; Robson, Mary Ann, by Askern Thomas 70; Seddon, Frederick, by John Ellis 170; Sheward, William, by William Calcraft 24–5; Smith, George Joseph, by John Ellis 176; Stratton, Albert, by John Billington 157 ; Stratton, Alfred, by John Billington 157; Webster, Kate, by William Marwood 78–9
Exter Prison 98, 100

Farrow, Ann 151, 152
Farrow, Thomas 151, 152

Index

Faulds, Dr. Henry 4, 154, 157
Faulkner, Julia 129
Federal Bureau of Investigation 5
Feltham, Inspector George 15, 16
Filey Royal Masonic Lodge 57
Findlater, Anthony 231
Fingerprint Bureau 5, 153, 155
Flatman Hotel 114
Flowers, J. 194
Flying Squad 5, 6
Foley, Police Superintendent 45, 47
Forensic Science Laboratory 6
Forest Home Cemetery 102
Foster, Campbell 87
Fox, Chief Inspector Frederick 5, 152
France 44, 97, 104, 111, 120, 177, 185, 220, 222, 233
Frankland Prison 219
Franks, Robert 128
Fremantle Prison 8
French, Dr. Frank 173
Froast, Chief Inspector Frank 3, 5
Fry, Helena 138
Fuerst, Ruth 222, 223, 228
Fulton, Forrest 124
Fyfe, David Maxwell 208, 217

Gala Day 51, 56
Gale, Sarah 16, 18
Gallery of Death 7
Gardner, Margery 197–8
Garibaldi, Giuseppe 53
Garret, Isaac 60
Garson, Dr. John George 154, 155, 156
Gay, Mr. 15
Gentleman Burglar 80
Gentleman Vampire of Bournemouth 195–201
George, Prime Minister Lloyd 166, 233
German Hanoverian Medals 91
Ghost Squad 6
Gibraltar Prison 81
Gibson, Richard 90, 91
Gifford, Solicitor General Sir Harding 77
Gilbert, William S. 10
Gill, Mr. C.F. 124, 148
Gillings, William 156
Girdwood, Mr. 14, 15
Gladwin, William 217
Glasgow, Scotland 37, 38, 44, 53, 128
Glasgow High Court 240
Glasgow Sentinel 43
Goddard, Brenda 212–3
Gold, Isaac Frederick 90, 93, 96
Goodacre, Reverend R.H. 35
Gore, Nurse 117
Gosling, Detective Sergeant John 6
Gough, Elizabeth 45, 48–9
Grange Cemetery of Edinburgh 55
Great Train Robbery 3
Great Yarmouth 19
Green, Dr. 109

Greenacre, James 13–19; execution 18; trial 17–8; *see also* Dismemberment Killer of Edgeware Road
Greenwich Police Court 85
Grey, Susan 86
Greyhound Inn 36
Gutteridge, Alfred 177
Gutteridge, Constable George William 177–82
Gutteridge, Muriel 177
Guy's Hospital 110

Habitual Criminals Register 8
Habron, John 82
Habron, William 82
Haigh, Emily 201
Haigh, John 201
Haigh, John George 10, 201–8; execution 208; trial 207–8; *see also* Acid Bath Murders
Hamilton, Margaret Evelyn 190
Hamilton Terrace 122, 127
Hammer, Betty 202
Hammersmith Bridge 75
Hampshire 51, 209
Hampstead 121, 231
Hand, Under Sheriff R.W. 35
Harber, Inspector 76
Harcourt, William 101
Hardy, Oliver 10
Hare, William 70
Harris, Captain 8
Harris, Elizabeth 99
Harris, Louisa (aka Lou Harvey) 131, 134
Harrison, Joan 253
Harrow Road Police Station 222
Havers, Cecil 232
Havers, Attorney-General Sir Michael 256
Havies, Florence 145
Hawkins, Justice Henry 85, 86, 141
Hayward, Greta 193
Heath, Neville George Clevely 195–201; execution 201; trial 200–1; *see also* Gentleman Vampire of Bournemouth
Henderson, Dr. Archibald 205, 207
Henderson, Police Commissioner Lt. Col. Sir Edmund 8, 9
Henderson, Rosalie 205, 207
Henry, Major Sir Edward Richard 4–5
Hertfordshire 120
High Court of Justiciary 56
Hill, Herne 105
Hill, Jacqueline 254
Hill, Jane 142
Hoban, Detective Chief Superintendent Denis 248
Hogg, Frank Samuel 121, 122, 123, 124, 126
Hogg, Phoebe 121–4
Hogg, Quintin 187
Hole in the Wall Tavern 75
Holland 162
Holland, Camille Cecile 144, 145, 146, 147, 148

Index

Holland, Ernest Legrand 147
Holloway Prison 232, 233, 234
Holmes, Detective Sergeant 92, 93
Holmes, Sherlock 10
Holmes, Willie 121
Home Office 100, 101, 110, 125, 147, 155, 198, 218
Home Secretary 217, 218, 219
Hopper, Dr. 117
Horfield Prison 214
Horsham Police Station 208
Hortham, Colony 211
Houdini, Harry 10
House of Commons 131
Howard, Michael 218
Howland, Detective Constable 91
Howlett, Detective Inspector 244, 245
Huddersfield 252, 254
Humble, John 253
Humphreys, Christmas 232, 235
Humphreys, Dr. Richard 114, 115
Humphries, Justice 208
Hunmanby, Scotland 52
Hurbert, W.E. de Bargue 200
Hutton, Arthur 124, 125
hyoscine 162

I Caught Crippen 165
Illinois 129
The Illustrated Police News 95, 133, 135
HMS *Implacable* 97
Inch, Dr. 236
India 209, 211, 243
Inglis, John 41
Inglis, Lord 56
Investigators: Anderson, Detective Constable 138; Arrow, Chief Inspector John 5; Atkinson, Sergeant Albert 152; Banister, Detective Inspector 123; Berrett, Chief Inspector James 179, 181; Bishop, Detective 183; Blockson, Police Constable Albert 179; Brinnand, Detective Sergeant Matthew 6; Bryning, Police Superintendent Isaac 118; Butler, Inspector Thomas 3; Cane, Chief Inspector Paul 5; Capstick, Detective Inspector John 6; Cherrill, Detective Chief Superintendent Frederick 192, 194; Child, Inspector John 244; Clark, Detective Inspector Nobby 6; Cock, Police Constable Nicholas 82; Cole, Police Constable Arthur John Hilton 243–4; Collins, Detective Inspector Charles Stockley 153, 156, 157; Conquest, Chief Inspector John 63; Crockford, Detective Inspector John 179; Cuthbert, Inspector 9; Dagg, Detective Sergeant Raymond Frederick 242–3; Davis, Inspector James 22; Dew, Chief Inspector Walter 5, 161–2, 163, 165; Donaldson, Chief Inspector Robert 183, 184, 185, 186; Feltham, Inspector George 15; Foley, Police Superintendent 45, 47; Fox, Chief Inspector Frederick 5, 152; Froast, Chief Inspector Frank 3, 5; Gosling, Detective Sergeant John 6; Harber, Inspector 76; Henderson, Police Commissioner Lt. Col. Sir Edmund 8, 9; Hoban, Detective Chief Superintendent Denis 248; Holmes, Detective Sergeant 92, 93; Howland, Detective Constable 91; Howlett, Detective Inspector 244, 245; Macnaghten, Assistant Commissioner Melville 152–3; Mattinson, Police Sergeant 180; Mitchell, Sergeant 163; Neame, Inspector 7, 8; Neil, Detective Inspector Arthur 175, 176; Oldfield, Superintendent George 253; Peglar, Police Constable 15; Pollard, Detective Superintendent 243; Randall, Police Constable 8, 9; Robinson, Police Constable 84, 85; Scott, Detective Sergeant 147; Souter, Detective Constable 199; Swanson, Detective Inspector Donald 94; Taylor, Police Constable Sydney 178; Tanner, Inspector Richard 3; Unett, Chief Constable Captain A.J. 182; Webb, Detective Inspector Albert 207; Whicher, Detective Inspector Jonathan 45, 47, 48, 50; Williamson, Detective Sergeant 48
India 241
Ingraham, Rose 120
Ireland 71, 77, 144, 227
Irish Sea 71
Isaacs, Attorney-General Sir Rufus 169
Isle of Wight 218
Ives, Mrs. 73, 75, 76
Ivory, Thomas 19

Jackson, Emily 248
Jackson, Henry 5
Jamaica 228
Jebb, Joshua 62
Joliet, Illinois State Prison 127, 128, 130
Jones, Bruce 251
Jones, William 151
Jordan, Jean 250
Jouannet, Doris 192, 194

Kaye, Violette 185–6, 188
Kendall, Captain Henry George, 162, 163
Kennedy, Ludovic 220
Kennedy, William Henry 178, 180, 181, executed 182
Kensington, Gladys 232
Kent, Constance Emily 45–51; *see also* Road Hill House Murder
Kent, Francis Savile 45, 49, 50
Kent, Mary Ann 46
Kent, Samuel Savile 46, 51
Kent, Williamson 48, 50
Kenyon, Mrs. 215–6
Key and Castle public house 21
Keyse, Emma 96, 97, 98, 99, 102, 103
Kidman, Louis 151
King, Peter Albert 242
The King of the Cat Burglars 79, 88

Index

Kings College Hospital, London 51
Kings Cross Rowton Houses 228
Kings Cross Station 183
Kirk, Harry 195
Knielands, Anne 236-7, 240

Labolmondiere, Assistant Commissioner Lt. Col. 8
Lambeth 130
Lambeth Poisoner 127-36
Lambourne End Station 178
Lanarkshire 238
Lane, Constance 206
La Neve, Ethel Clara 159-65
L'Angelier, Pierre Emile 38, 40, 41, 42, 43
Laurel, Stan 10
S.S. *Laurentic* 163
Lawler, Catherine 71-9
Leach, Dr. Alfred 107, 108, 110
Leach, Barbara 253-4
Lee, Adeline 102, 103
Lee, Evelyn 102
Lee, John Henry George 96-104; *see also* The Man They Could Not Hang
Lee, John, Sr. 97
Leeds 247, 248, 249, 250, 254
Leeds Assizes 87
LeFroy, John 88
Leicester Square 192
Leopold, Nathan 128
Lewes Assizes 187, 208
Light Trades House 255
Little Club 230
Littlefield, Henry John 154, 155
Liverpool 112, 114, 118
Lloyd, Margaret (aka Margaret Elizabeth) 174, 175, 176
Lockwood, Frank 87
Loeb, Richard 128
London Bridge Station 90, 94
London Government Act of 1963 6
Long, Maureen 250
Lopes, Justice 87
Louis Meier's Antique Shop 242, 243
Lovell, Dr. Edward 177, 179
Low Moorsley 63
Lowe, Margaret Florence 191-2, 194
Lower Broughton 81
Luftwaffe 192

MacDonald, Jayne 250
Mackenzie, Sir Francis 38
MacLennan, Hectorina 227, 228, 229
MacLeod, Norman 56
Macnaughten, Melville 125, 152-3
MacNiven, Dr. Angus 236, 239
Madame Tussaud's 126
Magdala Tavern 231
Maidstone Assizes 94
Maidstone Prison 176
Maloney, Kathleen 227, 228, 229

The Man They Could Not Hang 96-104
Manchester 80, 81, 250-1
Manchester Assizes 81
Manchester Royal Infirmary 252-3
Mancini, Tony 183-9
Manningham-Buller, Solicitor-General Sir Reginald 217
Manuel, Peter Thomas Anthony 235-41; execution 240-1; trial 240
Manuel, Teresa 236
Mapleton, Percy LeFroy 88-96; execution 96; trial 94-6; *see also* Murder on the Brighton Line
Marconi Telegraph 162
Marmon, Doris 139, 140, 141
Marmon, Miss 139
Marrist, Judge Henry 100
Marsh, Alice 132-3
Marshall, Doreen 199
Marwood, Chief Executioner William 78, 82, 88, 96
Marylebone 123
Masons 53, 57, 170
Massiah, Dr. Edward 184, 186, 189
Matthews, Charles 176
Matthews, Home Secretary Henry 119
Mattinson, Police Sergeant 180
Maurice, John Aubrey 102
Maybrick, Edwin 117
Maybrick, Florence 111-20; trial 118-9
Maybrick, Gladys Evelyn 113
Maybrick, James 111, 112, 115-7, 118
Maybrick, James Chandler 112
Maynards, J.G. Confectioners 60, 61
McCann, Wilma 247-8
McClure, G.B. 194
McEnreg, Father 78
McGill College, Montreal 128
McKinley, President William 119
McLeod, Mary 54, 56
McSwann, Amy 204, 205, 206, 207
McSwann, Donald 204, 205, 206, 207
McSwann, William 203, 204, 205
S.S. *Megantic* 164
Meier, Louis 241, 242, 244
Menhennick, Mr. 77
Mental Deficiency Act 211
Merstham 91
Metropolitan Police Act of 1829 3
Metropolitan Police Laboratory 234
Metropolitan Police Museum 86
Midland Bank 251
Millbank Prison 81
Miller, Bruce 158, 161
Millward, Vera 252
Milwaukee 102
Ministry of Health 214, 216
Minnoch, William Harper 39, 40, 44
The Mirror 235
Mitchell, Sergeant 163
Moat Farm Murder 143-49

Index

Monkwearmouth 66
Montague Place 190
S.S. *Montrose* 162, 163
Moore, Marilyn 251–2
morphine 108
Morris, Harold 155
Mount Vernon 239
Mowbray, Isabella 64, 65
Mowbray, Mrs. 64
Mowbray, William 64
Mrs. *Alice Gorton's Academy for Young Ladies* 37
Muir, Richard 156, 157, 164
Mulcahy, Katherine 193–4
Mundy, Bessie 171, 172, 173, 176
Murder on the Brighton Line 88–96
Murton 64
Murton Colliery Mine 64
Museum of Crime 9
Music Hall Ladies Guild 158
My Fifteen Lost Years 120

Nattrass, Joseph 65, 67
Nature 4
Neame, Inspector 7, 8
Neil, Detective Inspector Arthur 175, 176
Neil, Mary Ann 80
Nelson, Rita 227, 228, 229
Neve, Ethel Clara Le 159, 160, 165
New Orleans 44
New York City 44
New York Times 131–2
New Zealand 44
Newcastle upon Tyne 64, 238
Newgate Prison 10, 18, 125, 126, 128, 142
Newington, Stoke 105
News of the World 188, 218, 228
Nickolls, Lewis Charles 234
Nilsen, Dennis 10
Noll, Richard 195
Norfolk, Virginia 112
Norfolk Hotel 199
Norman Shaw Building 6
Norwich 21
Norwick City Gaol 23
Norwick Prison 25
Notting Hill 71
Notting Hill Gate 197
Nuremberg War Crimes 187

Oatley, Evelyn 191, 194
Old Bailey 61, 77, 99, 124, 141, 164, 169, 194
Oldfield, Superintendent George 253
On Poisons in Relation to Medical Jurisprudence 36
opium 55

Paddington 192
Paddington Railway Station 193
Page, James 15
Paget, Sir James 111

Palmer, Alfred Ernest 141
Palmer, Anna 32
Palmer, Arthur 140
Palmer, Freke 125
Palmer, Mary Ann 141
Palmer, Walter 31
Palmer, William 87
Palmer, Dr. William 26–37; execution 36; trial 32–4; *see also* The Rugeley Poisoner
Palmer, Willy 29
Palmerston 37
Panama Club 197
Park Crescent 188
Parkes, Dr. Peter 214
Parkhurst Prison 218, 257
Paterson, Dr. James 55
Payne, Mr. 17
Peace, Charlie Frederick 10, 79–88; execution 88; trial 87–8; *see also* Banner Cross Murders
Pearcey, Mary Eleanor Wheeler 120–7; execution 125–6; trial 123–5
Pearson, Yvonne 252
Peckham 83, 86
Peel, Sir Robert 3–4
Peglar, Edith 171
Peglar, Police Constable 15
Peglar, Samuel 13
Pentonville Prison 86, 165, 201, 245
Pepper, Professor Augustus Joseph 147, 148, 162, 164
Perry, Mary 39
Piccadilly Circus 112, 193
Pierrepoint, Chief Executioner Albert 195, 201, 208, 226, 229, 233
Pimlico 106
Pimlico Mystery 104–11
Pinchback Bridge 178
Pineapple Toll-Gate 13
Plimmer, Warder George 35
Plymouth, Devon 64
Plymouth Station 142
Pollard, Detective Superintendent 243
Portland Prison 102
Porter, Henry 75
Porter, Robert 75, 76, 77, 78
Potter, Edward 64
Pratt, Mary Dew 46, 47
Preston Park Station 90, 91
Price, Mr. 17
Priddington, Charlotte 121
Prince Phillip Playing Fields 248
Prisoner Property Store, 8
Prisoner's Property Act, 7
Pritchard, Edward William 51–7; execution 56–7; trial 55–6
Procurator-Fiscal 55, 236
Public House Murder 230–5
Pudsley 254
Putney Bridge 229

Index

Queen Street Station, Glasgow 55
Quick-Manning, John 68

R Division 186
Railway Police 91
Ralfe, Mathias 14
Randall, Police Constable 8, 9
Reading 138
Reading County Magistrate 216
Recovery, House of 65
Regent's Canal 13
Reivers, Olive 255
Renfield Syndrome 195, 201
Richardson, Irene 249, 252
Richmond Bridge 75
Richmond Police Station 77
Rickard, Royston 233
Riley, Thomas 68, 69
Ripper, Jack the 10, 94, 126, 128, 133, 136, 190, 193, 253
Rising Sun Tavern 75
Road Hill House Murder 45–51
Roberts, Paul 243, 244
Roberts, Warder George 35
Robinson, Police Constable Edward 84, 85, 86
Robinson, Isabella 66
Robinson, James 66, 67
Robinson, Mary Isabella 66
Robson, Mary Ann 35, 63–71; execution 70; trial 70; *see also* Dressmaking Serial Killer of Durham
Robson, Michael 63–4
"Rogues Gallery" 4
Rogulskyi, Anne "Annie" 246–7
Romford Police Station 179
Rooth, H. G. 155
Roper, Lt. Percy 96
Roundhay Park 249
Royal Air Force 189, 190, 193, 196
Royal Canadian Mounted Police 3
Royal College of Physicians and Surgeons 129
Royal Engineers 96, 143
Rugeley Poisoner 26–37
Rugeley, Staffordshire 26
Russell, Attorney General Charles 109, 119
Russell, Lord 131
Rytka, Helen 252

St. Albans Prison 120
St. Bartholomew's Hospital 111
St. George's Hall 118
St. Giles 24
St. Giles Hospital 234
St. John's Park 85
Saint Lawrence Seaway 163
St. Martin's Lane 243
St. Mary Churchyard 233
St. Mary's for Penitent Females 49
St. Nicholes Church 29
St. Peter Mancroft 24
St. Thomas's Hospital 129, 132

Salvation Army 138
Sambourne 210
Saunders, T.B. 48
Saville, Doris 187
Scindian 8
Scotland 129, 227, 235, 236, 237, 238, 240, 250, 258
The Scotsman 43
Scott, Detective Sergeant 147
Seddon, Frederick 10, 166–71; execution 170; trial 169–70
Seddon, Maggie 169, 70
Seddon, Mrs. 10
Seaham Harbour 65
Shawcross, Attorney-General Sir Hartley 208
Sheffield 79, 80, 81, 83, 86, 220, 227
Sheward, Martha 19–21; ghost 22, 23, 25
Sheward, William 19–25; execution 22–3; trial 24–5; *see also* The Tabernacle Street Murder
Shire Hall 148
Shockproof 213
Shrivell, Emma 131–2, 133
Sickert, Walter Richard 5
Simmons, Harry 139, 140
Simpson, Professor Dr. Keith 198, 199, 207, 242
The Sinner's Friend 35
Skylark Café 185
Sleigh, Warner 78
Slone Square 192
Smart, Doris 239, 240
Smart, Peter 239
Smethurst, Dr. Thomas 37
Smith, Frederick 131
Smith, George 35
Smith, George Joseph 171–6; execution 176; *see also* Brides in the Bath Murders
Smith, James 39
Smith, Janet 42
Smith, Madeleine Hamilton 37–44; trial 41–3
Smith, Mr. 3
Smith, Olive 247
Smith, William Henry 131
Souter, Detective Constable 199
South African Air Force 196
South East London 83
South Kensington 205
South Hetton Colliery 65
South Prison 56
Southampton 227
Spain 125
Spencer, Doris 215
Spilbury, Dr. Bernard Henry 162, 164, 165, 183, 186, 192
Spraque, Dr. 147
Stanton, Ellen 153, 155
Stapleford Abbotts 177
The Star 232
Steinback, Susan 33
Stepney 94
Stevens, Mr. 32
Stevenson, Judge 245

Index

Stevenson, Dr. Thomas 110
Storrs, Dr. 147
Stott, Daniel 129, 130
Stott, Julia Abbey 129
Stott, Robert 64
Straffen, John Thomas 209-19
Straffen, John Thomas, Sr. 209
Stratton, Albert 154, 155, 156, 157
Stratton, Alfred 154, 155, 156, 157
Stratton Brothers (Alfred, Albert) 10, 151-7, 10; executions 157; trials 154-7
Strong, Mr. 71
strychnine 32, 33, 61, 63, 128, 129, 130, 132
Sullivan, Arthur S. 10
Sun 219
Sunderland 66
Sunderland Infirmary 65
Surry 92, 119
Sussex County 241
Sutcliffe, Peter William 245-58; trial 256-7; *see also* Yorkshire Ripper
Swaine, Alfred 33
Swanson, Detective Inspector Donald 94
Sykes, Theresa 254-5
Symonds, Yvonne 197, 198
Szurma, Sonia 246

T Division 15
Tabernacle Street Murder 19-25
Tanner, Inspector Richard 3
Tasmania 88
Tawnton Assize Court 214
Taylor, Dr. 33
Taylor, Mary Jane 51-2, 54, 55
Taylor, Michael 55
Taylor, Mrs. 54, 55
Taylor, Police Constable Sydney 178
Teddington 72
Templar, Reginal Gwynne 103, 104
10 Rillington Place 222, 224, 225, 228
Thames River 136, 138, 139
Thames River Police 138
Thomas, Asken 70
Thomas, Julia Martha 72, 73, 74, 76, 77, 78, 79
Thornhill, Caroline Beatrice 171
Times of London 48, 49, 70
RMS *Titanic* 112
Tollard Royal Hotel 199
Trafalgar Square Riot 8
Tremouille, Adolphe Collot de la 104
Tudfil, Merthyr 225
Tyndall, Chief Justice 17

Uddington 239
Unett, Chief Constable Captain A.J. 182
University College, London 165
University of Manchester 65
University of Leeds 254, 255
Uxbridge Jail 221

Vaderland 120
victims: Atkinson, Patricia "Tina" 249; Bandara, Upadhya 254; Barker, Sidney Albert 61; Barrow, Eliza 167; Bartlett, Edwin 108, 109; Batstone, Cicely 213; Batten, Elisa May 242; Beard, Mrs. 58, 59, 60; Blakely, David 231-2; Bowyer, Linda 215-6; Brooks, Annie 30, 31, 32; Brooks, Flora Elizabeth 129; Brown, Hannah 15, 16, 17; Browne, Tracy 247; Burnham, Alice 173-4; Butcher, Christine 212; Christie, Ethel 227; Claxton, Marcella 248-9 ; Clover, Matilda 131, 134; Cock, Police Constable Nicholas 82; Cook, John Parsons 31, 32, 33, 34, 35; Cooke, Isabelle 238-9; Cotton, Charles 68, 69; Cotton, Margaret 67; Cotton, Robert 68; Crippen, Cora 160; Donworth, Ellen "Nellie" 130 ; Dunn, Sydney 288; Durand-Deacon, Olivia 206; Dyson, Arthur 83, 88; Eddy, Muriel 222-3; Evans, Beryl 225; Evans, Geraldine 225; Farrow, Ann 151-2; Farrow, Thomas 151-2; Fry, Helena 138; Fuerst, Ruth 222; Gardener, Kate 129; Gardner, Margery 197, 198; Goddard, Brenda 222-3; Gold, Isaac Frederick 90-1, 96; Gutteridge, Police Constable George William 178-9; Hamilton, Margaret Evelyn 190; Harris, Louise (aka Lou Harvey) 131; Haywood, Greta 193; Henderson, Archibald 205; Henderson, Rosalie 205; Hill, Jacqueline 254; Hogg, (baby) Phoebe 122; Hogg, Phoebe 121, 122; Holland, Camille Cecile 145; Jackson, Emily 248; Jordan, Jean 250-1; Jouannet, Doris 192; Kaye, Violette 185-6, 188; Kent, Francis Savile 45, 47, 49, 50, 51; Keyse, Emma 96, 98, 103; Knielands, Anna 236-7; L'Angelier, Pierre Emile 38, 40-4; Leach, Barbara 253; Lofty, Margaret Elizabeth 174-5; Long, Maureen 250; Lowe, Margaret Florence 191-2; MacDonald, Jayne 250; MacLennan, Hectorina 227-8; Maloney, Kathleen 227-8; Marmon, Doris 139, 140, 141; Marsh, Alice 132; Marshall, Doreen 199; Maybrick, James 118; McCann, Wilma 247; McSwann, Amy 205; McSwann, Donald 205; McSwann, William 204; Millward, Vera 252; Moore, Marilyn 251-2; Mulcahy, Katherine 193; Mundy, Bessie 173; Nelson, Rita 227-8; Pearson, Yvonne 252; Pritchard, Mary Jane 54, 55; Richardson, Irene 249; Robinson, Police Constable Edward 84-6; Robinson, Mary Isabella 66; Robson, Isabella 66; Rogulskyj, Anna 246; Rytka, Helen 252; Sheward, Martha 19, 20, 21, 23, 25; Shrivell, Emms 132; Simmons, Harry 139, 140; Smart, Doris 239; Smart, Michael 239; Smart, Olive 247; Smart, Peter 239; Stott, Daniel 129, 130; Sykes, Theresa 254; Taylor, Mrs. 54, 55; Thomas, Julia Martha 72-4; Walls, Marguerite 254; Ward, George 66; Watt, Marion 237; Watt, Margaret 237; Watt, Vivienne 237; Whitaker, Josephine 253

Index

Victoria, Queen 119
HMS *Victory* 51
Vincent, Howard 89
Vinnicombe, William Joseph 183
The Vonderashes 168

Wagner, Rev. Arthur 49
Wakefield Cathedral, High Church of 202
Wakefield Prison 81
Wales 225, 226, 230
Walker, Annie 105
Walls, Marguerite 254
Walworth 130
Walworth Police Station 22
Wandsworth Prison 72, 78, 194, 208, 217
Ward, George 66
Ward, Hannah 80
Ward, John 80, 85
Ward, Mrs. 66
Wardle, George 44
Warley Cemetery 182
Warren, General Sir Charles 9
Washington Post 62
Watt, Margaret 237–8
Watt, Marion 237–8
Watt, Mr. 238
Watt, Vivienne 237–8
Webb, Detective Inspector Albert 207
Webster, Kate 71–9; execution 78–9, 124; trial 77–8; *see also* Lawler, Catherine
Welles, Orson 10
West Auckland 67
West End Central Police Station 243-4
West London Mental Health Trust 62

West Sussex 205
West Yorkshire 246
Whalley Range 82
Wheeler, Janet 244
Wheeler, Thomas 120
Whibley, Charles 79
Whicher, Detective Inspector Jonathan 45, 47, 48, 50
Whitaker, Josephine 253
White Lion Inn 14
Whitechapel 9, 127
Whitehead, James 125
Widnail, Jane 26–8
Willcox, Professor 170
Wilson, Paul 257–8
Wilson, Robert 182
Wiltshire 45
Wimbledon 105, 106
Winchester 211
Windmill Club 191
Windsor Castle 62
Wisken, Mrs. 145
Woking Prison 119
Woolbest, Captain 71
World War I 5, 9, 177, 220, 230
World War II 6, 9, 187, 189, 196, 203, 222, 230
Wyman, Dr. Cuthbert 132

Yapp, Alice 114, 117, 118
Yellowless, Dr. Henry 208
York 83
Yorkshire 86, 87, 100, 219, 201
Yorkshire Ripper 241, 245–58